whole due 11 92

The
Home
Decorating
Sewing
Book

ELIZABETH J. MUSHENO

The Home Decorating Sewing Book

MACMILLAN PUBLISHING CO., INC. New York

COLLIER MACMILLAN PUBLISHERS London

Macmillan Publishing Co., Inc.
866 Third Avenue, New York, N.Y. 10022
Collier Macmillan Canada, Ltd.

Library of Congress Cataloging in Publication Data

Musheno, Elizabeth J
  The home decorating sewing book.

  1. Sewing. 2. House furnishings. I. Title.
TT715.M83   646.2′1   77-18987
ISBN 0-02-588190-6

First Printing 1978

Printed in the United States of America

This book is dedicated to my five daughters:
Sharon, Adelade, Yvonne, Cathay, and Deborah.

Acknowledgments

A project of this magnitude could not have been completed without the aid of many people who have shared their knowledge and given so generously of their time and talent.

The artists: Marie M. Martin, for her clear and concise technical drawings; Scott Hyde, who photographed the many projects I made.

My editor, Jeanne Fredericks, and my agent, Ray Pierre Corsini, both of whom gave encouragement just when it was needed.

The fabric and notions people who dispensed much valuable information: Herman Phynes of Fabrications, Jennifer Butler of Spring Mills, Leslie Warren of West Point Pepperell, Barbara A. Egner of Waverly Fabrics, Hilda D. Sachs of Window Shade Manufacturers Association, Lynne Hamer of Bloomcraft, Pat McCarthey and Judith Ross of Burlington, Helen Boyd of Crompton, Cecil Grant, Jr., of Glen Raven Mills, Inc., Thomas Reich of Donahue Sales, Edward Goodman of Conso Products, Rose Ann Fairchild of Kirsch Company, Julia Denny of Dupont, Mary Burke of Celanese, and Daniel Dannoff of Cohama.

My friends Anita and Joe Arnoso, who generously allowed me to use their beautiful backyard with pool and patio as a background for the outdoor photographs.

Family and friends who wielded paint brushes, hammers, and screwdrivers to aid this do-it-herselfer: Adelade and William Sullivan, Yvonne and Robert Leibrock, and Cathay Fulger and Robert P. Gleason. And my typist daughter, Yvonne Leibrock.

Contents

Introduction:
How To Use This Book

Whether you live in an apartment, private house, trailer, or van, *The Home Decorating Sewing Book* will help you enhance the beauty, comfort, and personality of your home. Even the novice will be able to follow the instructions for making simple draperies, pillows, and bedspreads. Those with more experience will find many challenging and rewarding projects.

I have included photographs to give you as many decorating ideas as possible and hundreds of step-by-step illustrations to clarify all the important procedures. Various shadings and tones in the illustrations are used to indicate the right and wrong sides of the fabric, stiffening, and the right and wrong sides of the lining.

I suggest you start by reading the first and last chapters so that you fully understand the preliminary steps and sewing terminology before beginning a project. In the first chapter, you will learn the fundamental steps needed to decorate your home with confidence: a careful evaluation of the room; where to look for ideas; how to find fabrics, trims, notions, and fixtures for your project; special tips on fabric selection; how to develop a color scheme that will work; budget and time considerations; and a plan for getting started. In the last chapter, you will find decorating terms and sewing techniques. Use this section to familiarize yourself with the sewing procedures needed for your project and, later, as a reference.

The Home Decorating Sewing Book attempts to introduce you to the wonders of sewing for your home. By adding your own imagination to the ideas and suggestions that follow, you will open up limitless opportunities for beautifying your home.

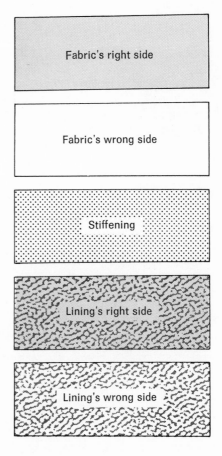

I
Practical Planning

Planning is the keynote to successful sewing for the home, whether it's a curtain for the kitchen, throw pillows for the bed, or draw draperies to cover a wall of glass. Haphazard planning could be your undoing, whereas careful planning starts you off properly and helps insure that you will complete projects that will be attractive additions to your home.

Think small for your first venture; don't overwhelm yourself. Make simple straight-hanging curtains, tieback curtains, or draperies for a one-window room. Or choose a knife-edge pillow for your sofa or a plain throw bedspread from a colorful fabric as a starter. By the time your first project is completed, you will probably want to try one of the others. Before you know it, you'll be ready to tackle any decorating project in this book.

Be innovative, but approach sewing for your home with an eye on your budget. Remember, you will need to purchase more than fabric to do a first-rate job. Don't splurge in one area and then skimp on the rest. You will have to plan carefully to allot your money properly.

Time is a factor many do-it-yourselfers fail to consider. Plan well in advance for any decorating projects. There's nothing more frustrating than starting a new project, on the spur of the moment, and giving yourself an impossible deadline. Then, as the work progresses, you will be aware that it's going to take longer to finish than you thought it would. When this happens, you have two choices: lay the project aside (if possible), or work much longer hours, borrowing time needed for other things. A little more time spent in planning a project can help you avoid a great deal of aggravation.

Think modern or traditional, but first consider your own tastes. Think about your family's requirements as to comfort and physical needs. Keep in mind your likes and dislikes and, most important, your life-style. Are you planning a formal dining room that will be a showplace and will receive only occasional use? Elegant silks, velvets, and brocades would be appropriate. But if a room is going to get constant use, you should think in terms of more durable decorator fabrics like sailcloth, textured cottons, or denim.

STEP ONE: WHAT DOES THAT ROOM REALLY NEED?

Begin by evaluating the room you want to redecorate. Look carefully at the room's construction as well as the proportions of the furniture you have. Consider the windows, doors, wall space, floor space, and focal points, if any. Each of these features will play an important role.

WINDOWS, DOORS, AND WALLS: Are there any structural problems caused by off-center windows or doors or by windows of several lengths and/or widths? Are the windows framed with wood or metal or are they unframed? Do the heating or cooling units need special consideration? What are the walls made of? Are they hollow with plaster, plasterboard, or metal coverings? Are

3

they solid masonry (stone, brick, or cinder block)? Are there several types of wall construction in the same room? This information is necessary when you hang curtain and drapery fixtures, pictures, and wall hangings. Make a record of all problems and special considerations as well as the measurements.

FLOORS AND FLOOR SPACE: The amount of available floor space influences how comfortable a room is for its inhabitants. An active family with children will need more floor space than a retired couple or a single person. Is the furniture arranged to utilize floor space in the best way for your life-style?

What is your floor made of? Is it wood or concrete? Make a note of any improvements you wish to consider, the construction of your floor, and of course room measurements.

FOCAL POINT: Every room should have a center of attraction that catches the eye as one enters. Does your room have a picture window that can be enhanced with curtains or draperies? Is there a fireplace or wall unit that could be brightened with a colorful framed fabric panel for a focal point? If not, create one by making a beautiful wall hanging or screens as described in Chapter VII (pages 168–169).

FURNISHINGS: Your present furnishings are probably quite usable, but they may be drab, the colors may clash, or their coverings may make them seem too large or too small for the room. Perhaps your window fashions need to be replaced. Do you need some accessories to liven up the room? Note the items you wish to change or where improvement is needed as you move on to the next planning step.

STEP TWO:
MAKE A PERMANENT RECORD

There are two things you should do next: Compile the information in a logical manner in a notebook that will fit in your handbag or pocket; and start a file for pictorial ideas. With notebook in hand, tour furniture stores and departments, go to decorator showcase houses or on house tours. Make notes or even simple sketches of ideas you might consider. But please don't do this in the establishment you're touring; you may be embarrassed if someone asks you to refrain. Have a cup of coffee and record your ideas a little later while they're still fresh in your mind.

Visit your library. You will find many maga-

Change the mood of a room with fabric—three ways. Fabric and accessories are used by designer Shirley Regendahl to create three different looks for the same room. For a traditional room, Waverly Fabrics' "Whitton Court" is used for the draw draperies over glass curtains, with a padded cornice, for the couch and loveseat slipcovers, and for the chair cushion and pillows.

zines and interior decorating books available for more ideas. And be a collector—if an idea in a magazine or newspaper interests you, cut it out and file it away. Don't save the whole thing or you'll spend endless hours looking for it when you need it.

STEP THREE:
GET ACQUAINTED WITH FABRIC

Fabric and related supplies can be quite costly, so it is well worth the time to do some extensive research. When you see a fabric you like, make a note of the width, cost, and colors.

Don't be afraid to look for unusual fabric sources—your attic, a thrift shop, or a friend's castoffs often yield enough usable fabric to sew many decorating items. Recycle old draperies, slipcovers, or bedspreads. Make them into new styles or add trim for a new look. Patchwork and pillows are great ways to use smaller, recycled fabric sections.

Sheets are another hot decorating fabric source, as are bedspreads and other bedding or fabric woven without seams. They are quite economical, as most are at least two yards wide, eliminating

the need to add seams for projects requiring very wide fabric sections.

At the Store
Proceed carefully as you look at fabrics. Feel the texture and weight. Be concerned about the quality—price does not always guarantee durable fabric. Threads should not shift when scratched with a fingernail, and the fibers should be of a uniform diameter without thin, weak areas. Rub the fabric together between your hands. If fibers come loose or a starchy residue is left on your hands, the fabric may not be serviceable. There are ways to make inferior fabric look good, but after it has been used for a time and has been washed or dry cleaned, the sizing is gone and the fibers are weakened. Such fabric will not withstand constant wear.

You should resolve the following questions about fabric selection for every type of home sewing project if you wish to insure satisfactory results:

• Has the fabric been treated to be stain-resistant or does it have soil-release properties for easy cleaning? This information is usually stamped on the selvage.

• Is the fabric crease-resistant? Permanent press

A contemporary room uses Waverly Fabrics' "Clementine" for the stationary lined-to-edge draperies over glass curtains, for the couch and loveseat slipcovers, and for the chair cushions.

For a more modern approach, Waverly Fabrics' "Shalimar" is used for the Roman shades with set-in flat cornices, for the couch and loveseat slipcovers, and for the chair cushions.

fabrics are usually crease-resistant, too. If you're not sure, try this test: Crush the fabric in a tight ball and then release. Do the wrinkles disappear in a short time or do they remain?

• Will the fabric withstand the wear it will receive? Use sheer, delicate, or luxurious fabrics in a room that does not have heavy traffic. Use tightly woven, medium- to heavyweight fabrics that are easily laundered for living rooms, bedrooms, and rooms with more than one function.

• Is the fabric preshrunk? If not, you should shrink it. (See Chapter VIII, "Terms and Techniques.")

• Is the fabric colorfast and fade-resistant? Ask the salesclerk or look on the cardboard tube or selvage.

• Stretch the fabric to see if it will give. You want a firm, unstretchable weave.

• Hold the right side of the fabric in the sunlight to see if the color is true under natural light and still compatible with your other colors. Next, hold the fabric up to the sunlight, with the right side facing you, to see if the color changes when the light shines through from the wrong side. This possible color change is important in matching drapery fabric to your other colors.

• Are plain-colored fabrics finished on the straight grain? The crosswise threads that run from selvage to selvage must be at right angles to the lengthwise threads that run parallel to the selvages. When fabric threads do not run in a straight line from selvage to selvage, the finished item will not drape in smooth folds from top to bottom and will have a tendency to curl at a curtain or drapery side hem edge.

• Does the print correspond with the grain? No matter how carefully it is matched, the design will not parallel the rods or flow in a straight line across a bed or couch if it is off-grain.

• Hold opaque fabric up to a bright light with the wrong side facing you. Depending on how much light, if any, comes through, the fabric may need to be lined for durability and privacy if it is used for curtains or draperies.

• Does your project require soft or crisp fabric? Soft fabrics hang straight down in small, soft folds when gathered on a rod or in a seam; they are sometimes called limp. Crisp fabrics will hang down in puffy, more deeply rounded folds when gathered on a rod or in a seam, and they are often described as stiff or rigid. Collect fabric in small folds in your hand about a yard from the end and let it hang straight. How will it gather, pleat, or drape?

• When you are using lining, lay a length of fabric on top of a length of lining and collect them in your hand to test the hanging characteristics as explained for soft and crisp fabrics above.

If you have answered all these questions satisfactorily but you are undecided about the color or print, buy a yard or two of the fabric. Take it home and hang it over a rod at a window or lay it over a bed, chair, or couch and leave it there for a day or so to see if you like it. This expenditure is small compared to what you might spend for the total yardage only to find you are stuck with a costly mistake.

Fabric Design Repeats

This design element that salespeople talk about is an important feature when selecting fabric. The design (sometimes called pattern) must be matched horizontally on each panel of fabric needed to make a pair of curtains, a bedspread, or a couch cover.

If you are choosing a fabric with a repeating design, see page 30 to figure out how much extra yardage is needed.

Depending on how you are using the fabric, there are some special visual considerations you should know about (see figure I-2).

1. For curtains or draperies, have the bottom edge of the design repeat fall close to the proposed hem turn-back. If a whole design is not needed to make the total length, it will be lost in the gathers or pleats.

2. For a bedspread, on a bed without a footboard, have the fabric design fall near the proposed hem turn-back.

3. For a bed with a footboard, center the design repeat over the pillow.

4. For a couch or chair cover, center the design repeats on the backrest and cushion.

Solid Color Fabrics

Most solid fabrics are great to sew, but be sure to mark the wrong side with a big **X**. Use chalk or a pencil or, if it would show through to the right side, indicate wrong side with safety pins. Mark every section as you cut it out. Also make sure the fabric reflects the light in the same way from all angles. If one way is dull and the other is bright, cut it as you would a napped fabric so it

1

2

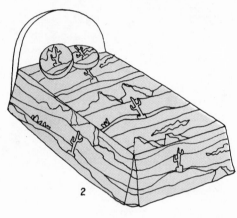

3

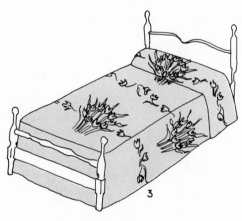

4

will have the same bright or dull look over the entire curtain, drapery, bedspread, or slipcover.

Storage

Fabric should be stored so it will receive a minimum of wrinkles. If you can get one of those heavy cardboard rolls from the storekeeper it will save you a lot of pressing. Otherwise, unfold the fabric and spread it out over a bed or table that is not being used.

STEP FOUR: INVESTIGATE TRIMS, NOTIONS, AND FIXTURES

Three important accessories to any home decorating project are trims, notions, and fixtures. Purchase these items with care so they will last the lifetime of the project.

Trims

So many trims are available that you may find it hard to decide on one. Whatever you choose, be sure the cleaning requirements of trim and fabric are compatible. Determine what technique to use to attach the trim—trim stitched in place by machine saves time, but it may detract from the overall appearance on an elegant fabric. Also note widths, colors, and prices of trims you like.

Notions

Thread, needles, pins, fasteners, cable cord, weights, tapes, measuring and marking tools, elastic, and more—there is a notion for every need. Visit stores that sell notions and find out what is available. If you are not a seamstress, you will be pleasantly surprised at all the variations of the basic sewing needs, but don't purchase anything at this time unless you need it; instead make a list of the items you may wish to purchase later.

Fixtures

Explore places that sell fixtures and hardware supplies; home improvement centers, hardware and fabric stores, or department stores and specialty shops are the best places to start. By doing this preliminary research, you will be able to find the fixtures required for particular projects more quickly. And since these stores often have brochures with decorating ideas, you may also discover some valuable ideas for improving your home.

TOP LEFT: *Designer G. Allen Scruggs uses a crewel-printed fabric for the flat cornice and hourglass curtains with Breneman's "Spice" translucent window shades for this unusually lovely deep-silled window treatment. Matching Conso trim is glued to the shade edges. The window fabric is used for chair cushions at the table as well as for the wing chair to complement the other furnishings and to create an eclectic provincial room.*

BOTTOM LEFT: *Waverly Fabrics' "Deveron" is used by Mary Kay Baldwin to complement the traditional furnishings. A self-fabric-covered plywood lambrequin accents the pinch-pleated café curtains. Floor-to-ceiling self-covered plywood panels add columns of color throughout the room and the slipcovered couch completes the total look.*

BELOW: *This eclectic living room was designed by the author. The fabric (from Fabrications in New York City) at the indented, off-center windows with a heating/air conditioning unit is used to create the color scheme: red, kelly green, and black. The window is framed with a padded cornice and stationary draperies to hide the boxed-in steel beams, then window seats are added to fill in the remaining space for perfect viewing of the ships on the Hudson River. Bloomcraft's "Sunset" in kelly green is used to cover the island couch and sleigh bed (see "Fabric, foam, and wood furniture" in Chapter VII). The window fabric is laminated to the coffee table. The director's chairs, covered in Sunbrella® canvas from Glen Raven Mills, Inc., and the matching laminated Parsons table complete the conversation area.*

LEFT: *An elegant, sophisticated, modern dining room by designer Mary Kay Baldwin has a traditional window treatment for the unusually shaped windows—pinch-pleated stationary draperies with tiebacks made from Waverly Fabrics' "Fredericksburg."*

RIGHT: *Today's hybrid kitchen–dining area even has sleeping space for a guest. Designer Ann Heller, ASID, uses a red, white, and blue Early American theme. The cornice and couch are covered with J. P. Stevens sheets and "Colony" striped shades by Joann Western Mills Co. are used at the windows. A polka-dot table cover with gingham napkins completes the country look.*

BELOW: *The ambience that glows in this classic living room designed by Mary Kay Baldwin will never be outdated. "Wright Farm Coverlet" from Schumacher's Old Sturbridge Village Crafts Collection is used on the walls, at the window for pinch-pleated stationary tieback draperies, and for the fronts and cushions for the slipcovered wing chair and couch. Waverly Fabrics' solid colored "Manor House Velvet" is used for the contrasting backs of the slip covers, for the other wing chair, and for the window seat cushions and pillows.*

STEP FIVE:
PLAN OUT YOUR BUDGET AND TIME

Sewing for the home requires budget considerations and a time evaluation. You should make a realistic budget to give yourself an idea of how much money is available for the project. Even if you are willing to spend a great deal to express your individuality, you should make a budget and stick to it. If you are budget-minded, do not buy inferior quality materials to save money. Shop around or wait for sales to find serviceable fabric, notions, trims, and fixtures that will suit your needs. Be sure to match quality—don't spend all your money on one item and then skimp on the rest.

The time factor is hard to calculate as you will be doing something for yourself and no two individuals will work at the same pace. But by planning logically and reading project instructions step by step, you should be able to arrive at a realistic calculation of the time needed to complete a project.

If you're doing a whole room, divide the work into several stages; it will be less confusing, and the room (if you have to live in it) will develop right before your eyes. If you think one stage will take a week of your spare time, add a day or two for the unforeseen. For most decorating projects the actual sewing does not take a lot of time; it's cutting, matching, and pinning, adding trim, pressing, and hanging that take longer than planned.

STEP SIX: THINK ABOUT COLOR

Color can be used to set a mood, improve work efficiency, induce relaxation, or create excitement. To use color to the best advantage, you should first understand some basic principles about color and how it works.

Color is divided into four groups. The first three groups make twelve basic colors or hues: red, yellow, blue, green, orange, purple, red-orange, red-violet, yellow-orange, yellow-green, blue-violet, and blue-green. Then a mixture of these hues makes the remaining three colors— black, gray, and white—for a total of fifteen. Add tints and shades, and you can match any of the thousands of colors nature has provided.

PRIMARY COLORS: Red, yellow, and blue are the only pure colors, and all shades and tints are produced from them.

SECONDARY COLORS: Equal parts of two primary colors produce a third color. There are three of these secondary colors: green, orange, and purple, and they are made by mixing yellow and blue, yellow and red, and red and blue, respectively.

TERTIARY COLORS: When equal parts of a primary and a secondary color are mixed, six more colors are created. Red and orange make red-orange; red and purple make red-violet; yellow and orange make yellow-orange; yellow and green make yellow-green; blue and violet make blue-violet; and blue and green make blue-green.

NEUTRALIZING COLORS: Black and gray are made when all the primary colors are mixed. White appears to be a color without hue to most laymen's eyes, but the substance used to make the color usually contains 10–20 percent gray color to permit it to reflect light.

SHADE: Take any of the 12 basic colors and add black to make a shade of that color. The more black added, the darker the shade will be.

TINT: Add white to any of the 12 basic colors to make a tint of that color. The more white added, the lighter the tint will be.

VALUE: The shade or tint is a darker or lighter value of the basic color.

COLOR INTENSITY: Any color can be made bright or dull. Retain the color, shade, or tint that is close to the three basic groups for a bright color that will reflect its intensity, or neutralize it by adding black to make it become a duller or less intense hue.

COLOR HARMONY: Learn to analyze the components of each color you select. Because several colors are mixed together for most hues, you are choosing hues as well as colors. For example, there may be several greens among your fabric swatches, but one shade could have too much yellow, blue, or black in its dye, and it would therefore clash with the rest of your color scheme.

Optical Illusions Created by Color
Now that you have a better understanding of color and realize that colors may clash or harmonize with each other by the simple addition of black, white, or one of the primary colors, the next step is to learn how to use color effectively.

Blue, green, and violet are considered to be cool colors; they remind us of the sky, rolling hills, and shady nooks. Use these colors in various shades and tints when you want a relaxing, comforting room. Red, yellow, and orange are the warm colors; they suggest sunset, autumn leaves, or the warming flames of a fire. Pale tints of the warm colors will tend to make a room seem inviting and relaxing; darker shades create a mood of excitement.

When using color, consider what it can do for a room. In a bright, sunny room, you can soften the mood with cool or neutral colors, but take care not to suppress the light and lovely feeling a room like this evokes. Brighten a darker room with warm colors, but retain the relaxed, cool feeling by using pale tints rather than the darker shades.

Cool, receding colors give an illusion of distance; use them on the walls of a small room to make it seem larger than it actually is. Use these colors to slipcover large furniture to make it seem smaller.

Warm, advancing colors give the illusion of closeness. Use them on the two narrow end walls of a room that is much longer than it is wide; the room will look wider. Or make a ceiling that is too high seem lower by painting it with an advancing color. In a room with a minimum of furniture, slipcover some of the furniture in warm colors as a welcoming feature.

When you combine colors, be aware of how they interact. Choose colors that are compatible so they do not clash. The value of each color will affect the total color scheme; some will look lighter, duller, or more intense than when used alone. Dark colored walls or floors will absorb light; light colors will reflect it, so how you light a room is influenced by the colors you use.

To make a room seem wider, use a dominant color or fabric to stop the eye where you want it to stop. Hang draperies across an entire wall to create an illusion of greater width. If you want to minimize structural flaws, paint walls a cool, light, or neutral color and cover furniture with bright pillows and slipcovers or use other accessories to draw attention away from the walls. Treat walls broken up by doors the same way, adding accents in the corners, on the doors, or in spaces between for a total, unbroken look.

Develop a Color Scheme

Plan carefully. First decide what colors will be best for you and your family—any color harmony that feels right is the way to go. If you need some inspiration, use the hues in a favorite picture that may later become a focal point; a length of fabric or even a pot of flowers could be your inspiration.

Before you start, determine what your color scheme must help you do:

• What is the mood and function of the room? Is it quiet or active, formal or casual; is it used for study, conversation, listening to music, watching TV, eating, relaxing, sleeping, or a combination of several activities?

• Are the room's size and shape adequate? Is it too small? Too large? Is it structurally satisfactory? Are there structural flaws to camouflage? Structural assets to accentuate?

• Where is the room located? Does the room get heavy traffic? Is it isolated? Does it have a view? Is the view to be accented? Camouflaged? Which direction does the room face?

When you have answered these questions, you are ready to choose the right formula for your room. The next step is to make a color scheme chart, using the notebook you started in step one. Set up two facing pages as shown (figure I-3). For the furnishings you already have (and plan to use), color swatches are needed for the chart. If none are available, cut appropriate colors from magazines, fabric, or other sources that match. To compile this information in a logical way, prepare your color chart in this manner: Cover both pages with the wall color or covering. This will represent the background color of the room. At each upper corner allow space for window fabric. Draw a strip across the bottom for carpeting and a narrow strip above it for woodwork. Draw in the shape of a bed or a couch and make spaces for chairs and any wooden furniture. Add smaller spaces for accessory pieces such as lamps, figurines, etc. Place existing samples on your chart. When shopping or researching, you will have a record of all the colors you must work with. As you select fabric to complete your color scheme, you may choose a large print that is not in proportion with the other color swatches—don't panic! Simply remove the other color samples from the chart and lay them on the print to see if they harmonize.

When you have selected samples that seem to work with your chart, be sure to test them with the colors in the room, since the pattern or color of the fabric or the light in the room may require something with a lighter tint or a darker shade.

Look at your swatches in both natural and artificial light; each type of light casts a different color and will change the shade or tint of the selected color.

Examine the completed chart carefully.

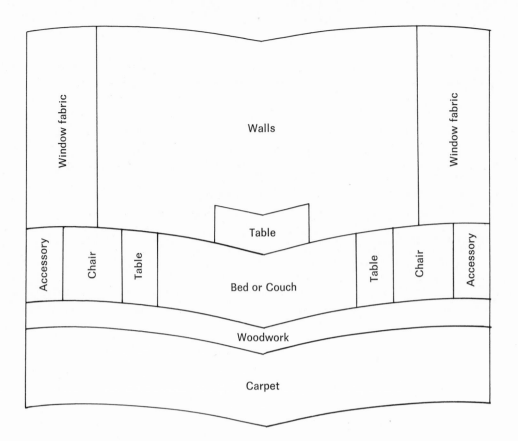

• Do you have a simple, contrasting color scheme of two colors? Or do you have three colors, called a triad?

• Do you have a monochromatic color scheme of one color used in the pure color with shades and tints?

• Do you have a closely related (analogous) color scheme in which two colors from the primary or secondary colors, such as blue and green, are used?

• Do you have an accenting color scheme in which neutral shades or pale tints are used throughout with accent colors that contrast or relate to the background?

• Perhaps you would like an eclectic color scheme, which combines aspects of several of the classic formats.

Be concerned with the total impact of the room. Experiment with different color schemes if you are not certain which color is best for the room. Hang a length of fabric or a colored sheet on the wall or near a window, or drape it over the furniture to see how that shade, tint, or design will look in the room. Live with it for a day or two. This should help you decide which color to use. The expense would be small com-

pared to the outlay for the full yardage, particularly if you are unhappy with the choice.

If your color scheme is working well but you feel that the room needs some pizzazz, perhaps all that is needed is a strong accent color. A few throw pillows, a framed fabric print, or a slip-covered chair may provide that added touch of color. Set the mood and sew a colorful room that's just right for you, your family, and your friends.

STEP SEVEN: GET STARTED!

Get ready to take the plunge. With pencil and paper in hand, start the actual step-by-step process. Begin with a rough scale drawing of your project and the room dimensions. Make a shopping list and then plan your project in stages. When you have compiled these vital statistics, review the chapters that will help expedite these crucial planning stages.

Scale Drawings
Make a rough scale drawing of your floor space and the four walls. Add the windows, doors, and all the measurements. Make small-scale shapes of the furniture and accessories you plan

to keep. Graph paper will make this step easier. You may prefer to skip the scale drawing and move the actual furniture around, but it's much easier to see the possibilities of rearrangement when you have all the information at your fingertips. Accurate measurements are a must. Imagine making a picture or wall hanging and finding out it is too large or small to make an impressive addition to your total plan.

Itemized Shopping List

Make a detailed list of every item you need to complete each article and complete your color scheme chart. Read through all the steps outlined in each chapter, making detailed notes and compiling the estimated fabric and trim yardages. Make tiny drawings of the number of fabric lengths you will use (two and one-half panels for each drapery, the lengths for the top of a bedspread, and the way the fabric must be cut for the drop, etc.) so you can allow for the fabric repeats. The more information you have, the easier your shopping will be. Add to your list all the notions you need: thread, needles, pins, cable cord, stiffening, stuffing materials, zippers, etc. Be sure to inventory your own supply of notions and itemize those needed and in what quantities.

Project Planning

Most working plans for any article require at least five steps: working out the design by making a pattern or using measurements; cutting the fabric; stitching the article together; pressing; and hanging or positioning the finished item in the room. When making several additions, you must do the five steps for each.

It doesn't matter if you're doing one small project, one large project, or a group of projects for your home—plan carefully to work in stages and your room will blossom right before your eyes. For example, nine individual projects were used to redecorate my living room. Some were extensive: creating a window treatment with a flat cornice, stationary draperies, and window seats; constructing a sleigh bed (see page 161) and then an island couch (see page 163); refinishing two end tables; constructing a coffee table (see page 167). Some were not nearly as extensive: sewing seven decorative pillows and bolsters, making a floor-length tablecloth, and covering five plastic Parsons tables. With planning, it took me four months to complete that one room in my "spare" time. You should be able to do the same—maybe even in less time, depending on how extensive your redecorating plan is.

Start your first project while you're still inspired with the various ideas found in this book. The pride of accomplishment and the pleasure you and your family or friends derive from one small project will help launch you on a more ambitious sewing program to decorate your home.

II
Window Variations—
The Easiest Home-Sewing
Project

Sew a dramatic statement for your windows—from stark simplicity with white sheer panels to luxurious draperies of silk with graceful swags, or any style in between. The straight hems and seams used to make most curtains and draperies, along with accurate measurements, are the only requirements, so even if you have little sewing experience, your first decorating project can be surprisingly easy. And if you are budget-minded, you can make a distinctive window treatment for considerably less than custom or ready-made designs would cost and you won't have to compromise on fabric or style. Think cost *versus* fashion; gracefully draped curtains created by many yards of inexpensive material will make more of an impact than the skimpy use of expensive fabric.

Decide what your windows should do for the room, and remember they are meant to provide light and air. Windows are the eyes of your home—a light in a window welcomes a guest, and on the inside windows are an expression of you. A personalized window variation will set the mood for the whole room. It can enhance a pictorial view or mask an unappealing one, minimize structural flaws or conceal heating and cooling units when not in use.

Consider the options and analyze your needs. There are hundreds of combinations possible—you are limited only by your imagination.

Think about the room. Are the window proportions to your liking or would you like to increase the height, width, or both? To add dimension to a low ceiling, extend curtains or draperies from floor to ceiling, or add width to a narrow window by framing it with fabric. Large rooms are the place for bold patterns and contrasting colors; small rooms need window treatments that blend with the walls to make the room seem larger.

Think energy, light, and acoustics. Tests show that shades and/or insulated draperies can reduce by as much as 21 percent the energy required to cool a room in the summer and can reduce by about 8 percent the amount of heat lost through windows in the winter. Sheer and loosely woven fabrics can cut down on daytime glare and help prevent fading of furniture coverings. Draperies, shades, blinds, and shutters control light and privacy. The ample use of fabric affects the acoustics in a room and helps reduce noise.

Do some research as suggested in Chapter I before starting. Then choose a window treatment from the following pages to match your decor. The instructions are given step by step to speed you on your way.

WINDOW TYPES

Nearly all window types have some kind of indentation when placed in a wall. The classic window has a wooden frame around the side and top edges and a little shelf, called a *sill,* at the bottom edge. The strip of wood that is placed underneath the sill for support is called the apron. Today, due to the cost of lumber, many builders are eliminating the wooden trim around the windows, finishing the window indentation the same as the walls.

It is important to know the type of window you have and how it was finished. Some windows will need special considerations. For example, casement windows that swing inward and sliding glass doors that serve as windows present a problem. Window fashions for these types must be hung in such a way that they won't interfere with the use of the window. Short, wide clerestory or ranch windows usually look best with sill-length curtains or draperies that don't overwhelm their size. Be aware that the type of window you have will affect the outcome of your finished sewing project.

1. *Double-hung sash:* Opens at both top and bottom. Each sash may have one pane or may have mullions holding smaller panes. They may be placed alone, in pairs, in groups of three, or in corners. Any type of window treatment may be used.

2. *Picture:* One large stationary framed window with a double-hung or casement window on each side for ventilation. Draw draperies and curtains should clear window for ventilation.

3. *Indented sliding glass:* These windows slide on tracks to open or close and usually have, instead of wooden trim, a plastered recess with a sill. Short café curtains and priscillas are good choices.

4. *Casement:* A window that opens inward or outward on hinges by hand or crank. Sheer curtains can be attached to window sash. Other styles of curtains or draperies should clear inward-swinging windows.

5. *Clerestory or ranch:* Wide shallow windows placed high for privacy. Sill- or apron-length curtains are a good choice.

6. *Jalousie or louvered:* A group of narrow horizontal windows that open to any desired angle by a crank. Treat as you would a double-hung sash window.

7. *Bow or bay:* Three or more windows set at angles to each other and extending beyond the main wall. Cut-to-measure rods are available for this type.

8. *Sliding glass doors:* Treat as a wall of glass, using extra-wide styles that will clear doors when used.

9. *French doors:* These also serve as windows and may open inward or outward. Inward-swinging doors need curtains or draperies that don't interfere; outward-swinging doors can be treated the same as any window.

10. *Windowed entrance doors:* These outer doors with windows let in light and also allow someone on the outside to look in. Curtain with fabric that will ensure privacy or allow you to look out to screen visitors.

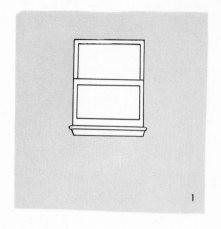

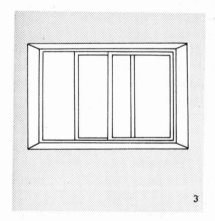

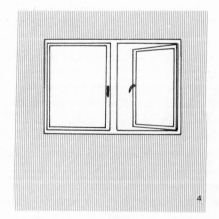

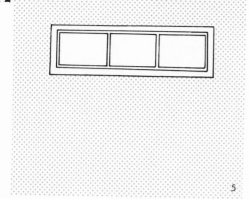

5

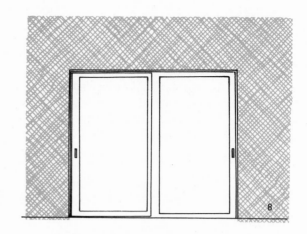

8

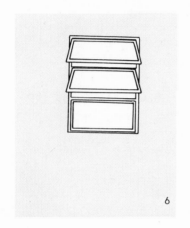

6

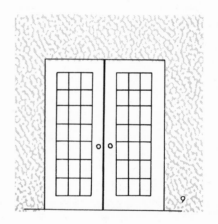

9

7

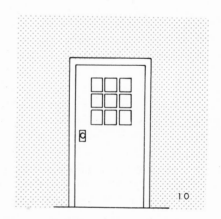

10

WINDOW TREATMENTS FOR
ANY LIFE-STYLE

Give your windows the decorative touch they deserve. Choose fabric that will work well with the type of curtain or draperies you plan to make. Color, too, will add a special note. Plain or fancy, casual or formal—select a window treatment just right for your home.

Curtains and draperies have some sewing procedures in common—they are made in pairs with narrow side hems, a wide bottom hem, and a top finish, called a *heading*, that is constructed so they can be hung on a rod.

Curtains have a tunnel of fabric stitched in place that is called a *casing*. It is open at both ends so the rod can be inserted. *Plain casings* have a fold at the top of the curtain that rests on the rod. *Casings with a heading* have a narrow fold of fabric stitched in place above the casing. The heading extends above the rod, with the stitching resting on the rod, and looks like a narrow ruffle when the curtain is gathered on a rod.

Curtains separated at the center and held to the side of the window with some kind of tie are called *tieback* curtains. Curtains that are placed on the lower sash of a double-hung window are called *sash* curtains. *Café* curtains are usually placed on the lower half of the windows, but they are placed on the outside of the indentation with fancy rods.

Pinch-pleated headings, hung on the rod by means of hooks, are frequently used for draperies, but today's ingenious decorators are using many other styles as well. Throughout the book, you will see draperies that have various hanging devices: pleater tape and hooks to look like stitched pinch pleats, casings with a heading, tabs, and others.

Cornices, swags, and valances are used at the top of a window as a decorative accessory, as a way of tying several windows together or to hide structural flaws. *Cornices* are usually wooden frames that are covered with fabric. *Valances* are made from fabric. These two window toppers can be as long or as short, simple or ornate, as you like. *Swags* are lengths of fabric draped loosely across the top of the window, with short ends hanging down at each side.

You may choose any type of heading, hem, or window top accessory for the curtains or draperies you plan to sew. Just be sure to allow enough fabric for the custom finish suggested.

Now that you have some idea what design elements are available, here are just some of the ways you can combine them for different effects.

1. *Glass curtains:* The primary function of this type of curtain is to diffuse light. Make from sheer fabric and hang directly in front of glass. When used alone, these curtains usually end at the sill. When used with draperies, they should be the same length as the draperies—sill, apron, or floor. Cornices, valances, and swags are used to top off sheers, too.

2. *Casement curtains:* These serve the same purpose, but they have rods at both ends of the

II-3

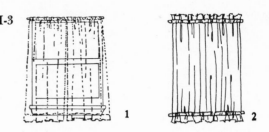

1

2

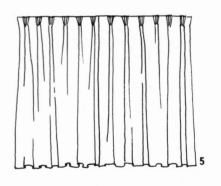

3

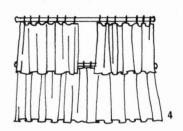

4

5

6

sheer panels. Use on windowed doors and casement windows. Or break with tradition and use them in the kitchen or bathroom—anywhere it pleases you.

3. *Tieback curtains:* The greatest variety of window treatments can be made with this style. The tops may be pleated, scalloped, or shirred and hung with rings or hooks, or they may have a casing with or without a heading. Measure from the top of rod to the proposed hem length. If they are hung with rings, however, measure from the bottom of ring.

Embellish the opening and hem edges with ruffles (self or contrasting), fringe, or decorative tape trims. Have them meet at the center; part them in the middle to show off a valance or fancy rod. A double rod will hold a valance across the entire window over tiebacks. Use them with matching or contrasting café or sash curtains across the lower half of the window. When tieback curtains are used over full-length sheer curtains or are made of the heavier decorator fabrics, they are correctly called *stationary draperies.*

Priscilla curtains are the favorite tieback for sheer fabric, with generous ruffled edges and the tops gathered on the rod with a casing. Sheers may meet at the center or crisscross when a double rod is used.

4. *Café curtains:* Hung from rings on metal or wooden rods, these straight panels can be plain or fancy. Café curtains originally were used on the lower half of the window for privacy, while allowing light to come in on the upper half. Café curtains are meant to be stationary, but they may be opened or closed by sliding the rings along the rod. Measure from the bottom of the rod to the desired hem length. Use with draperies, valances, swags, or in tiers. When making tiers, be sure that each panel hem overlaps the tier below it by the same amount.

Sash curtains: They are hung on the window sash next to the glass, with a sash or door curtain rod. Use a casing with or without a heading and measure from the top of the sash to the sill.

Draperies can help set the mood of your room from casual to formal; the style possibilities are endless. There are two basic types:

5. *Draw draperies:* These ensure privacy when closed and let the daylight stream in when opened.

6. *Stationary draperies:* These draperies are decorative and cannot be drawn.

Either type can be used alone or with sheer curtains, valances, or cornices. Stationary draperies can meet at the center or be straight panels at the outer window edge; either style can have tiebacks. The tops are usually pleated and hung from rings and tabs or are hooked into place. The hem can end at the sill, apron, or floor. Line draperies for extra insulation or, when used alone, to provide a continuity of color from the outside of your home.

Cornices, swags, and valances are three great means of camouflage (figure II-4). Use them to hide window top irregularities, to tie two or more windows together, to hide curtain and drapery fixtures, or, by placing them high above the window frame, to add height.

II-4

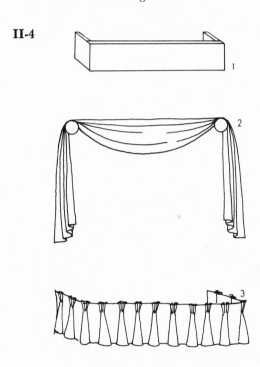

1. *Cornices* are usually made of wood or a combination of wood and buckram and decorated to match or contrast with curtains or draperies.

2. *Swags* are free-flowing folds of fabric draped over rods, pulled through rings, or hung over a decorative ornament.

3. *Valances* are short, decorative curtains usually hung on a rod. Elaborate valances of heavy fabric or heavily trimmed ones will need the support of a board attached to the wall with angle irons.

Shades, shutters, and screens are three more novel treatments that may be used alone or with other window dressings (figure II-5).

II-5

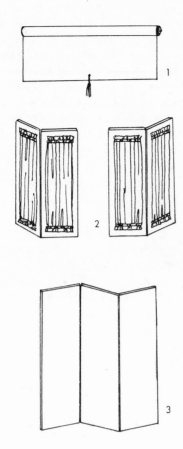

1. *Shades:* Made today with designer fabrics, the lowly roller shade has become an exciting decorating feature. Also increasing in popularity are the Austrian and Roman shades. If you are not familiar with the construction of these shades, turn to the shade section, page 60, for descriptions.

2. *Shutters:* May be used, with their own curtains, across and below the window to conceal cooling or heating units when not in use.

3. *Screens:* May be used in place of side panel draperies or to conceal an unsightly pipe or wall. They can be totally covered with fabric or have frames with curtains.

RODS, FIXTURES, AND ACCESSORIES

Rods play an important role in any window treatment. I am going to discuss the classic uses, but there's no law that says you can't use a thick café curtain rod at the top of your window to hold up tieback curtains or use a combination of several types of rods at the same window. How you like the result is the important factor. Curtain rods can be hidden or highly visible. Most rods are adjustable, wooden rods being the ex-

ception. The type you have selected and how you plan to place them must be considered before measuring for fabric. Be sure the rods will support the weight of the fabric.

Fixtures are the devices used to hold curtain and drapery rods in place, and accessories are the gadgets needed to hang the fabric. Fixtures may be decorative or hidden. Besides the clamp-type fixtures used at each end of the rod, you need additional support for both curtains and draperies when they cover wide areas. Select fixtures according to the type of rod and the fabric's weight; select accessories according to the style of heading you wish to use.

FLAT CURTAIN RODS: The most practical and economical way to hang glass or tieback curtains and stationary draperies. The rods are available in two types and two weights (figure II-6). Both the single and double rods come in standard and heavyweight. Choose the weight suitable for your fabric. Fixtures may be nailed to the window frame for lightweight fabrics. Screws will be needed for heavier fabrics. The only accessory used with these rods is a hook for draperies; the hook is inserted into the heading and clipped over the rod.

II-6

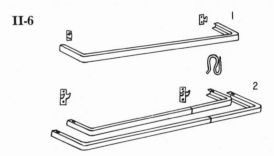

1. *Single rods* may also be used for tier curtains or to hang a valance above café or sash curtains.

2. *Double rods* are used to hang crisscross curtains, stationary draperies, and sheers, or curtains with a valance.

SASH AND DOOR RODS: Use for lightweight curtains that are hung close to the glass (figure II-7). There are two styles:
1. round
2. flat

II-7

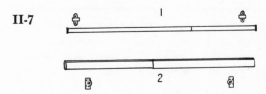

24

For casement curtains, French doors, and windowed entrance doors use two rods, one at the top and one at the bottom of the glass. Fixtures are usually mounted with nails.

CAFÉ RODS: Always visible, these rods can be as plain or as fancy as you desire (figure II-8). The three most popular types are made of white enameled metal, brass, and wood. The rods may be smooth or fluted; they come in a variety of thicknesses and with a wide choice of finials. In most cases, the finial extends beyond the window frame; there are, however, a few styles designed to be used on the inside edges of the frame closer to the window. Mount fixtures to window frame so the finials extend beyond it.

II-8

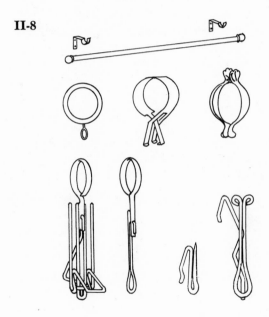

Accessories are a very important part of the café rod. There are rings of every size and shape. Some have eyes so you can use hooks in them or sew them to the fabric; others are clipped onto the fabric. There are also rings with hooks to be used with pleater and scallop tapes.

TRAVERSE RODS: A wide variety of styles, weights, and lengths are available and prices can range from quite modest to expensive (figure II-9). These rods have sliding brackets with holes, attached to the cords on the inside of the rod, that are used to hook the draperies in place. Extra-wide fabric panels will draw more easily if a cord tension pulley is installed on the baseboard or floor. Rods usually have a center opening so a panel hangs on each side of the window. One-way rods are also available for corner windows and doors.

1. *Hang-back rods:* When draperies are drawn open, you may want them to hang back from the window over the wall and frame, clearing the glass. Measure glass section of the window or door before purchasing rod. At the store, select a rod of approximate length and pull to the open position. Measure from the end slide to the tip of the overlap slide bar. Fabric folds will create a space between the slides—allow 1/4″–1/2″ for each space, depending on the fabric weight. Calculate the additional width. Add this measurement to the slide measurement and you will have the hang-back width needed to clear the glass. Double this width and add to the glass width for the rod length needed. For example: Slide and bracket measurement, 10″; fabric allowance for medium weight, 3″; hang-back doubled, 26″ + glass width 48″ = 74″. Purchase a rod that will extend to 74″.

2. *Conventional traverse rods:* Hidden when draperies are closed.

3. *Decorative traverse rods:* Meant to be seen.

There are several other types of traverse rods to consider:

4. *Traverse rod with flat curtain rod:* For draw draperies and glass curtains.

II-9

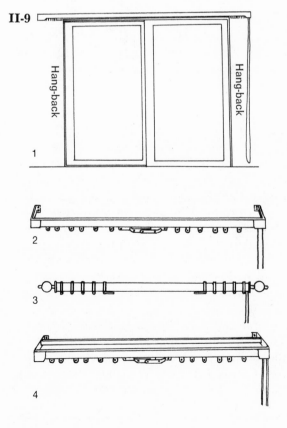

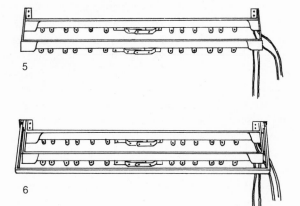

5

6

5. *Double traverse rods:* For opaque and sheer or insulation draw draperies.

6. *Double traverse rod with flat curtain rod:* For valance and two pairs of draperies.

Fixtures used to mount traverse rods must be attached securely to walls or ceiling. (Read installation tips on page 27). Accessories for traverse rods include hooks that are pinned onto curtain, others that are slipped under facing for self-pleated headings, or hooks designed for use with pleater tape.

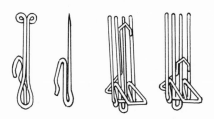

SPECIALTY RODS: For unique window fashions there are some very special rods (figure II-10):

1. *Wooden rods:* May be used with panel, tie-back, or café curtains or with stationary draperies. They may be indented or have finials; used with or without wooden rings.

2. *Swing rods:* Intended to be used in pairs. Mount at each side of the window frame. They cover only a small portion of the window when used for side panel draperies, but they should meet at the center of an inward-swinging casement window or cover each narrow window when used in pairs.

3. *Canopy rods:* Two single rods placed the desired distance apart with the shallower rod on the top and the deeper one on the bottom.

4. *Curved flat rods:* They hold curtains and stationary draperies in an arc and may be single or double.

5. *Tension rods:* These are gaining popularity for use with lightweight curtains. They are placed across an indented window and do not need fixtures.

II-10

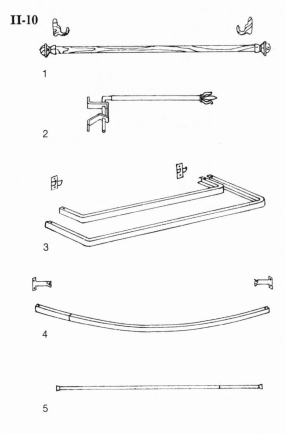

1

2

3

4

5

There are both traverse and flat curtain rods designed specifically for bay or bow windows and corner windows. They usually have to be specially ordered. A new bendable rod is also available that will bend to fit these windows.

Weights may be used on the hems of any type of curtain or drapery to help improve the hang of the fabric. 1) Round, 2) square, or 3) triangular sew-on weights, 4) covered weights that may be pinned or sewn on, and 5) tape-covered shot weights are available in various weights and sizes (figure II-11).

II-11

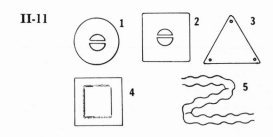

Installation Tips

Find out what kind of walls you have—hollow or solid—and what material the walls are made of. There are several types of anchoring devices that will enable you to attach the hardware to hollow, plaster, wallboard, metal, solid cement, or masonry walls (figure II-12).

If your walls are hollow, look for a wooden stud where you want to attach the rod fixtures. Either rap with your knuckle on the wall until you find the less hollow, more solid sound that indicates a stud, or buy a stud finder at the hardware store. If there are studs where you need them, just attach the rod fixtures with screws. (You can also use screws to attach rod fixtures to wooden window or door frames.) But if the studs are not where you must attach the rod fixtures, you will have to use hollow wall anchors or bolts. If you need some expert advice, you'll be able to get it from the hardware store, but don't go in during a rush hour if you need guidance. Here are the three most commonly used types of hollow wall anchoring devices.

II-12

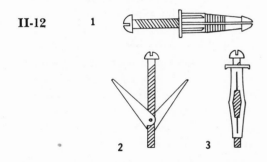

1. *Plastic hollow wall anchor:* For most situations, this is sufficient for plaster or wallboard. Drill a hole smaller than the screw; tap anchor into hole with hammer; place fixture over plug and insert screw. The anchor will spread, holding the screw in place.

You can also use a lead anchor in the same manner for cement or masonry walls.

Metal walls such as those found in recreational vehicles may need only a drilled hole.

2. *Toggle bolt:* For heavier draperies. To insert, drill a hole large enough to push bolt and toggles through; insert bolt through fixture; position fixture over hole and insert bolt into hole with wings held close to bolt. When bolt is tightened, toggles will open up and hold securely.

3. *Molly bolt:* For heavier draperies. To insert, drill a hole large enough to accommodate the slotted sheath; position fixture over hole; tap molly bolt in place with a hammer. As you

tighten the bolt, the sheath ends will draw together, spreading the sides to hold it securely.

FABRIC: A WINDOW'S BEAUTY SECRET

Fabric used at windows is like makeup on a woman's face: it must blend with or accent the basic color scheme and furnishings. Do you want the windows to blend with the walls as a blusher would on the cheeks or be accented as an eye enhanced with eyeliner? Fabric at windows can help to highlight good features or create a sense of space.

Proceed carefully as you look at fabrics. Be sure to review the fabric section in Chapter I before you make your final selection—quality and performance should be the deciding factor. For help in determining which fabric will be just right for your sewing project, consult the following categories. But don't be intimidated by the breakdown—some fabrics are suitable for many window styles.

GLASS CURTAINS: Dotted swiss, organdy, batiste, ninon, marquisette—sheer and semisheer fabrics are the classics; many types similar to those mentioned above are available under trade names, including new burn-out, open-weave, embroidered, and flock designs. Soft and crisp fabrics work equally well; make crisp fabrics double the width of the window; soft fabrics look great tripled.

CASEMENT CURTAINS: The same sheer and semisheer fabrics recommended for glass curtains are suitable. For privacy, on windowed entrance doors, use triple fullness whether fabric is soft or crisp.

TIEBACK CURTAINS: Use any sheer, light-, or medium-weight fabric your decor demands. You may even want to line fabrics that were not designed specifically for decorating, such as yard goods made for clothing or sheets.

CAFÉ CURTAINS: Fabric selection for café curtains is almost unrestricted. Try gingham, denim, ticking, chintz, or corduroy for a casual room, or consider one of many decorator fabrics, including satin, brocade, or velvet, in a formal setting; in fact, just about *any* sheer, semisheer, light- or medium-weight fabric may be used.

SASH CURTAINS: Usually made of sheer or semisheer fabrics.

DRAPERIES: The major requirement for drapery fabric is that it hang in loose, even folds. Semisheers, open-weaves, or light, medium, and heavy fabrics are used. Sheers are often made as draw draperies instead of glass curtains and used in combination with either stationary or decorative draw draperies so you can have an unobstructed view or cut down glare when necessary.

Lining will extend the life of any fabric and give your windows a uniformity of color when viewed from the outside. It will also prevent light from showing through loose weaves so the color will be more pronounced. Off-white or eggshell lightweight cotton sateen is the classic fabric for lining, but any durable lightweight lining that does not interfere with the hang of the draperies may be used. Make sure the lining has the same cleaning requirements as the drapery fabric. For washables, use preshrunk lining or shrink it according to the instructions in Chapter VIII.

Insulated lining fabric is available, but it is slightly rigid; you may want to use a double traverse rod with the insulated fabric made into draperies and used next to the window behind decorative overdraperies.

CORNICES, SWAGS, AND VALANCES: Adornments at the top of windows may be simple or formal. Use with matching or contrasting fabrics; these narrow trimmers may have decorative edges, too. Cornices may be covered with closely woven fabric of the same weight as the curtains or draperies. If your curtain fabric is sheer, use an opaque contrasting fabric for the cornice. Swags may be used alone or with any type of curtain or drapery. Fabric should drape and cascade in smooth, rounded folds. Fabrics suggested for tie-back curtains or draperies are good choices. Valances are made of the same fabric as curtains and draperies when hung with a rod and may be smooth or gathered on the rod as the fabric dictates. Fabric used for intricately draped or gathered valances should have the properties needed to achieve softly rounded draped folds or gathered ripples.

SHADES, SHUTTERS, AND SCREENS: When decorating with these unique devices, select your fabric carefully. There is a wide fabric choice for shades. Roller and Roman shades work best when made of tightly woven cotton, linen, rayon, or blends in a medium-weight fabric. Austrian shades should be made of sheer, semisheer, or lightweight fabrics that gather nicely.

For shutters with curtained inserts, choose a fabric that blends with the walls or a bright colored one. Semisheer or lightweight fabrics are suitable.

Screens can be solid or have curtained inserts. Solid screens should be covered with tightly woven medium- to moderately heavyweight fabrics; for screens with curtailed inserts use light- or medium-weight fabric that gathers softly on a rod.

MEASURE WINDOWS ACCURATELY

Precise measurements are needed to ensure good results. When making curtains and draperies that hang free at the bottom edge, there are three lengths that should be considered for the most aesthetic proportions: The hems should just touch the window sill or floor, or they should be parallel with the bottom edge of the apron. If your window does not have an apron and you want to use this length, have the hem fall 2"–3" below the bottom edge of the window. Floor-length curtains may end at the top of a baseboard heating unit to prevent heat loss, but that length is visually less attractive.

The measurements described below will be used to calculate the yardage needed for each pair of curtains or draperies. Some measurements are standard while others will change with each style. The measurements explained in this section also appear in a chart that follows and have corresponding numbers for faster calculating.

The finished length and width measurements must be established first, although they are not numbered in that order on the chart. That way the specific allowances for rods, style, and window variations can be added to these primary figures in a more logical order for the chart.

• Mount rods before taking any measurements.

• Use a metal tape measure or a folding wooden ruler; a cloth tape may stretch and make your measurements inaccurate.

• Measure every window that will have the same treatment, even if they seem to be the same size.

• Write down each measurement as you work —errors can be costly.

Finished Length Measurement (Measurement #1)
Curtains and draperies are made in three lengths: sill, bottom edge of apron, or floor (figure II-13). Each length complements structural lines.

Finished Width Measurement (Measurements #8, 9, and 10)
Measure front span of rod between the outer rounded or square corners (figure II-14). Measure each return (ends between outer corner and win-

II-13

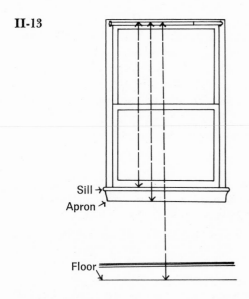

Sill →
Apron ↗

Floor ↙

II-14

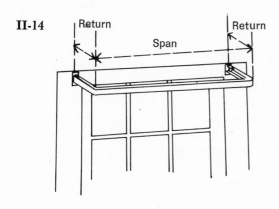

Return | Span | Return

dow frame or wall). Add the two return measurements to the span measurements for the width needed.

Rod and Window Variation Measurements

For some rods and windows, you must make adjustments to arrive at the correct finished measurement.

DOUBLE RODS: Measure the width of both rods when using a valance with curtains.

SASH AND DOOR RODS: These rods are mounted close to the glass and do not need a return measurement. Measure length as instructed in figure II-13; measure width between brackets.

CASEMENT WINDOWS, FRENCH DOORS, AND WINDOWED ENTRANCE DOORS: Measure the length from the top of the upper rod to the bottom of the lower rod.

CAFÉ CURTAIN RODS: These rods do not need a return measurement. Position lower rod first; place it at the center of window or glass, at the

lower edge, or anywhere in between these two positions. For two or more tiers, mount top rod on the wall above the window frame. The finials should be lined up along the frame edge. If you are using tieback curtains or stationary draperies, you may want to extend the top rod at each end so the curtain or draperies will not hang over the café side edges. Measure the length for the lowest tier from the bottom of the slider portion of rings or clips to the desired hem length. Any remaining tier lengths should be measured from the bottom of the slider portion of rings or clips to the same spot on rod below. Rods may be exposed if you like. Measure widths between finials. For indented rods, measure widths between rod ends.

TRAVERSE RODS: These rods should be placed at least 4″ above the glass. For conventional traverse rods, measure as instructed in figures II-13 and II-14. To the length measurement, add at least ½″ so draperies will extend above top of rod. The length measurement may change depending on the type of hook (or pleater tape) used. To determine what the amount of change is, place the hooks in the slider holes on the rod. They may extend above the rod or drop below it. Measure the amount the hooks are above or below the rod, and adjust the measurement for the finished length accordingly (measurement 1). Measure the length of the overlapping and underlapping slider bars (that overlap when the draperies are closed). Add these numbers to the width measurements (measurements 8, 9, and 10). For decorative traverse rods, measure from bottom of the slider ring to the desired hem length. To the width measurement, add the measurements of both the overlapping and underlapping bars. For one-way traverse rods, measure width across the span between outer corners and one return.

WOODEN RODS: Rods should be placed about 4″ above the glass when used at the top of the window. For café curtains, position rod as directed in *café curtain rods*. For length measurements determine hem length first. Start measuring from the top of the rod if you are not using rings and from the bottom of the rings if you are using them. Panel, tieback, and café curtains do not need a return for their width measurement; measure between finials or rod ends. For stationary drapery width measurement, measure rod span between finials.

SWING RODS: For the length measurement, measure each rod as instructed in figure II-13.

For panel drapery width measurement, measure rod span. For casement curtains width measurement, measure rod span: do not measure return.

CANOPY RODS: To find the length, measure from the top of shallow rod to bottom of the deeper rod. To find the width, measure the deeper rod as instructed in figure II-14.

CURVED RODS: Measure the width from wall to wall around the curve.

TENSION RODS: Measure length as instructed in figure II-13. For the width, measure across rod between the sides of the window indentation.

When the measuring is completed, some modifications must be made. Allowances for the top headings and lower hems must be added to the finished length, and fullness, seam allowances (if needed), and side hems added to the finished width.

The actual yardage required cannot be calculated until you have selected the fabric, since widths may vary from 35″ to 70″ and fabric design repeats must be considered as well.

Total Length Requirement

To the finished length measurement add the amount needed to finish the heading, the bottom hem edge, and, if necessary, the amount needed for each fabric design repeat. Extended trims and ruffles will require some length adjustments, too. The total length calculation is for one panel.

Heading Finishes (Measurement #2)

Casings should be at least ½″ deeper than the rod is wide; adjust suggested measurements, if necessary.

CURTAINS, PLAIN CASINGS: Add 2″ (1½″ for the casing and ½″ to turn under the raw edge).

CURTAINS, CASING WITH A HEADING: Add 4″ (2″ for a 1″ heading—doubled—with a 1½″ casing and ½″ to turn under raw edge).

CASEMENT CURTAINS: Two casings and two headings—this finish is needed at both the top and bottom of the curtain to be anchored with two sash rods for casement windows, French doors, and windowed entrance doors. Add 8″ for the two casings with headings. Each heading will be 1″ wide (doubled), the casings 1½″ wide, and each has ½″ to turn under raw edges.

CAFÉ CURTAINS: For a 3″ plain or self-pleated heading in opaque fabrics, allow 3½″ (½″ to turn under raw edge). For sheers, allow 6″ (3″ for heading and 3″ turn-under for support). When using straight pleater tape, add 1″; for

scalloped pleater tape add ½″; when making your own scallops, add 3½″ (3″ for heading plus ½″ to turn under raw edge).

DRAPERIES: For lined draperies add ½″ for a seam allowance. For unlined draperies with pleater tape, add 1″. For self-made pleats, use stiffening 3″ or 4″ wide and add 3½″ or 4½″ to match stiffening width with ½″ to turn under raw edge.

Hem Finishes (Measurement #3)

The allowances needed for hems vary with the type of trim or finish you're using. Hems are usually 3″ deep to add some weight at the bottom.

SHEER FABRIC CURTAINS: Add 6″, for a 3″ hem and 3″ to turn under to support the hem.

OPAQUE FABRIC CURTAINS: Add 3½″, for a 3″ hem with ½″ to turn under raw edge.

DRAPERIES: Add 6″, for a 3″ hem and 3″ turn-under to stiffen hem. It's also a good thing to allow this much in case there is unanticipated shrinkage when draperies are cleaned. For very long draperies in heavier fabrics, use a deeper hem (up to 5″) with the same amount for a turn-under.

Trim and Ruffles that Extend Beyond the Panel Hem Edges (Measurement #4)

Adjustments must be made in the length requirement. Subtract the trim width (portion that extends beyond the straight edge or seam allowance), then add ½″ for applied trim or ruffle or 1″ for a plain self-made or purchased ruffle.

Fabric Design Repeats (Measurement #6)

This must be decided at the time the fabric is selected. The designs must be matched on each panel needed to make a pair of curtains or draperies. Examine the fabric design. Make a fold from selvage to selvage at the top and bottom of the design feature that is repeated along the full length of the bolt. Measure the distance between the folds: add this amount to the length of each panel.

Total Width Requirement

Now that you have established the exact length of each panel, you will need to calculate the total width requirement. To the finished width measurement add the fullness, the side hems, and the seam allowances for each seam needed to join fabric widths together to make each half of a pair of curtains or draperies. Extended trims and ruffles will require some width adjustment after the fullness is determined.

Fullness (Measurement #12)

The rule for fullness is to double the finished measurement—anything less will result in skimpy, unattractive curtains or draperies. For light- and medium-weight fabrics, double the width measurements; for heavy and semisheer fabrics, allow two and one-half times the measurements; for sheers, triple the measurement.

Pleater tape headings will save time and a lot of aggravation when pleated curtains and drapery tops are desired. Purchase tape and hooks before you establish the exact fullness requirement. For café curtains and other curtains or draperies without returns and overlaps, buy the regular pocket tape 2, 2½, or 3 times the rod span, plus 6″ for each window. For curtains or draperies with returns and overlaps, buy regular pocket tape, 2 times the rod span plus ½ yard for each window. For extra fullness, buy multi-pocket tape 2½″ or three times the rod span, plus ½ yard for each window.

Pleat tape with hooks for half the rod (figure II-15). A pocket is needed at each end of the tape plus a ½″ turn-back. Pin turned-back ends in place.

1. For draw draperies, include the return and overlap. Stationary draperies that meet at the center need only the return. For café curtains, a return or overlap is not usually used.

II-15

2. For draw draperies, a pleat should be placed at each front corner of rod by the return and at the spot where the overlapping bar begins.

3. For stationary draperies and curtains, place a pleat at the front of the corner by the return and about 2″ from the center opening edge.

4. For café curtains skip two pockets at each end and then divide pleats evenly.

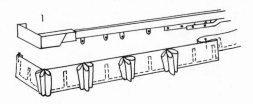

Remove hooks and trim tape turn-back to ½″. Measure tape between the turn-back ends to determine fullness needed for each half of a curtain or drapery pair.

For self-pleated headings, plan the fullness needed for each pleat and space now for one-half of a curtain or drapery pair. For draw draperies, a pleat should be placed at each front corner of a rod by the return and at the spot where the overlapping bar begins (see figure II-15, step 2). For stationary curtains and draperies with a return, place a pleat at the front corner by the return and 2″ from center openings (see figure II-15, step 4).

Pinch and French pleats may be 4″–5″ deep (4″ is average); box pleats are 4″ deep. Spaces may be anywhere from 2½″ to 4½″ wide (4″ is the most commonly used measurement), depending on the fullness desired. Measure rod span between corner and center, allowing for overlapping at opening for draw draperies. Subtract return and center opening space, then divide remaining width into equal spaces; add amount for each pleat. (See figures II-27 and II-28 for actual construction of pleats.)

Trim and Ruffles that Extend Beyond the Center Opening Edges (Measurement #13)

After you have determined fullness, subtract 2 times the trim width (portion that extends beyond the straight edge or seam allowance) from the total fullness requirement; then add 1″ for applied trims or ruffles or 2″ for a plain ruffle. (See Chapter VIII, page 205 for construction.)

Side Hems (Measurement #14)

On each pair of curtains or draperies you will have four side hems: one on the left, two in the middle where the panels meet, and one on the right.

For opaque fabrics, add 8″—1½″ for each hem with ½″ to turn under raw edge or to use as a seam allowance when lining draperies.

For sheer fabrics, add 12″—1½″ for each hem and 1½″ to turn under raw edge for support.

For casement curtains, add 2″—½″ for a hem on each side of the panel with ½″ to turn under the raw edges.

For curtains that will have center opening edges finished with extended trim or ruffles, divide the amount needed for sheer or opaque fabrics in half.

Seam Allowances (Measurement #16)

When you need several fabric widths to make each curtain or drapery, half the fabric must be joined with seams. If the selvages are flat and not distorted, add 1″ for each seam. Check fabric at store to see if unprinted edges may be wider than ½″. If they are, double the measurement and add that amount for each seam. For unusable selvages, allow 2″ for each seam. Trim away selvage and then use a French seam (see Chapter VIII, page 202).

Some fabric widths may not require a seam to make a pair. Frequently, one and one-half fabric widths are needed. Join the half-widths to the edges that will hang near the frame and use the two whole widths for the center meeting edges.

MAKE AN ESTIMATED YARDAGE GUIDE

The measurements you will calculate for steps A, B, and C should be worked out on paper in a logical manner so you can take this information with you when purchasing the fabric. If there is time, you may want to do Step D at the store or with help of the salesclerk. Use the guide below to compile your statistics.

Step A: Length
1. Finished length   _____
2. Heading finish   + _____
3. Hem finish (if needed)   + _____
4. Subtract extension width of trim or ruffles then add seam allowances (if needed)   − _____
5. Fabric panel length   = _____
6. Repeat length (if needed)   + _____
7. Total fabric panel length   = _____

Step B: Width
8. Rod span width   _____
9. Return width (if needed)   + _____
10. Overlap width (if needed)   + _____
11. Finished width   = _____

Step C: Fullness
12. Multiply finished panel width by 2, 2½, or 3. For pleats, use pleater tape length or predetermined fullness for self-made pleats   _____
13. Subtract extension width of trim or ruffle (2 times) for center opening edges   − _____
14. Side hems (4 hems for plain edges; for panels with extended trim or ruffles, allow for 2 standard width hems at the side edges and 2 seam allowances to apply trim)   + _____
15. Total width needed for each window (without seam allowances)   = _____

Step D: Fabric Yardage
16. Determine the number of fabric widths needed for each window by dividing total width (item 15) by your fabric width. For a partial width, purchase a full width of fabric. If you are making more than one pair, the extra will be utilized. Or use it to give added fullness, or for pillows, etc.

_____ ÷ _____ = _____
width (item 15)   fabric width   number of widths needed

17. Divide the total width (item 15) by 2. Each half will make a pair of curtains or draperies.

_____ ÷ 2 = _____
width (15)   width of each single curtain or drapery

18. Add seam allowances, as directed, for each seam and adjust the width (item 17) needed to make each extra-wide single curtain or drapery.

_____ + _____ = _____
width (17)   seam allowance   extra-wide single curtain or drapery width

NOTE: Adjust fullness, if necessary, for several inches only.

19. To find out how much fabric is needed in inches for each pair of curtains or draperies, multiply the length (item 5 or 7) by the number of fabric widths (item 17 or 18).

_____ × _____ = _____
length (5 or 7)   number of fabric widths (17 or 18)   total inches needed of fabric

20. To convert inches to yards, divide the total number of inches by 36.

$$\underline{\hspace{3cm}} \div 36 = \underline{\hspace{3cm}}$$

| fabric in inches | yards of fabric |

NOTE: Purchase about ¼ yard extra fabric for straightening the ends. When figuring yardage, select the nearest eighth-yard.

Example

One pair of finished draperies 48″ wide and 87″ long made up in 54″-wide fabric, or two twin-size sheets (72″ × 108″).

1. 87″
2. 87″ + 1″ = 88″
3. 88″ + 6″ = 94″
4. not needed
5. 94″
6. not needed
7. not needed
8. 39″
9. 39″ + 6″ = 45″
10. 45″ + 3″ = 48″
11. 48″
12. 48″ × 2″ = 96″
13. not needed
14. 96″ + 8″ = 104″
15. 104″
16. 104″ ÷ 54″ = 1 width + 50″ (2 fabric widths)
17. 104″ ÷ 2 = 52″
18. not needed
19. 94″ (item 5) × 2 (item 16) = 188″
20. 188″ ÷ 36 = 5 yards 8″ + 9″ = 17″

TOTAL: 5½ yards of 54″-wide fabric. When using twin-size sheets, you will have excess fabric from both sheets.

Example

One pair of finished glass curtains 90″ wide and 90″ long, with doubled hems, made up in 48″-wide fabric, or four twin-size sheets (72″ × 108″).

1. 90″
2. 90″ + 4″ = 94″
3. 94″ + 6″ = 100″
4. not needed
5. 100″
6. not needed
7. not needed
8. 86″
9. 86″ + 4″ = 90″
10. not needed
11. 90″
12. 90″ × 3″ = 270″
13. not needed
14. 270″ + 12″ = 282″
15. 282″
16. 282″ ÷ 48″ = 5 widths + 42″ (6 fabric widths)
17. 282″ ÷ 2 = 141″ (2 seams for each curtain)
18. 5 widths 42″ + 4″ for seam allowances = 46″ (6 widths)
19. 100″ (item 5) × 6 (item 18) = 600″
20. 600″ ÷ 36 = 16 yards 24″ + 9″ = 33″

TOTAL: 16⅞ yards of 48″-wide fabric. When using twin-size sheets, you will have very little fabric left over.

Example

One pair of finished tieback curtains with self-fabric ruffles with a heading, 3″ extension, and tiebacks; 40″ wide and 50″ long, made up in 45″-wide fabric, or one double bed sheet (81″ × 108″).

1. 50″
2. 50″ + 4 = 54″
3. not needed
4. 54″ − 2½″ = 51½″
5. 51½″
6. not needed
7. 51½″
8. 40″
9. not needed
10. not needed
11. 40″
12. 40″ × 2 = 80″
13. 80″ − 5 = 75″
14. 75″ + 4 = 79″
15. 79″
16. 79″ ÷ 45″ = 1 width + 34″ (2 fabric widths)
17. 79″ ÷ 2 = 39½″
18. not needed
19. 51½″ (item 5) × 2 (item 16) = 103″
20. 103″ ÷ 36 = 2 yards 31″ + 9″ = 40″

TOTAL: 3⅛ yards.

Additional fabric is needed for ruffles (see Chapter VIII, page 205) and tiebacks (see figure II-19). To find the ruffle strip length, add the panel length (item 5) 51½″ to single curtain width (item 17) 39½″ = 91″. For 1½ fullness, multiply 1½ × 91″ = 136½″ for each curtain. For both curtains, a strip 4½″ wide and 273″ long is needed. Divide 273″ by the fabric width 45″ = 6 fabric widths. 4½″ × 6 (fabric widths) = 27″ or ¾ yard. From the strip cut away from the curtains, cut 4 strips 3″ wide and 21″ long for 2″ by 20″ finished tiebacks.

TOTAL: 3⅛ yards for curtains + ¾ yards for ruffles = 3⅞ yards of 45″-wide fabric. When using a sheet, you will have some excess fabric.

CURTAINS: PLAIN AND FANCY

For your first curtain project, start with a plain, straight-edged style. As your proficiency improves, add trimming details and other decorator touches. The first curtains described are called glass curtains: they are sheer, unadorned panels that make an excellent first project because they're so straightforward. The tieback curtains, which are explained on page 39, start with the same straight panels but use a narrower turn-under from the hem. Immediately following the tieback curtains, you will find café curtains—these two styles are great for beginners, too.

You don't have to limit yourself to sheer or semisheer fabrics; sheets are an excellent mate-

ABOVE: *White accents are used by designer Carol Weil to broaden the limited horizons of a small bedroom that must accommodate twin beds. Charming sill-length embroidered fabric by Kent-Bragaline, Inc., is tied back with grosgrain ribbon to show the Graber Manufacturing Company's "Bolero" window shades. The white heirloom bedspreads are topped off with ruffled pillow shams and color-coordinated crocheted afghans.*

LEFT: *A simple tieback curtain edged with jumbo-sized rickrack and hung on a wooden rod is used by designer Shirley Regendahl to complement the new "Sunchex" shade by Joanna Western Mills Co. She glues on medium- and baby-sized rickrack to form the diamond pattern on the shade. The rosettes are made from rickrack. Take note all you needleworkers: These shades may be decorated with embroidery. A wicker chair with matching seat cushion helps to brighten the corner, too.*

Designer Mary Kay Baldwin uses the simple elegance of Priscilla curtains as companions for one wing chair slipcover made from Waverly Fabrics' "Milford" print.

35

Crisp greens and chalk whites are used by designer Abbey Darer to create this garden look. Plain paneled tieback curtains are hung on a matching fabric-covered wooden rod; the same fabric is used to trim the "Plissé" window shade by Joanna Western Mills Co. The double-clothed dining table is first covered with a round cloth with cording for a hem edge, then topped with a scalloped square of seersucker that looks very much like the shade that is trimmed to match.

Designer Michael Sherman pairs pinch-pleated draw draperies made from
an abstract shell design by Connaissance Fabric, Inc., with Breneman's
"Kristan" window shade accented with Conso trim. The same fabric is used
to line the bookshelves and panels on the storage wall.

The traditional entrance hall is dramatized by designer Mary Kay Baldwin
with Waverly Fabrics' "National Toile" for the pinch-pleated stationary
tieback draperies over sheer glass curtains and for the casement curtain for
the window alongside the door.

rial to use for these styles. When using sheets for plain, straight-hemmed panels, use the wide sheet hem as the bottom hem of the curtains. Cut sheets to the proper length and width. Then turn the side hems over the wide hem, using the selvage edges as an inner hem edge, if they have been retained. Make the heading, and the panel is completed. The striped tieback curtains with matching valance shown in Chapter VII, page 166, were made with three sheets. The ruffled sheet hem was used for the opening edges, with plain hems on the side and bottom edges, and a plain casing at the top under the valance. The valance was made with the ruffled sheet hem as the bottom edge, plain side hems, and a casing with a heading at the top. The excess sheet fabric was used to cover the desk.

NOTE: If your floors are uneven, it's a good idea before completing floor-length curtains to make the heading first and just pin the hem in place. Make any adjustments and then stitch hem in place as instructed.

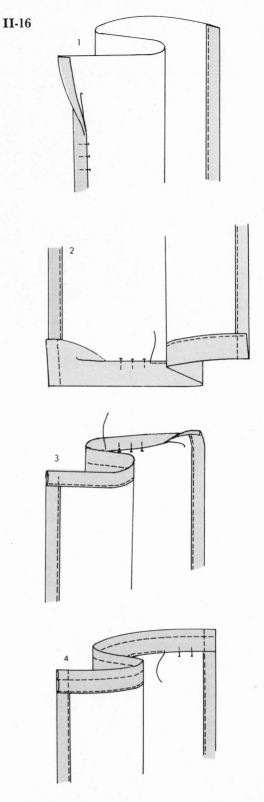

II-16

Glass Curtains

Sheer, free-hanging, unlined panels hung from flat rods, in pairs, with a casing at the top and hems at the side and bottom edges.

Most sheer and semisheer fabrics are easy to sew. Use a size 11 or 14 machine needle and polyester thread. For fabrics that do not feed easily through the machine, hold the material taut in front and back of the needle while stitching, being careful not to stretch or distort fabric. To join fabric widths for wider curtains, trim away selvages and make narrow French seams (see Chapter VIII).

CONSTRUCTION (figure II-16): Shrink fabric, if necessary (see Chapter VIII, page 206). Straighten ends. Cut out as many panels as needed. Stitch any seams needed for wide panels.

1. Make side hems first. Turn the long side edges 3″, wrong sides together; press. Open hem allowance and turn in the raw edge to meet the fold; press hem flat; pin. To hold hems in place, stitch close to inner fold. Hems may be blind-stitched with special sewing machine attachment or hand-sewn with slip-stitch method #1 (Chapter VIII, page 206).

2. Make bottom hem by turning up lower edge 6″; press. Turn in raw edge to meet fold; press again. Pin hem in place, making sure ends do not show on the right side of the long side hems. Stitch close to fold.

3. Make a plain casing if your curtain tops will be totally covered by stationary draperies, cornice, or valance. Turn down top edge 2″ (or predetermined amount); press. Turn in raw edge ½″; press and pin, making sure side edges do not

show on the right side of the curtains. Stitch close to inner fold to form casing.

4. Make a casing with a heading if your curtains will be used alone. Turn down top edge 3″ (or one-half the predetermined heading width plus the casing width); press. Turn in raw edge ½″; press and pin, making sure side edges do not show on the right side of the curtains. Stitch 1″ from outer fold to form heading and again along inner folded edge to form casing.

Casement Curtains

These curtains have a casing with a heading at the top and bottom edges with narrow side hems. One continuous panel is used for each casement window, French door, or windowed entrance door.

CONSTRUCTION (figure II-17): Shrink fabric, if necessary. Straighten ends. Cut out panel as directed.

1. Make side hems first. Turn in long side edges 1″, wrong sides together; press. Turn in raw edge to meet fold; press and pin. Stitch side hems in place close to inner fold.

2. Turn in top and bottom edges 3″; press. Turn in raw edges ½″; press and pin, making sure ends do not show on the right side of the curtain. Stitch close to inner fold to form casing.

II-17

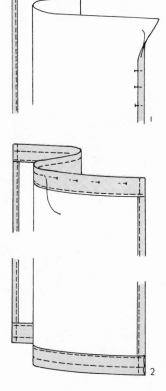

Test heading width before stitching by placing a row of pins 1″ from folds at the top and bottom. Insert rods and hang. Curtains should be taut; adjust pins if necessary. Make headings narrower or wider, dividing adjustment equally between the top and bottom. Remove rods. Form headings by stitching along line marked with pins.

Tieback Curtains

Expand the basic techniques used to make plain glass curtains. Tie back the panels away from the center of the window to form graceful folds with fabric, ribbon, rope, or decorative clips. You can also decorate the center opening and hem edges with purchased trim, fringe, or ruffles or with self- or contrasting ruffles you have made. Plain sheer, semisheer, or opaque panels made like glass curtains may become tieback curtains with the simple addition of a tieback.

If trims extend beyond the center opening and hem edges, be sure to make adjustments in the length and width requirements before you cut.

If you are making curtains with ruffles, be sure to consider the fabric weight when planning the fullness. For sheer, semisheer, and lightweight fabrics, make the ruffles two times the finished length and width for fullness. For other fabrics, make 1½ times the finished length and width. Calculate the additional yardage required and add to curtain yardage for self-ruffles.

Style variations are unlimited—plain or fancy edges and tiebacks; top with a casing and heading or make a plain casing to be used with a cornice, swag, or valance; opening edges may meet at the center, or they may be separated and used with a valance or ruffle, or the exposed rod may be covered to match curtains; one of the decorative top edges recommended for café curtains can be made and hung with rings from round wooden or metal rods.

CONSTRUCTION: Shrink fabric, if necessary. Straighten ends. Cut out as many panels as needed. Cut out tiebacks, interfacing (see figure II-19), and self-trim, if used.

1. For plain-edged panels (figure II-18), stitch side hems in place by turning in the long edges 2″, wrong sides together; press. Turn in raw edges ½″; press and pin in place, making sure ends do not show on the right side of the curtain.

2. Stitch bottom hem in place.

NOTE: Any trim that becomes a part of finished

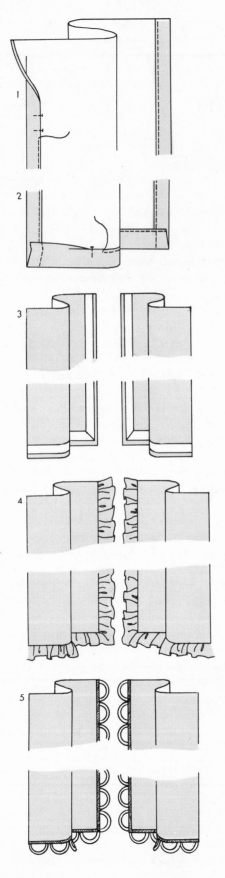

edge must be stitched in place along center opening and bottom edges after hemming and before making the casings (figure II-18).

3. For decorative band trims, stitch in place along the center opening and bottom edges before making the casing. Choose appropriate casing and make same as for glass curtains.

4. Attach purchased or self-made ruffles to center opening and bottom edges in same manner.

5. Attach fringe or any other extended trim to center opening and bottom edges as directed in Chapter VIII, page 201.

When center opening and bottom edges are finished and the casings are completed, make tiebacks to match or contrast. Self-fabric tiebacks are the favorite; long bands with buttonholes or rings to hook behind the curtains are easy to construct. Make tiebacks as narrow or as wide as you like. Use plain or decorate to match curtains. Calculate the additional fabric required for either self- or contrasting fabric.

To make two 2″-wide finished tiebacks (figure II-19): cut four 3″-wide fabric strips at least one-half as long as the finished width measurement and two 3″-wide interfacing strips the same length.

II-19

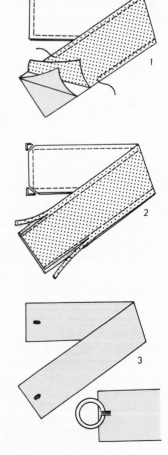

1. Place two fabric strips right sides together, then place one interfacing strip over them. Pin all three layers together along the long edges. Stitch long edges and one end in a ½″ seam, leaving one end open for turning and adjustment.

2. Trim interfacing seam allowance close to stitching and trim across corners to eliminate bulk. Turn right side out through open end; press.

When curtains are completed and hung, wrap tieback around curtain and anchor to frame with a pin. Reposition or shorten tieback until the desired effect is achieved. Mark position for hook.

3. Turn in raw edges of unfinished ends ½″; pin. Stitch folded edges together. Make a machine buttonhole at the center of each end or sew on a small bone ring. Secure to the wall with a cup hook.

Café Curtains

These versatile window coverings make the strongest statement at the top—pleated, scalloped, or plain with rings or fabric loops on a decorative rod. The hem edges are usually straight, but there is no reason why you can't add ruffles or scallops. Fabrics can be anything from sheer to medium-heavy decorator fabrics. If café curtains are used with lined stationary draperies, they should be lined, too, using the same technique. Stiffening (called crinoline) sometimes is used in café curtain headings to support most fabrics. Use organdy or permanent-press interfacing for sheer fabric stiffening. Select the weight and width most compatible with your fabric or as directed for the style heading. Café curtains may be used alone, in tiers, or with swags, valances, shades, and screens.

Shrink fabric if necessary. Straighten ends. Cut out as many panels as needed. Cut out any companions, such as valances or swags, too.

CONSTRUCTION WITH PLAIN HEADING (figure II-20): Prepare each panel by pressing the side and bottom hems into position. For opaque fabrics, turn in side edges 2″; press. Turn under raw edges ½″; press again. Turn up hem 3½″; press. Turn under raw edges ½″; press. For sheer fabrics, turn in side edges 3″; press. Turn under raw edge to meet fold; press again. Turn up hem 6″; press. Turn under raw edges to meet fold; press.

Cut a strip of 3″-wide stiffening, as long as each panel is wide between side hem creases. Open side hems.

1. For opaque fabrics, place one edge of stiffening ½″ from top of panel; pin. Stitch stiffening to fabric ¼″ from the inner edge. Turn raw edge over remaining stiffening edges; stitch in place.

2. Turn side edges over stiffening along

II-20

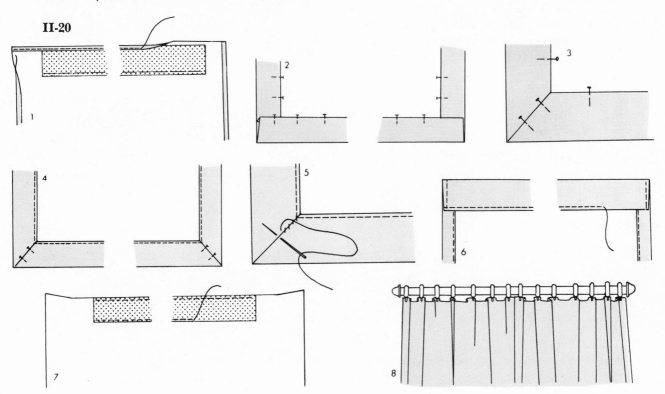

41

pressed edge; pin. Turn up hem to pressed position; pin.

3. At corners, turn in hem ends on an angle to form a miter where side and hem edges meet; pin.

4. Stitch side and hem edges to curtain in one continuous stitching.

5. Slip-stitch miter fold in place. Miter may be stitched in place by machine. Hems may be blindstitched with special machine attachment or slip-stitched in place (see method #1 in Chapter VIII, page 206).

6. Turn heading down along stiffening; pin, making sure edges do not show on the right side of the curtain. Stitch inner edge in place through all thicknesses.

7. For sheer fabrics, open side hems. Place stiffening along top edge of panel; pin. Stitch ¼" from each long edge of stiffening. Complete hems and heading same as for opaque fabrics.

8. Clip or sew on rings, using an uneven number. (You use an uneven number because rings are sold in uneven numbers of pairs.) Curtains will hang in soft, rolling folds on the rod.

CONSTRUCTION WITH PRESSED PLEAT HEADING: Prepare café curtains the same way as for plain heading (figure II-20, steps 1–7). Allow about 2" for each pleat, starting 3" from each end. Divide each panel into an uneven number of pleat folds, making the first fold for a pleat at the center. Press across heading as each pleat is made. Hold pleats together with clip rings by placing double prong in the front and single prong in the back (figure II-21).

II-21

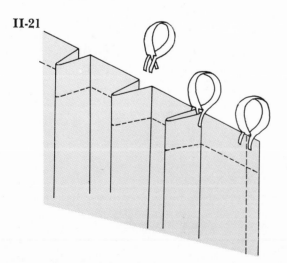

CONSTRUCTION WITH PLAIN SCALLOPED HEADING (figure II-22): Press side and bottom hems in place same as for plain heading. Cut a 3"-wide strip of stiffening the length of each panel between the side hem creases. Make a paper pattern the same size. Plan to use an even number of scallops no deeper than 2". Draw scallops and spaces on paper using a saucer or a compass. Cut out scallops and transfer outlines to stiffening.

1. Open side hems and place stiffening 3¼" from top raw edge; pin securely.

Complete side and bottom hems same as for plain heading (figure II-20, steps 2–5).

2. Turn heading hem, right sides together, along stiffening; pin. Stitch along the scallop markings. Trim each seam allowance to ¼" of stitching. Trim stiffening close to stitching. Clip each curved seam at ¼"–½" intervals so scallops will lie flat when turned right side out.

3. Turn heading hem right side out, making sure corners of ring tabs are square; press. Turn in raw edges ½"; press. Stitch in place.

4. Sew rings to tabs or clip on; hang curtain.

II-22

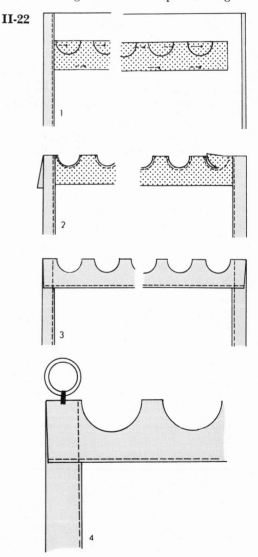

CONSTRUCTION WITH PLEATER TAPE HEADING: The straight- and scallop-edge pleater tapes provide a faster way to make pleats than by hand for opaque fabric café curtains.

Press and stitch the side and bottom hems as instructed in plain headings (figure II-20, steps 2–5), disregarding references to stiffening.

For straight-pleater tape (figure II-23):

1. On the right side of the fabric, lap top edge of the premeasured tape ½″ over top raw edge of panel (with pocket opening edge free). Line up one pocket with each side hem. Stitch top edge of tape to panel.

2. Turn tape to the wrong side along top of tape; press. Turn in ends so they do not show on the right side; pin. Stitch along ends and across remaining long edge of tape.

3. Insert pleater hooks into pockets, forming pleats. Sew or clip on rings, or use pleater hooks with decorative rings attached.

For scalloped pleater tape (figure II-24): Make side and bottom hems the same way as for plain headings (figure II-20, steps 2–5), disregarding reference to stiffening.

1. Place wrong side of tape on right side of panel with scalloped edge ¼″ below raw edge. Stitch ¼″ from edge of tape. Cut away excess fabric and clip scallop curve to stitching at ¼″–½″ intervals.

2. Turn tape to the wrong side, making corners flat; press. Turn in side edges of tape so it doesn't show on the right side. Stitch along ends and across remaining long edge of tape.

3. Insert pleater hooks into pockets, forming pleats. Sew or clip on rings, or use pleater hooks with decorative rings.

II-24

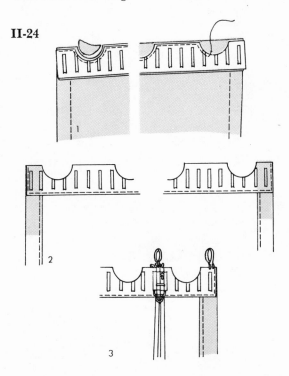

II-23

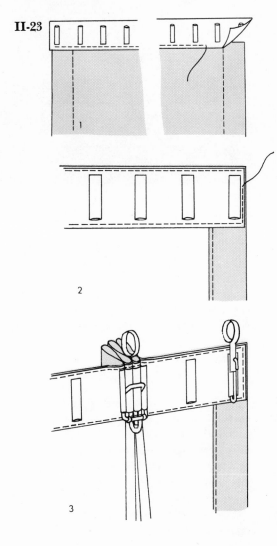

CONSTRUCTION WITH SELF-PLEATED HEADINGS: For pinch-pleats, French pleats, or box pleats, make panels the same way as for plain headings (figure II-20, steps 1–5), stitching only the ends of the heading in place. Then follow figures II-27 and II-28 for pleat construction.

DRAPERIES: CASUAL OR FORMAL

Believe it or not, draperies can be made as quickly and as easily as plain curtains. Draperies have straight hems on three edges and may be made entirely by machine. Make draperies from denim, ticking, kettle cloth, sheets, or an ap-

ABOVE: *This impressive formal living room by designer Shirley Regendahl emulates the elegance of a paneled drawing room. Waverly Fabrics' "Beacon Hill" print is used for the pinch-pleated stationary tieback draperies, the slip-covered couch, and part of the slip-covered wing chairs. Waverly's "Glen Royal" in a solid color is used for the contrasting chair sides and back.*

LEFT: *Four casement windows with glass curtains on swinging rods are framed with tab-hung, box-pleated stationary draperies with a matching valance and café curtains. This window dressing was designed and constructed by the author using "Maxime" fabric from Cohama. All hems are machine-stitched in place, including the miters.*

propriate print or textured fabric in a casual room that gets a lot of use. Use antique satin, a sophisticated decorator print, or damask for a touch of luxury in a more formal room.

Draperies, unlined or lined and hung on a traverse rod that allows you to open and close them at will or on a rod in a stationary position, are usually floor length. Draperies nearly always have pleated headings—the classic self-pleated heading is the least expensive, but takes more time to make than if pleater tape is used.

Draperies may be used alone or with a cornice, swag, or valance; they may be used in tiers with or without decorative tops. Rods may be concealed or decorative. Glass and café curtains are favorite companions for stationary draperies.

For your first drapery project, start with an easy-to-sew fabric that does not have a fabric design motif requiring matching. Don't be skimpy with fabric—fabric sections are easy to seam together. Why not make the easy, machine-sewn, unlined draperies (described below) with sheets—sheets are easy to sew and quite economical. Read the tips for quick draperies from sheets at the end of the instructions.

For those odd-shaped window tops that you want to accent, make a paper pattern the exact shape of each window. Work out the top of draperies in muslin or an old sheet to see what shape the top will need when pleats are spaced evenly across each heading.

Follow the step-by-step measuring instructions and use the Yardage Guide Chart. You will need diligence to calculate precise measurements. If you find this incompatible with your personality, it may be wise to forgo this type of sewing project—incorrect figures could be costly.

Your iron, an ironing board, and a metal ruler will speed up the hemming procedure.

NOTE: If your floors are uneven, be sure to check the drapery length before hemming permanently. Pin hem in place; do not press, then you won't have a crease to worry about if adjustments prove necessary. Complete the heading. Hang draperies, making adjustments if required, and then let hang (for twenty-four hours, if possible). Complete hem as instructed.

Machine-Sewn Unlined Draperies

If saving time is important to you, use pleater tape for both draw and stationary draperies. When you hang tape on the rods to find the exact fullness, the pleat positions will be established as well.

CONSTRUCTION (figure II-25): Straighten fabric ends. Cut as many panels as needed to complete the draperies, using the measurements from your Yardage Guide Chart calculations. Join any seams needed for extra-wide panels. Use the selvage as a finish, or zigzag raw edges of the trimmed seam.

1. Turn in long side edges 2″, wrong sides together; press. Turn under raw edges ½″; press and pin. Stitch close to inner fold to hem in place.

2. Turn up hem edge 6″; press. Turn under raw edge to meet fold; press and pin, making sure the ends don't show on the right side. Stitch hem in place.

3. Stitch premeasured pleater tape to top raw edge to form the heading (see café curtains, II-23, steps 1 and 2). Insert end and multiprong hooks in pockets to form pleats.

II-25

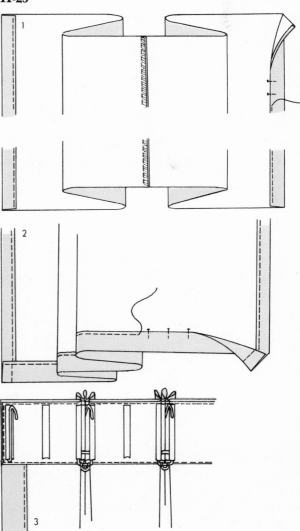

45

Tips for quick draperies from sheets: Use the wide sheet hem as the drapery panel's bottom hem, cutting each panel as long and as wide as needed, retaining the selvages when possible. Turn in the side edges over the wide hem, stitching the selvages in place, if retained. Add pleater tape and your draperies are ready to hang.

Basic Unlined Draperies

This method is a satisfactory finish for even the most costly or luxurious fade-proof fabric. The following instructions are for a self-pleated heading; but if you decide to use pleater tape, follow figure II-23, steps 1 and 2.

CONSTRUCTION: Straighten fabric ends. Cut as many panels as needed to complete the draperies, using the measurements from your Yardage Guide Chart. Join seams needed for extra-wide panels. Trim away selvages and stitch in a French seam, matching fabric designs if necessary.

Turn in the long side edges in the same way as directed for machine-sewn draperies (figure II-25, steps 1 and 2), ending the ½″ turn-under 7″ above the hem edge. Press hem edge and pin all hems into position. Do not stitch hems in place.

Pleater tape does not need the stiffening, but the top edge of self-pleated headings must be stiffened to be firm enough to support the pleats (figure II-26). To stiffen heading for self-pleats, use width of stiffening needed. Cut a strip of stiffening for each panel to fit between the creases of the side hems at the top edge.

1. Open out the side hem folds near the top. Place stiffening ½″ from raw edge; pin. Stitch stiffening to panel ¼″ from inner edge. Turn raw edge over remaining stiffening edge; stitch in place through all thicknesses.

2. Turn top edge to the wrong side along stiffening edge; press. (NOTE: The inner edge is not anchored. Pleats will hold heading in place. The pockets formed may be used to slip hooks in place instead of pinning.) To eliminate bulk at corners, trim away side hem along the stiffen-

II-26

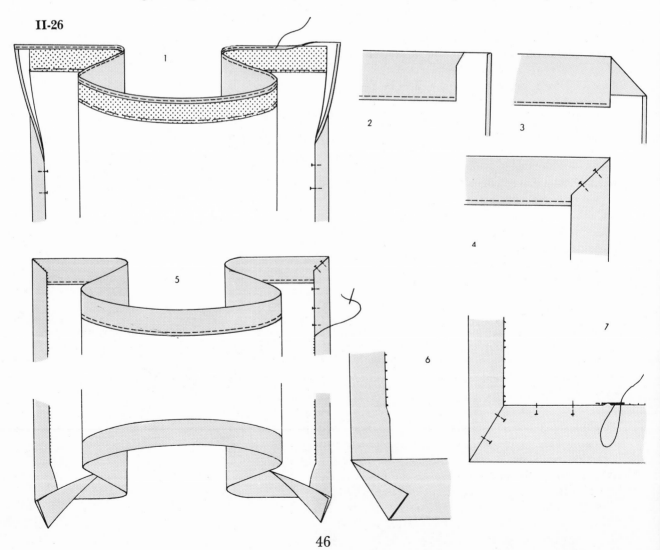

ing to within ½" of the top fold; cut diagonally to top fold, continuing along top fold to outer edge of hem.

3. To form miter, turn in top edge diagonally to meet hem crease.

4. Turn side hem over stiffened heading; pin.

5. Slip-stitch miter. Finish off draperies with either self-made pleats or pleater tape pleats in the same manner. Slip-stitch long side hems of panel to the top of bottom hem. Hems may be blind-stitched by machine or machine-stitched close to edge.

6. To miter bottom hem corners, turn in ends diagonally to meet side hems.

7. Pin and slip-stitch miters and bottom hem in place. Do not trim away bottom hem corners.

Add weights (see figure II-35, steps 1 and 2) or sew weights to inner folds of hem before sewing the hem in place.

Self-Pleated Headings

Three types of pleats can all be made from the same pleat base: pinch pleats, French pleats, and box pleats.

The measurements you used to purchase fabric are used again at this point (see page 28). Use measurements #8 for rod span and #9 for return measurement. For draw draperies, use overlap measurement #10. Divide the total finished width (measurement #11) in half to establish the finished width of each drapery panel.

CONSTRUCTION (figure II-27): Mark one panel at a time, starting with the left half. Use long pins (the sort used for corsages). With a pin mark the return measurement at the left side and the center opening. (For stationary drapery panel allow 2" and for draw drapery panel about

3¼".) Pin a pleat in place at these two points. Use the predetermined pleat depth and space width with which you calculated measurement #12. Use 4"–5" for pleats and 2½"–4½" for spaces.

For a stationary drapery panel. Use an uneven number of pleats.

1. Pin a pleat fold beyond the return and opening spaces. Fold panel in half, matching end pleats, and pin another of equal depth at the center.

2. Divide the remaining two spaces into an equal number of pleats, making all spaces the same width.

3. Mark and pin the remaining panel and then place the panels wrong sides together, making sure the return spaces fall together for the left and right window frame with the narrower opening spaces at the center. Repin pleat folds with two pins pointing toward the top, making sure the heading width is correct (measurement #11). Keep folds straight with vertical lines parallel and perpendicular to the top.

For a draw drapery panel. Mark return and center opening as directed for stationary panels. Pin a pleat fold beyond the return and opening spaces. Divide remaining space into pleat folds and spaces as planned for measurement #12; you may use an even or uneven number of pleat folds.

4. Mark and pin remaining panel and then place panels wrong sides together, making sure the return spaces will fall together for the left and right window frame with the overlapping spaces at the center. Repin pleat fold as described in step 3.

5. To stitch pleats, start at right edge. Turn

II-27

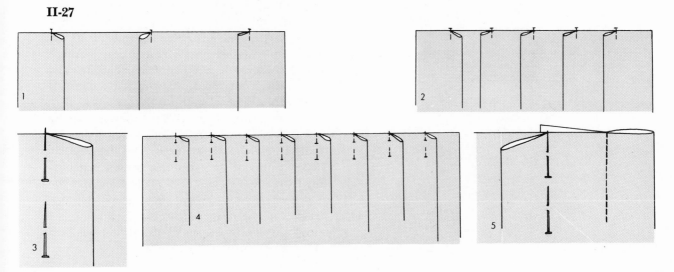

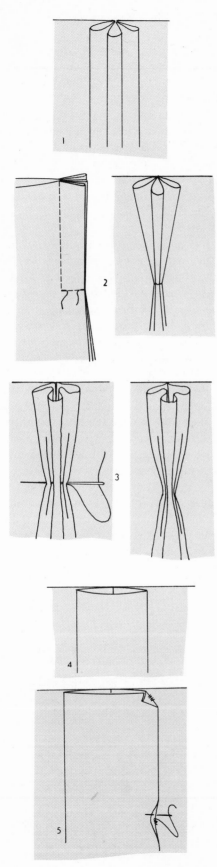

side hem under panel and make pleat fold flat, keeping top edges of pleat fold and space even. Stitch $\frac{1}{32}''$–$\frac{1}{16}''$ inside the pin markings to allow for "shrinkage," since fabric weight and tension of the pleat stitching will reduce the total width when all pleats are stitched and shaped. Backstitch at beginning and end, removing pins as you work. End at inner edge of stiffening.

To make pinch-pleats (figure II-28). Divide the large pleats into three smaller pleats of equal size.

1. Flatten side pleats against the stitching, then pull up the center to form a third pleat with the inner folds close to the crease formed over the stitching.

2. Bring pleats together at this point. Pinch fabric tightly and press. Stitch across the bottom, along the inner facing edge or sew the folds securely by hand.

3. To make French pleats: Divide large pleat into three equal smaller pleats, as described in step 1. Use heavy matching thread to gather the folds of the pleats at the base of the stitching. Pull up gathers and stitch back and forth through folds to hold gathers.

4. To make box pleats: Divide large pleat in half over stitching; press lightly.

5. Sew invisibly (see slip-stitching in Chapter VIII) to panel at upper corners and at the edge of the stiffening.

Classic Lined Draperies

Lining draperies saves a lot of hand sewing because the side hems are pressed into place. Use the Yardage Guide Chart to estimate how much lining fabric you'll need. In step A, allow $\frac{1}{2}''$ for the heading finish. Do not add for a hem finish since lining is shorter than drapery. In Step C, subtract the finished side hem width from the total width needed (measurement #15). Follow step D to calculate number of fabric widths and total yardage required, allowing an additional $\frac{1}{4}$ yard to straighten ends.

CONSTRUCTION (figure II-29): Straighten lining and drapery fabric ends. Cut as many drapery and lining panels as you need. Join drapery fabric seams needed for extra-wide panels, matching any fabric designs, and press open. Raw edges do not need a finish when covered with lining. Stitch lining fabric widths together in a $\frac{1}{2}''$ seam; press seams open. Turn up lining hem $1\frac{1}{2}''$; press. Turn in raw edge $\frac{1}{2}''$; press and pin. Machine-stitch in place close to inner fold.

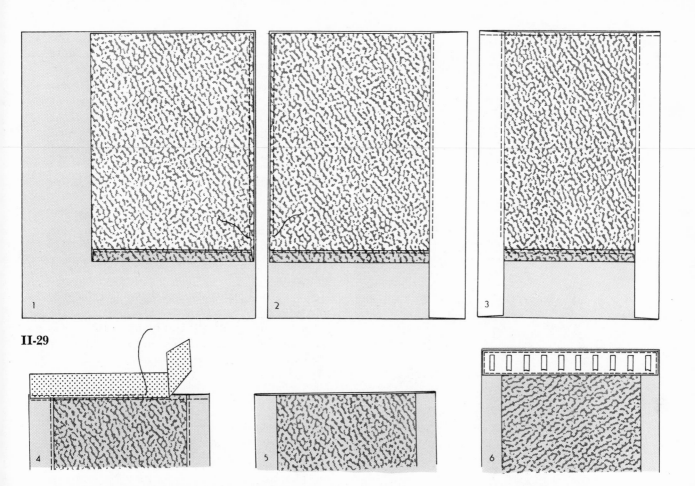

II-29

1. With right sides together and upper edges even, pin lining to drapery panel at one long side edge. Stitch in a ½″ seam, ending 2″ above bottom edge of lining.

2. Bring lining to opposite long side edge. Pin and stitch lining to drapery panel the same way.

3. Press seams toward lining. Center lining over drapery panel; pin. Stitch upper edges together in a ½″ seam.

4. For a self-pleated heading, cut a 3″- to 4″-wide strip of stiffening the length of the panel. Lap over seam allowances with long edge along seam stitching; pin. Stitch to seam allowance.

5. Turn panel right side out. Press top and side edges, making sure lining does not show on the right side of the top edge.

Finish headings before hemming.

6. For a pleater tape heading, pin premeasured tape to top of panel, over the lining, turning in ends ½″. Stitch along all edges through all thicknesses.

Make self-pleats in heading as directed in figures II-27 and 28.

Check hem lengths before continuing. Pin drapery panel hems in place. Insert pleater tape hooks or self-pleat hooks and hang on rod.

Make any hem adjustments needed, and you are now ready to finish off the hems (figure II-30).

1. Open hems. Sew a weight to each side hem.

2. Sew a weight to each seam.

II-30

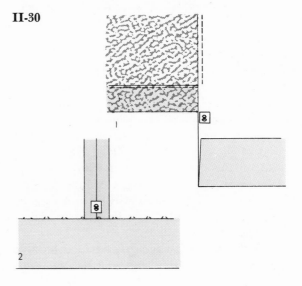

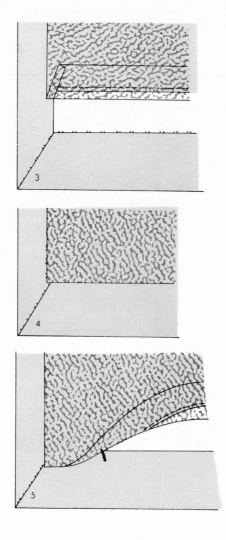

amount for the contrasting layer. In step A of the chart, be sure to adjust the casing with a heading width to accommodate the rod and allow 6″ for the hem. In step C, add ½″ for each side hem (2″ for the total width needed for measurement #15). Seam if necessary, following step D to calculate the number of fabric widths needed and total fabric required. Allow an additional ¼ yard to straighten ends.

CONSTRUCTION OF LINED-TO-EDGE DRAPERIES (figure II-31):

1. Place right sides together: pin long side edges and upper edges together. Stitch long side edges together in a ½″ seam and the upper edges together in a ¼″ seam. Press open the long open side seams.

Turn panel right side out. Press flat the side and top edges along the seam.

Make casing as directed in figure II-16, step 4, omitting the ½″ turn-under, and stitch close to the stitched edges to form casing.

2. Make hems by turning up bottom edges 6″; press. Turn in raw edges 3″ to meet fold; press

II-31

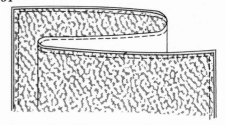

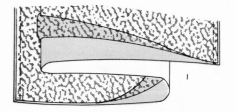

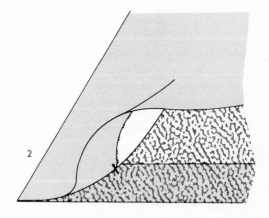

3. Hem drapery panel as directed in figure II-26, steps 6 and 7 for unlined drapery.

4. Slip-stitch remainder of lining in place.

5. Anchor lining to drapery at 10″–12″ intervals with French tacks so lining and drapery fabric will act as one layer.

Latest Drapery Styles

Two newcomers in stationary drapery fashions are lined-to-edge draperies and draperies with box pleats and tab hangers (instead or rings); both styles are hung on wooden rods.

Lined-to-edge draperies are made with two layers of decorator fabric of equal weight, one a print and the other a contrasting solid. The draperies are tied back to show the contrasting side, and a casing with a heading is used to complement the wooden rod. These draperies are shown over glass curtains on page 5.

Use the Yardage Guide Chart to determine yardage for one fabric layer, and buy the same

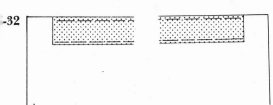

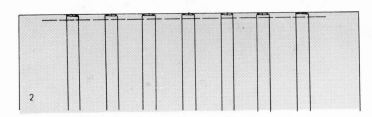

and pin. Slip-stitch hems in place. Fasten hems together wtih French tacks at 10″–12″ intervals to hold the two layers together. Make tiebacks as directed in figure II-19, steps 1, 2, and 3.

Tab hangers with box pleats are great for both draperies and café curtains, and they cut down the fixture cost. The photograph on page 44 shows a way to combine café curtains and draperies. The tabs featured are 2½″ long—from the top of the rod to the drape. A 7″-long and 5″-wide strip was used for this length, but you can adjust the length as you desire.

Use the Yardage Guide Chart to estimate yardage. In step A, subtract at least 2½″ from the total finished length to allow for tab hangers and use a regular hem allowance. In step C, plan pleats as directed to establish fullness for the total width needed (measurement #15). Seam if necessary, following step D to calculate number of fabric widths and total yardage required. Allow additional fabric for the tabs—one tab 5″ wide and 7″–11″ long for each pleat and one for each side hem—and for heading facing 5″ wide the width of each panel after it has been pleated, plus ¼ yard to straighten ends.

CONSTRUCTION OF A PANEL (figure II-32):

1. Machine-baste a strip of stiffening to top edge of panel between side hem allowances.

Make box pleats in top edge following directions for self-pleated heading (page 43), allowing the same width space for side and center openings (no return used). Do not sew pleat fold in place.

2. Machine-baste upper edges of pleats to panel.

CONSTRUCTION OF TABS (figure II-33): Cut a 5″ × 7″–11″ tab for each pleat and each side hem.

3. Fold lengthwise and stitch in a ½″ seam. Press seam open, being careful not to press creases in tab.

4. Turn tabs right side out. Center fabric over seam; press flat.

5. Fold tab in half with seam on inside: baste to panel over each box pleat and at side edges.

CONSTRUCTION OF FACING (figure II-34): Turn in long side edges of panel over stiffening. Cut a 5″-wide fabric strip to face pleated heading; it should be the length of top between side edges plus 2″.

6. Turn in lower facing edge ½″; stitch. Stitch facing ends to side hem edges in a ½″ seam. Press seams toward sides.

7. Stitch facing to heading over pleats and tabs in a ½″ seam.

II-34

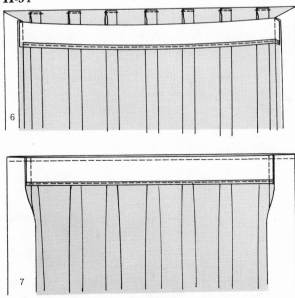

II-33

51

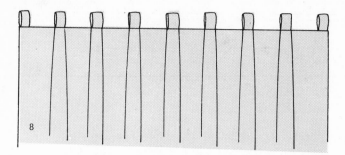

8

8. Turn facing right side out; press.

For some fabrics, it may be necessary to stitch across each space to hold the facing in place. If so, stitch ⅛″ from the top edge between each pleat.

Finish side and bottom hems as directed as for *basic unlined draperies* (page 46).

Drapery Tips

Here are several tips to aid you in achieving a professional look.

FABRIC-COVERED WEIGHTS (figure II-35): There are several types of covered weights available, or you can make your own coverings.

To make weight covers in fabric to match your draperies:

1. Trace around the weight on the wrong side of the fabric. Use two layers and stitch together alongside the tracing, leaving an opening large enough to insert weight.

Turn cover right side out; insert weight. Sew opening shut.

2. Sew weight to hems at each corner and seam. (Purchased covered weights are sewn or pinned in place at the same spots.)

To insert covered chain weights in a hem for sheer and lightweight fabrics, use weights the same length as the finished panel.

3. Insert weights into hem with a safety pin. Tack weight at side hems.

4. Tack weights in place at any seams.

ANCHOR SIDE EDGES (figure II-36): Stationary draperies with fabric that touches the wall or window frame should hang taut and in a straight line.

1. If your fixture does not have a hole for a hook to secure heading ends, screw a cup hook into the wall and sew a small plastic ring to the heading.

2. To secure a hem, use a cup hook on baseboard or floor and sew ring to hem to hold in place.

II-36

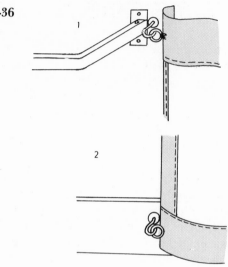

SET DRAPERY FOLDS (figure II-37): In order to have fabric hang in soft, rolling folds, the pleats must be set from heading to hem. Pressing is not satisfactory because it forms too sharp a crease.

1. For stationary draperies, form the pleats in a tube below the heading pleats. Do not attempt to make the individual stylized folds that match each one for a pleat. Work down the fabric to the hem, forming each pleat tube with pins. Spaces between the pinned pleats should be nearly the same width as those in the heading.

II-35

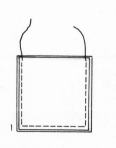

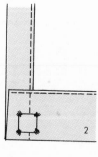

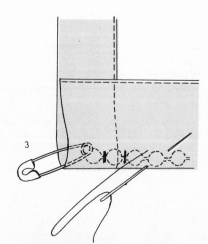

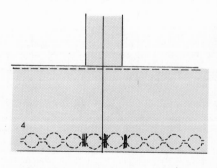

II-37

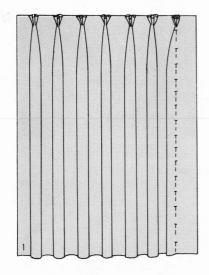

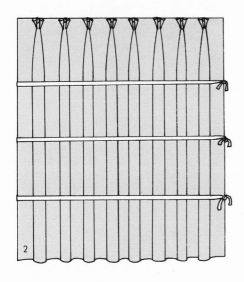

material, you can purchase it cut to measure. After the wooden frame is made, it is covered with fabric. The most popular way to cover it is with a layer of padding (flannel, batting, or a thin layer of polyurethane foam) and a layer of decorative fabric that is permanently stapled, tacked, or glued into place. For a removable cover, buckram and Velcro® are used. Cornices may be made in a box form, to enclose the side and front edges of curtains or draperies at the top, or flat, to cover a wall area from corner to corner. You will find examples of both types throughout this book.

CONSTRUCTION OF BOX CORNICE (figure II-38): Use ½″-thick wood and make a three-sided box about 3″–5″ wider and longer than the rod it is to enclose. NOTE: Wooden trim with one decorative edge may be substituted. Be sure to match the design at the corners.

II-38

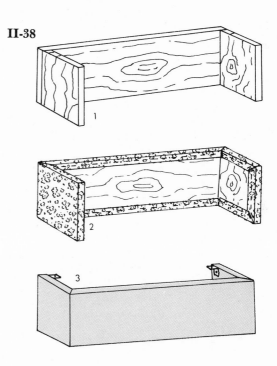

Allow to hang with pins for two or three days.

2. For draw draperies, you may want to set the folds with the draperies drawn (open for tighter folds). Set the folds below the heading as directed for stationary draperies (step 1 above). Then tie draperies with a soft strip of fabric or tape loosely at 12″–18″ intervals, making sure the side hems and folds are smooth and flat. Allow to hang this way for two or three days.

CORNICES

Decorative toppings for curtains and draperies—cornices—may be as simple or as ornate as you desire. They are great helpers when you have irregular windows, a group of windows, or if you want to tie a whole wall together as a focal point.

These rigid structures are made of pine or plywood. If you don't want to saw your own

1. Cover the ends of wood that are to be butted together with Elmer's® glue. Place the long section on top of the short ends and nail together with finishing nails. Allow glue to dry according to manufacturer's instructions.

2. To cover box with your choice of padding, cut padding the width and length of the frame (including ends) plus 1½″ on all edges. Use more than one layer of padding if you want more rounded edges. Staple, tack, or glue padding to cornice on the back, clipping so any inward

curved or pointed edges will lie flat. Cut away excess padding at corners.

3. To cover padded box with fabric, lay a length of fabric over the long front of cornice, centering any design motif. Anchor fabric with push- or T-pins, making sure the top edge of the cornice is on the straight grain of fabric. Cut out fabric about 1″ wider than padding. To staple, tack, or glue fabric to the back of cornice, start at the center of the top edge and work toward each end, pulling the fabric taut. Fold in fullness at corners. Do the same at the bottom edge, clipping any inward curves or points so the fabric will lie flat. Make sure the fabric is smooth and wrinkle-free across the padding. Do the ends last.

Leave cornice plain, trim with rows of decorative upholstery tacks, or attach trimming with fabric glue, using rust-proof pins to secure trim until glue dries.

Attach angle irons to cornice at the top ends with screws. Position rod fixtures before permanently attaching cornice to the wall.

CONSTRUCTION OF FLAT CORNICE (figure II-39): Use ½″-thick wood the length of the wall or window indentation, less about ½″ for padding and fabric thicknesses on each end. Use three or more angle irons to support.

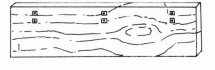

II-39

1. Before covering, drill holes through board, using angle irons as guide for hole positions. Insert bolts through holes and fasten with nuts.

2. Attach padding to the flat cornice as di-

rected for the box cornice, figure II-38, step 2. NOTE: When attaching padding and fabrics, support long cornices on the backs of straight chairs covered with towels.

3. Cover flat cornice with fabric as directed for box cornice, figure II-38, step 3. Attach angle irons and hang.

The flat cornice looks great with thick self-fabric cording on both long edges. Cut fabric the width of the padding board plus 1″ for seam allowances and the length recommended above. Cut two strips this same length and wide enough to stitch in a corded seam and pull to the back and staple or tack.

Position rod fixtures on walls before attaching cornice to ceiling.

CONSTRUCTION OF REMOVABLE CORNICE COVER (figure II-40):

1. Use buckram for stiffening. Cut desired

II-40

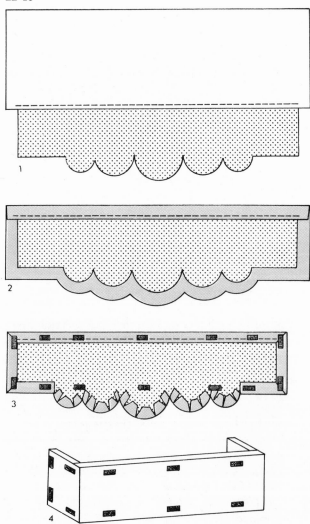

54

shape from buckram, making any shaped edge extend below cornice wood. Cut fabric about 2″ longer and 4″ wider than buckram, centering any design motifs with upper long edge on straight grain. Lap fabric over upper edge of buckram 2″; machine-baste ½″ from raw edge through both thicknesses.

2. Wrap fabric around buckram, pulling it taut; hold with push- or T-pins. Trim edge into shape.

3. Clip into corners and points. Glue fabric to buckram, folding in fullness along curve evenly. Trim away excess fabric. Hold in place with rust-proof pins until glue dries. Glue 3″–6″ strips of Velcro® (loop side) at 6″ intervals at the upper edge and above shaped edge.

4. Glue or staple hooked strip of Velcro® to cornice, matching strips on buckram. Place cornice cover on frame, keeping upper edges even.

SWAGS

Decorate your window with a garland of fabric draped across the top and held in place with rings, posts, or decorative rod. Swags, with their soft, draping folds, are great toppers for glass and café curtains as well as formal draperies. Select soft, lightweight fabric. Position ornamental holders at top of window. Measure span between holders or brackets and down along each side of the window to where you want the swag tip to end; add 1″ for seam allowance. Line swag with a self- or contrasting fabric and trim the edges if desired. Make swag 18″–45″ wide when finished. Cut two lengths of fabric the desired length and width.

CONSTRUCTION (figure II-41): If trim is to be used, baste it to the ends and to one or both long edges of one fabric section (see Chapter VIII).

1. With right sides together, stitch long edges and ends, leaving an opening on one long edge to turn right side out.

Trim corners; turn right side out. Sew opening shut; press.

2. Drape swag over posts or rod or through rings, folding fabric carefully at these points to make soft, draping folds across the window with softly pleated ends. A few pins anchored strategically in the fabric folds at the back of the holders will keep the fabric from shifting with breezes or jarring.

To make the pouffed swag shown in the photograph of a child's room, use a single layer of 44″-wide fabric the length of both sides and top of window, plus 36″–48″ extra to drape the pouffs.

Hem edges with extended trim as directed in Chapter VIII, page 205. Use a flat curtain rod, 4 cup hooks, 2 decorative ties, and 1⅓ yards of narrow twill tape. Drape swag over rod and make a cascade with decorative ties. Fasten cup hooks at even intervals at sides of window. Use 12″-long strips of tape to gather swag into a tight tube. Spread out fabric and hang swag to cup hooks, draping pouffs as shown.

II-41

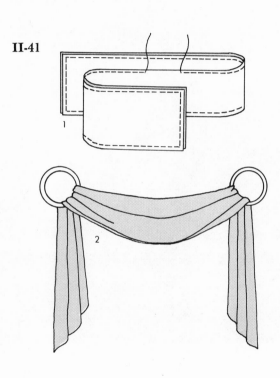

VALANCES

These short, ornamental curtains or draped festoons may be plain, fancy, smooth, pleated, gathered, or draped with jabots or draped scallops. Valances may be used at windows or hung as a canopy. The classic styles are hung with a rod, but the heavier, more ornate draped ones need a board for support. They can be as narrow as 6″ or as deep as 18″—it's your choice.

For ideas on how to decorate a valance, see discussion of ruffles as an edge finish, extended trim as an edge finish, and decorative band trim in Chapter VIII, or appliqués in Chapter VII.

Classic Valances

Favorite companions for these short, curtain-like valances are tieback curtains, café curtains,

ABOVE: *Tie up a swag to frame an indented sliding glass window for the nursery, kitchen, or bath. Designed and constructed by the author. A length of 44"- to 45"-wide apparel fabric is trimmed with Conso's ball fringe and matching ties with tassels to hold the top cascade. At even intervals alongside the window, cup hooks are used to hold the pouffed cascades in place.*

RIGHT: *A calico print from Spring Mills, Inc., sets the mood in a kitchen with a Pennsylvania Dutch theme. A shaped-ruffled valance is cut with side panels that extend to the apron edge. The same fabric is used for a tablecloth with matching napkins. Designed and made by the author. You will find instructions for the shaped ruffle, tablecloth, and napkins in Chapter VII under "Table toppings for every room."*

56

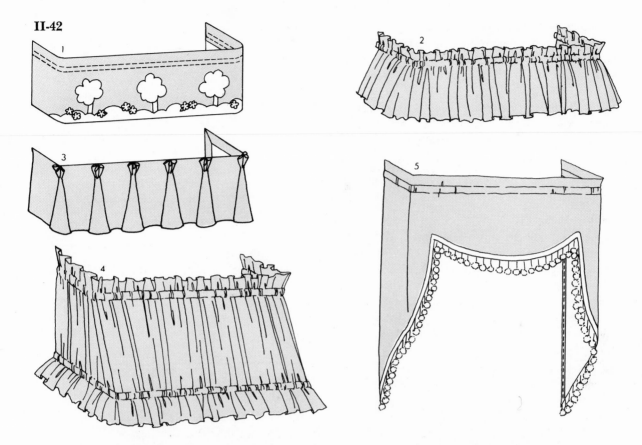

and stationary draperies. They may also be used as a canopy. The following styles are hung on a rod (figure II-42).

1. PLAIN, SMOOTH VALANCE: Make valance the length of the rod including returns, plus 2″–4″ for ease, and as deep as desired. Use a casing with a heading at the top and add 1½″ for side and bottom hems. Decorate with appliqués or band trim if desired.

2. GATHERED VALANCE: Make valance two or three times the length of the rod, including returns, as deep as desired. Use a casing with a heading (to gather valance on rod), 1½″ for side and bottom hems. Add ruffles or trim as desired.

3. PLEATED VALANCE: Follow Yardage Guide Chart for self-made pleats or pleater tape, making valance as deep as required. Make heading and pleats as instructed for draperies (page 47). Hang valance with hooks and anchor top with hook and ring as shown in figure II-36, if used on a curtain rod.

4. CANOPY VALANCE: Two rods are used for this show-stopper. Make fabric at least twice the length of the rod with the deepest return. Use a casing with a heading on both edges. Allow 1½″ for side hems. A plain casing may be used on the bottom edge of the length of the deepest re-

turn plus 2″ for ease. Make casing ½″ wider than needed for rod so a decorative edge, such as a ruffle with a heading or fringe, may be applied to the smooth-fitted bottom rod.

5. SHAPED VALANCE: Most often used with sash curtains, this valance can be used alone or with glass or café curtains. The shaped calico valance (shown on page 56) was used alone on an indented sliding glass window. The only window in the kitchen, it was opened and closed frequently, so sash curtains were not practical. The shaped ruffle was used on a matching tablecloth that is featured in Chapter VII. Directions for the ruffle are on page 177.

To design a shaped valance, make a pattern with newspaper, shaping inner top and side edges as desired. Tape pattern on the rod, including the returns, and check proportions. Remove pattern and modify as directed below.

For a smooth valance, add about 4″ to the width and 1½ or 2 times the width for a gathered valance. Distribute the extra allowance evenly, adding one-fourth the amount to each long side edge and the remaining one-half the amount to the short center strip.

Add casing requirements to the top of the pattern, 1½″ for 1″-wide finished side hems on the long, straight outer edges, and ½″ seam allowances on all remaining edges. Decorate the inner shaped edges with ruffles or extended trim, subtracting the finished trim width from these pattern edges.

Use pattern to help determine yardage, allowing additional fabric for self-ruffles when used.

After valance is cut out, apply trim to the inner shaped edges. Makes the hems on the long, outer side edges, and make the casing as the last step.

Draped Valances

These beauties are most often used with glass curtains or stationary draperies. The two most popular styles are the draped valance with jabots and the draped valance with scallops. These heavier valances have decorative trimmed edges and are attached to a valance board above the curtain or drapery rods, to support the weight of the draped fabric.

Make a pattern from muslin or an old sheet before cutting into your valance fabric. When shaping the valance fabric into draped folds (after testing the pattern and using it to cut out the fabric), steam the fabric. Hold a steam iron over fabric and steam along the folds—do not rest iron on fabric. Shape fabric with fingers as it dries.

CONSTRUCTION OF VALANCE BOARD (figure II-43): Use a ½″-thick board, 2″–5″ wider and longer than the mounted rod. Anchor three angle irons to board with screws and mount board on wall above rod. Measure front of board and the two ends (returns) to establish length of valance needed.

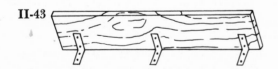

II-43

PATTERN FOR DRAPED VALANCE WITH JABOTS (figure II-44): This is the most popular type of draped valance.

1. To make the center valance cascade pattern, use a piece of fabric about 24″ deep (lengthwise grain) and the width of the board (crosswise grain) less 8″. Valance cascade may be deeper for wider windows.

Draw a line through the center of the fabric

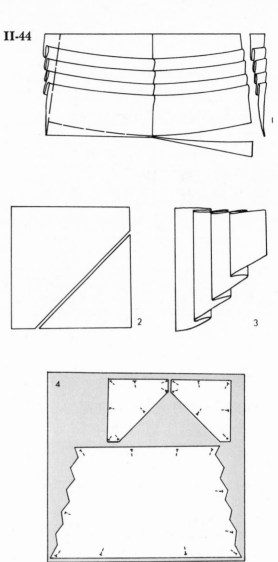

II-44

pattern. Measure down this line 4″, pull up a 2″-deep fold over ruler; pin. Shape fold to the left and right in a slight arc to within 1″ from top edge; pin outer ends only. Make three more 2″-deep folds, placing folds 1″ apart. Lower edge will measure about 3″ from last fold at center line. Measure and mark 3″ along last fold for the shaped hemline. At the top, measure in 1″ and make a diagonal line to hem corner. Cut along this line.

2. To make a jabot pattern, use a piece of fabric the desired finished length (jabots may be 18″ to 30″ long). Use the lengthwise grain hanging down and the crosswise grain along the top edge. The width should be three times the measurement of the valance board end (return) and about 6″ at the side of the cascade. About ½″ of the cascade should extend under the finished edge of the jabot.

58

On one long edge, mark the length of the pleated side edge of the cascade. At the lower opposite corner, mark the depth of the board end plus 2″. Draw a line between these two points and cut away the excess fabric.

3. Starting at the narrow upper end, measure in 4″, fold and make a 2″-deep pleat; pin. Make as many pleats as needed and test with the cascade.

Pin jabot and cascade pattern to board, lapping jabot ½″ over the cascade. When proportions are satisfactory and necessary changes made, remove all pins from pattern. For the valance cascade, add ½″ to all edges. For the jabot, add 1″ to the long side edge and the short center edge. Add ½″ to the top and diagonal edge.

4. Pin pattern to valance fabric. Be sure to cut a left and right jabot.

CONSTRUCTION OF VALANCE AND JABOTS (figure II-45):

1. Attach trim to lower edge of cascade valance. Mark center with basting thread and shape folds as you did for the pattern. Stitch ¼″ from raw ends. Fold 1″-wide twill tape in half; press. Encase ends with twill tape, turning in lower ends; stitch.

2. Lap 1″-wide twill tape over upper edge ½″, turning in ends ½″; stitch.

3. Hem side and center edges of jabot. Turn in these edges 1″; press. Turn in raw edges to meet folds; press and stitch hems in place. Attach trim to diagonal edge. Make pleats as you did for the pattern; baste. Lap 1″-wide twill tape over upper edge ½″; pin. Turn in side edge ½″; wrap tape around front edges for 2″. Stitch in place through all thicknesses.

4. Fasten valance and jabots to valance board with Velcro® tape or snap tape. For Velcro®, attach hook section of fastener to board with staples or tacks; stitch loop section to underside of twill tape to jabots, ending where it meets the valance and encasing raw edges between Velcro® and twill tape. Pin jabot overlaps to valance. Apply snap tape to valance and jabots in the same manner, mitering corners, placing ball section on the board and the socket section on the jabots and cascade.

PATTERN FOR AND CONSTRUCTION OF DRAPED VALANCE WITH SCALLOPS (figure II-46): Use three or more draped scallops for each window or use with jabots. Attach valance board to wall above draperies or curtains. Measure board along both ends and the front. Divide this measurement by

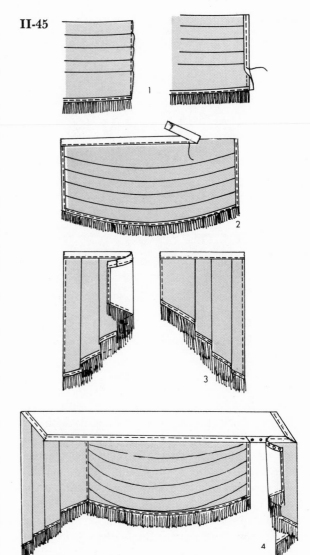

II-45

3. Each scallop should be the length across the top from finished edge to finished edge, plus 1½″ for ease and lapping. A strip of fabric 24″ deep (lengthwise grain) and 39″ wide (crosswise grain) folds into a 34″-wide scallop. Adjust these measurements to your needs.

A cutting board with 1″ grids is helpful when draping. Anchor center of valances to a flat surface padded with newspapers if you don't have a cutting board. Draw a line on the papers the length of scallop, and mark spaces as for a cutting board.

1. Draw a line down the center of the pattern. Measure down this line 3″, pull up a 1″-deep fold over ruler; pin. Make the same fold at each end of the fabric. Make six more 1″-deep folds along the center and at each end, making folds 1″ apart. Lower edge will measure about 1½″ from last fold.

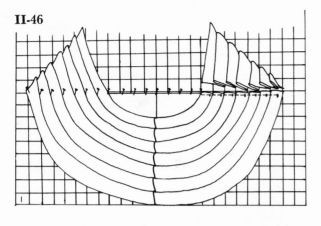

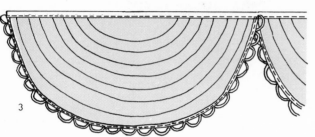

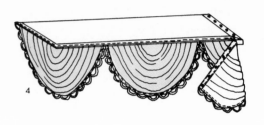

Swing lower edge corners up in line with the center. It is now apparent how much more fabric must be worked into each fold. Starting with the first fold, shape into a curve at each end. Shape one side first, repinning and refolding as needed. Flat area across the top may ripple slightly. This will be eased in later. Shape opposite side to the same measurements. Anchor edge of each fold and distribute fullness across flat area, pinning in place. Draw a line across the scallop. Trim away excess fabric along this line. Test draped scallop on the valance board. When proportions are satisfactory and necessary changes made, remove all pins. Add ½" to all edges and cut out three scallops. If trim is quite wide, you may need to adjust the scallop width.

2. Pin pattern to valance fabric and cut out.

3. Attach trim to lower edge of each scallop. Mark center with basting thread and shape folds same as for pattern. Stitch ¼" from upper edge, easing in excess fabric. Lap ends of scallops ½"; pin. Stitch 1"-wide twill tape to long straight edge, lapping ½" over raw edges; turn in ends.

4. Fasten valance to board with snap tape. Miter twill tape at corners; stitch. Attach ball section of tape to board with staples or tacks, mitering tape at corners between two snaps. Stitch socket section of tape to valance, aligning snaps and mitering corners to match; encase raw edge between snap tape and twill tape. Hang valance.

SHADES

Each year decorators use innovative techniques to renew bygone favorites to make them more suitable for the easygoing life-style of Americans. The old green or white plain roller shade has been transformed into a colorful window fashion. The trend toward fabric roller shades has brought the Roman and Austrian shades to the forefront as well.

These important window accents are available in a wide choice of colors and styles for those interested in purchased shades to complement their newly made curtains and draperies. There's a new shade available for the needleworker, too. It resembles canvas and can be embroidered with a border or design. Purchased shades may be decorated with trims or appliqués attached with fabric glue. Do not attempt to stitch these trims in place as you will damage the shade. Lay shade on a flat surface when applying trim and keep flat until completely dry.

Roller Shades

There are several ways to make fabric roller shades. Use light- to medium-weight, smooth, and tightly woven fabric. Textured, thick and thin, sheer, open-weave, or stretchy fabrics are not suitable. To aid you in this new adventure there are kits containing all the material needed to transform fabric into a shade, or you may use iron-on nonwoven interfacing and a replacement rod. The kits may be purchased at a shade and curtain shop or any department store or shop that carries home decorating supplies. The interfacing can be purchased anywhere dress goods are sold.

The kits have a backing that is laminated to the fabric and are available in many widths, including extra-wide. One kit uses a pressure-sensitive backing to make the fabric adhere; the other kit has a heat-sensitive backing. Both kits are easy to use if you follow the manufacturers' step-by-step instruction booklets. Write to the Window Shade Manufacturers' Association, 230 Park Avenue, New York, New York 10017, if they are not available in your area.

Purchase a roller and install brackets (figure II-47). Reverse-roll mounting brackets should be used so shade will roll on the outside away from the window, unless a cornice or valance is used to hide the plain color of the backing on the roller. Each type of installation requires a specific pair of brackets.

Measure carefully; use a metal tape or a wooden carpenter's ruler to ensure accuracy. Measure from the top of the roller to window sill for the finished length of the shade. To find the length of the rod needed and finished shade width:

1. Measure between window jams with inside mountings.

2. Measure between bracket bases for those placed on frame or wall.

3. Measure between bracket bases for those placed on the ceiling.

CONSTRUCTION OF ROLLER SHADE WITH IRON-ON NONWOVEN INTERFACING (figure II-48): Purchase fabric at least 1″ wider than roller and 12″ longer than the length requirement for rolling so shade won't tear off the roller. Interfacing should be 3″ longer than fabric. Make a pattern for any decorative edges, then add this amount to the basic fabric and interfacing yardage. To use a brass café curtain rod or a bamboo pole as a slat, add 11″ to both yardages.

II-48

You will need fabric, iron-on nonwoven interfacing, roller and brackets, stapler or tacks. For optional finishes, choose wooden slat, café curtain rod, or bamboo pole for hem; decorative pulls and trim; and the tab hem needs foldover braid.

Work on a smooth, flat surface large enough to hold entire length of interfacing. Straighten interfacing and fabric ends. Press any creases out of fabric. Draw a line 3″ below one straightened end of the interfacing and a line down the center. Mark center of fabric with tailor's chalk. Now pad surface with several layers of sheets.

Lay interfacing on padded surface with bond-

II-47

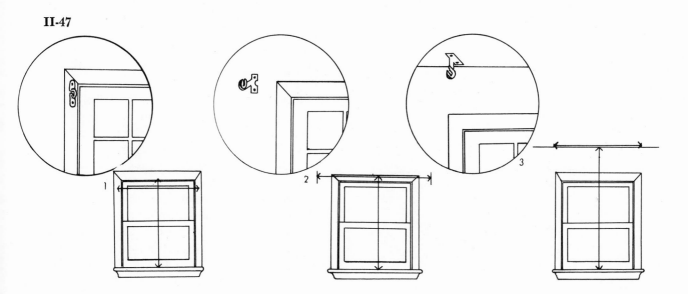

61

ing agent up. Place fabric, wrong side down, on top of interfacing, with one edge along the 3″ line. Match center lines of fabric and interfacing. Bond fabric in place, following manufacturer's instructions for heat and time. Work from center to the outer edges. Start at the top and work toward the bottom, making sure both layers are wrinkle-free.

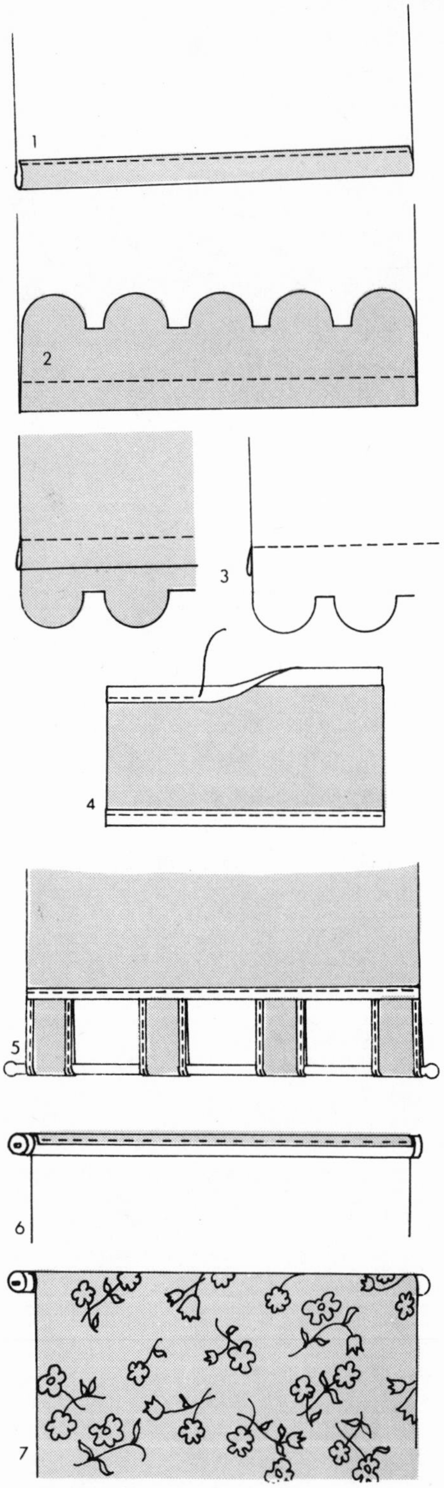

Trim shade to ⅛″ less than the roller measurement, keeping fabric design motifs centered.

For any type of fabric shade, make one of following hems (figure II-49).

To make a casing to hold the wooden slat:

1. Turn up lower edge 1¾″ from cut edge. Insert slat and attach a pull at center of shade.

For a decorative edge, cut out design with pattern.

2. To make casing to hold wooden slat, fold shade wrong sides together at desired distance from edge. Stitch 1½″ from fold.

3. Insert slat and pull down decorative edge. Trim or braid may be glued or fused to the shaped edge.

For a tab and rod or pole edge:

4. To make tabs, cut four or more tabs 11″ long and 4″–12″ wide. Encase the long tab edges with foldover braid.

5. Fold tabs wrong sides together and place on wrong side of shade. Encase tabs and shade edge with fold over braid. Insert rod or pole through tabs.

6. & 7. Attach shade to roller with staples or tacks, making sure it will roll as planned.

II-49

Roman Shade

This handsome window style hangs smoothly when closed and draws up into pleats when the cords are pulled. It is by far the easiest shade to make and it is comparatively easy to hang. Fabric should be firmly woven. The stitching from the ring tape may be hidden with bands of trim to complement the fabric. Decorative rods may be used at the hem edge, held in place with trim or tabs made with self-fabric. The Roman shades in the Chapter I photograph showing a room decorated three ways were made with a facing, using the fabric designs as the guide for the tabs.

Shade may be hung with a board or a pressure-tension curtain rod. Use a board that will fit between the window jambs at the top and about 2″ wide or as deep as the indentation and at least ¾″ thick. Fasten board to jambs with an angle iron at each end. A pressure-tension curtain rod may be used if you have a window indentation that will hold the screw eyes securely.

MATERIAL NEEDED TO MAKE SHADE:

Fabric—2″ wider than indentation or window, and 4″ longer for a board or 5½″ longer for a rod. For wider width shades, plan seams so they will fall under the tape.

Roman shade tape—each tape should be the same length as the fabric, including hem. Use one tape for each side edge of shade and additional tapes for each 10″–12″ intervals across the fabric.

Traverse cord—the same length as tape, plus the width of the window and enough to hang down at least 3′ at one side of the window for each tape used.

Velcro® or snap tape the width of the board.

One ⅜″ brass or metal rod to hold shade flat. It should be ½″ less than the width of the finished shade.

Screw eyes large enough to hold all cords, one for each tape.

Small awning cleat.

Board with two angle irons and screws or a pressure-tension rod.

Band trim and decorative rod is optional.

CONSTRUCTION OF ROMAN SHADE (figure II-50): Cut fabric to required measurements.

1. Turn in side edges 1″; press. Turn in top edge ½″ for board or 2″ for rod and press.

2. Turn up bottom edge 3½″; press. Turn in raw edge ½″; pin. Stitch upper edge of hem in place and side hem edges together at each end.

3. Place tape over one side edge with a ring over the hem edge and the tape extending 2½″ below; top of tape should end below pressed edge so the last ring will be at least 2″ from the board or rod. Cut all tapes to this measurement, making sure the rings are at the same position for each strip. Use a zipper foot to stitch tapes in place. Turn up bottom tapes 1⅜″ and pull up ring. Stitch securely in place below ring (detail). Place tape ½″ from sides, covering raw edges. Stitch down along one edge, across the bottom and loop, and up the other edge. Divide remaining width equally between the tapes needed and stitch in place in the same manner, making sure the rings line up across shade on all tapes.

4. Stitch one section of Velcro® or snap tape to the wrong side of shade over ½″ pressed-in edge.

5. Staple or tack remaining half to front edge of board. For a rod-hung shade, turn in raw edge of casing ½″ and stitch in place.

Cut traverse cords and knot securely to each ring at the bottom of the shade, threading cord up through all the rings on the tape. Slip rod into loops at the bottom.

6. Fasten shade in place and mark position for screw eyes for each cord where it emerges. Remove shade; install screw eyes and the cleat at a comfortable position on the right side of the window. Thread cords through corresponding screw eyes to the right side. Lightly knot together all cords and test to make sure they all pull evenly.

7. Make a tight knot and cut off all cords but one; use that one to wrap cord around cleat.

II-50

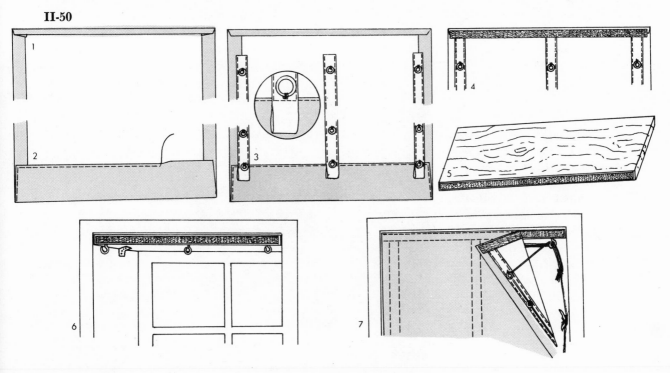

Designer Carl Fuchs creates this pleasant and practical nursery as a guide for new mothers with a flair for decorating and for fathers with a little handyman know-how.

Tailored lambrequins made from plywood frame corner windows with Lanscot-Arlen's Mayfair Collection; the "Mayfair Striped" is stapled in place to match the laminated shades by Stauffer Chemical Co. The same stripe is used on the doors and drawers, and for added interest is used on the bias for the screen. The plaid, "Mayfair Madison," is used for the crib spread and on the floor. The door fronts and drawers are made durable and serviceable with polyurethane varnish.

Matching fabrics and wall covering by Vice Versa are used in a beach house living room by designer Eleanor Cash. A reverse-roll window shade is laminated with fabric that matches the fabric-covered plywood panels and pinch-pleated tieback stationary draperies to create a wall of fabric. Matching chair seats and cushions for the wicker furniture are covered with an abundance of throw pillows for lazy afternoons.

Austrian Shade

At one time these filmy shirred shades with graceful fringed scallops were used exclusively in formal rooms, but now they are seen in every room, including the kitchen and bath, or are used as a valance in a shorter version. Sheer, semi-sheer, or lightweight fabric that gathers into soft folds works best. Preplanning is necessary. Measure the length of window between jamb and sill and the width between side frames. To figure yardage, double or even triple the length for soft sheers. To find the total fabric width needed for each shade, divide the width into two or more equal widths of 8″–10″. Each section will become a scallop. For each scallop, add 2″–4″ (none should be wider than 12″) and 3″ for the side hems. For wide width shades, plan seam so it will fall over a tape, since scallops will not drape correctly if seamed. Example: For three scallops, add up to 15″ (12″ for scallops; 3″ for side hems) to the fabric width requirement and use four tapes. For six scallops, add up to 27″ (24″ for scallops; 3″ for side hems) to the fabric width requirement and use seven tapes.

MATERIAL NEEDED TO MAKE SHADE:

Fabric—use as measured, adding 2″ to yardage for rod cover.

Austrian Ring Shir-tape—buy the required number of strips, the length as needed for the shade fabric.

Fringe—the length of the shade fabric width.

Tassels—the same number as tape strips, if desired.

Traverse cord—the same length as for tape, plus the width of the window and enough to hang down at least 3′ at one side of the window for each tape used.

Small awning clamp.

One ⅜″ round brass or metal rod to hold shade flat. It should be ½″ less than the finished shade width.

Screw eyes large enough to hold all cords, one for each tape.

Board with two angle irons and screws, or a pressure-tension rod to hang the shade.

Velcro® or snap tape the same length as the front length of the board.

CONSTRUCTION OF AUSTRIAN SHADE (figure II-51): Cut fabric to required measurement. Seam if necessary, stitching in a ¼″–½″ seam; press open. Raw edges will be covered with tape.

1. To hem side edges, turn in 1½″; press. Turn in raw edges ½″; pin. Stitch hem in place.

II-51

Turn in top edge ½″ for board or 2″ for rod; press.

2. On the right side, turn up bottom edge ¼″–½″ (width of fringe heading must cover raw edge); press. Place fringe over raw edge, stitch to shade along both edges of heading, forming hem.

3. To attach tape to shade, place it over one side hem so a ring starts about 3″ below the

65

pressed edge of the top with tape extending above the top pressed edge and 1½" beyond the hem; pin. With a blunt, pointed object, separate tape weave over the cords and pull out the cords. Tie cords together at the top and bottom so they don't pull out. Cut all tapes to this measurement, making sure the rings are at the same spot for each one. Turn up ends 1½" to form loops for a rod. Use a zipper foot to stitch tapes in place. Stitch both edges of tape in place, with side tapes ¾" from outer edges, stitching across tape about 1" above bottom hem. Stitch remaining tapes in place, keeping sections equal; make sure all rings are lined up across shade.

To cover rod so shade won't shift, cut a 2"-wide self-fabric strip 1" longer than finished shade width. Fold in half lengthwise. Stitch across one end and long edge in a ½" seam. Turn right side out and insert rod. Sew remaining end shut. Slide covered rod through tape loops at shade hem. Tack at each end.

4. On the right side, make pleats on each side of center tapes and one at each side tape so shade is the required finished width at top; pin.

On the wrong side, stitch one Velcro® section over pleated top and attach other section to board as directed for Roman shade (figure II-50, steps 4 and 5).

For a casing, open pressed-down edge; pin pleats in place for about 6" and then make casing by turning in raw edge ½"; stitch to shade; pleats will be held in place at this point.

5. To shirr the shade, pull up the two cords of each tape equally to the finished length, including the trim. Tie cord securely, but do not cut off. Cords may be released to clean. Tie ends out of the way; distribute the shirring evenly along all the tapes, keeping the rings parallel. Sew tas-sels to back of shade below each tape loop, if desired. Cut traverse cords in lengths as directed. Knot securely to each tape loop. Thread cord up through all the rings on each tape. Hang shade as directed for Roman shade (figure II-50, steps 6 and 7).

SHUTTERS

There are many styles that may be used as a shade or a draw drapery substitute. Shutters are often used in combination with shades and decorative valances. The style that requires casement curtains is a decorator's favorite. Two shutters are needed for each window. Make your own with pine strips. Have strips cut to measure for convenience. Artist's stretcher frames may also be used.

Easy Shutters

Very little skill is required to make these easy shutters, especially if you have the wooden strips cut to measure. The corners may be mitered or straight.

MATERIALS NEEDED TO MAKE TWO SHUTTERS:
4 long pine strips ¾" × 1" for sides
4 short pine strips ¾" × 1" for two top supports and two bottom supports
Corrugated nails
Elmer's® glue
4 sash rods
4 hinges
2 knobs
Fabric the length of the shutter opening, plus allowance for two casings, and twice as wide as the opening

CONSTRUCTION OF SHUTTERS: Select the better side of the wood for the front of the shutters, which will be painted or stained (figure II-52).

II-52

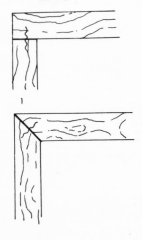
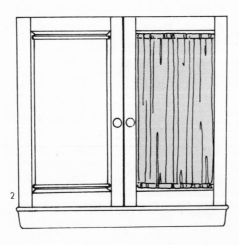
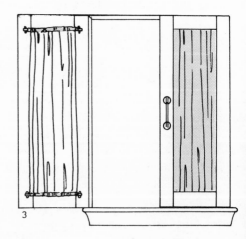

RIGHT: *A master bedroom's dormer-window sitting room alcove is shaded and shuttered by designer Ann Heller, ASID, in matching wallpaper and fabric with Breneman's "Kristan" shade with a border and cornice from the wallpaper. The shutters are filled in with casement curtains. Polka-dotted slipcovered furniture and a double-covered lamp table add to the coziness of the arrangement.*

BELOW: *Designer James R. Patterson concentrates bold interest at the window wall of his own bedroom-study, producing a space-widening result with decorative ease. "Brave Arrow," a Stockwell fabric, and matching wall covering help to create the built-in look. A quilted couch cover with matching wedge-shaped bolsters starts the look. Window Shade Manufacturers Association's laminated shade with matching tabs and a brass rod covers the window. The wall covering is used to cover the screen and flat cornice.*

1. Before nailing the two long strips to the two short strips, spread glue on each end. Place front sides down and align the rectangle. With the corners square, keep edges butted tightly together and in alignment; fasten strips with corrugated nails. Allow glue to dry at least 24 hours. Sand and finish as desired.

Make casement curtains as directed on page 39.

2. Attach the knobs to the center strips that will meet and the rod fixtures on the back or in the narrow indentation. Attach hinges to the shutters.

3. Hang the shutters by attaching hinges to window indentation.

SCREENS

Used at windows with shades or curtains or as dividers, screens are a great way to hide structural imperfections or add a seasonal touch. For those of you who like to change your decor each spring and fall, you might like to use screens at the windows in place of draperies in the winter months and use light, airy curtains alone for the warmer months. A screen may be used to help create a secluded hideaway or to separate one area from another. Use a two-panel screen at each side of a window; three or more panels for a divider.

Purchase a screen and cover it with fabric by gluing or stapling it in place. The staples won't be noticed if they are used on the inner edges. Or you can make screens to your precise measurements.

Use a firmly woven medium- or heavyweight fabric, fake leather or suede, patchwork, appliqués, or any kind of appropriate coverings for your screen. Sheets are one of the most economical ways to make beautiful screens.

Screens for Special Uses

These screens are quite easy to make, but they are time-consuming. Make simple wooden frames that are padded with flannel or an old sheet for reinforcement, and then cover with a decorative fabric. Instructions are given for fabric hinges, but you may use any type of suitable metal hinges instead.

MATERIALS NEEDED: Frames should be 12″–18″ wide and as long as needed. Short screens will need one center support; screens that reach from floor to ceiling will need at least three supports.

2 pine strips 1″ × 2″, the length of the finished screen for each panel

2 pine strips 1″ × 2″, the length needed for the top and bottom supports less 4″ (the width of the two long upright strips) for each panel

1 or more short strips the same length as the other supports—as center support for each panel

Corrugated nails

Elmer's® glue

Staples or tacks

Decorative upholstery tacks

Masking tape ½″ wide

Flannel or a substitute to reinforce both sides of each panel

Decorative fabric (allow extra fabric to match design repeats when calculating yardage)

Hinges—6″-wide strips of matching fabric, or 3″-wide grosgrain ribbon, or metal hinges

CONSTRUCTION OF SCREENS (figure II-53): To make a frame for each panel of your screen, join wooden strips as directed for shutters, figure

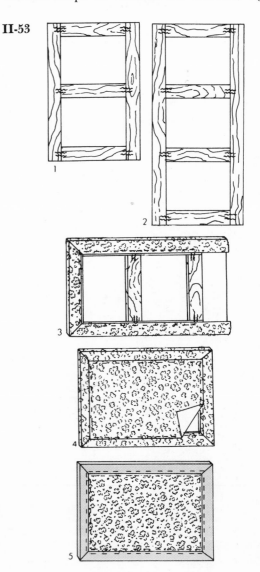

II-53

II-52, step 1. Use 2 corrugated nails to fasten each support.

1. Center support for shorter screens.
2. Space supports evenly for longer screens.
3. To reinforce each panel, cut one flannel section as long and as wide as frame, plus 3″ on all edges for the front and one flannel section about 1″ smaller than the frame on all edges. Lay frame over larger flannel section and wrap around to other side of frame. Staple or tack near inner frame edge, starting at the top and working to the bottom on one side, keeping fabric taut. Then do the other side the same way, pulling flannel taut across the frame; staple. Fasten ends, working from center toward corners. Miter corners, keeping them flat; staple.
4. Center backing strip over frame and staple in place over front flannel raw edge.

To cover panel front with decorative fabric, cut one section of decorative fabric the length and width of each panel, plus 2½″ on all edges. For each panel back, cut another section of decorative fabric ½″ larger than the panel on all edges, matching design with front if necessary.

5. Center panel on wrong side of larger fabric section with the stapled back facing you. Wrap one long edge over panel and staple. Work from top to bottom and keep fabric taut. Do the same for the other long edge, pulling fabric taut across the front without distorting the design. Staple both ends in place, keeping them taut and flat as you did with flannel.

CONSTRUCTION OF HINGES (figure II-54): For a fabric hinge:

1. Cut a 6″-wide strip the length of the panel, plus 1″. Fold strip lengthwise, right sides together, and stitch ends in a ½″ seam. Turn; press, keeping raw edges even. Place strip on back of panel with top and bottom edges even; staple.

For a grosgrain hinge, cut ribbon the length of the panel plus 3″. Turn up ends 1½″; press. Turn in raw edge ½″ and stitch hem in place. Attach ribbon hinge to panel as directed for fabric hinge.

If you are using metal hinges, attach after panels are completed.

2. To finish back of panel, tape wrong side of smaller fabric section edges with masking tape, keeping corners free of tape. Turn in all edges a scant ⅝″, folding a miter at each corner.
3. Center panel back over panel with turned-in edges about 1/16″ from outer edges. Fasten back in place with decorative tacks, keep-

ing fabric taut and making sure the edges do not extend beyond the back panel edges.

4. Make another panel in the same manner. Align both panels when joining fabric hinge.
5. For a screen with three or more panels, reverse edges to be hinged on center panel, so the three panels can be folded flat. To do this, make a seam on the front right edge of the center panel and the front left edge of the third panel to insert the fabric hinge; allow a ½″ seam allowance on each edge. Stitch hinge to these front panel covers first. Install the front covers on all panels before tacking the backs in place. Cover the third panel, then the second, and then the first as instructed for a double screen. Make seams line up with panel edges and staple panel seam allowances and hinge to frame before pulling fabric taut across the front of the panel.

II-54

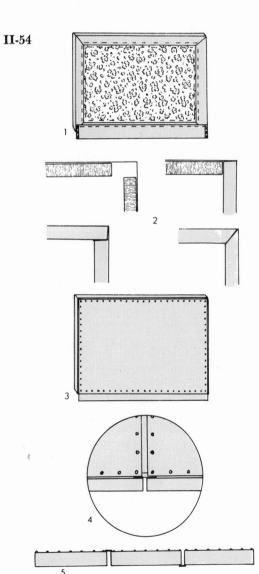

III
Pillows, Cushions, and Bolsters— Easy-to-Make Decorating Jewels

Crown your new decor with a colorful assortment of pillows, cushions, and bolsters sewn in jewel-like hues, using fabric textures and designs or a needlecraft project to add a personal touch. Indulge in expensive strips of fabric (since you're saving by sewing) or keep costs to a minimum. Just match the fabric to the use it will receive. Use silks, satins, velvets, or other delicate or luxury fabrics in a formal room and employ chintz, homespun, corduroy, sailcloth, denim, cotton blends, or any durable fabric that will withstand the wear received in a busy room.

Pillows and cushions can be made in just about any shape—round or square, oval or oblong, triangular or crescent—or they can take the form of an animal or a flower. Bolsters, on the other hand, are usually round, square, triangular, or wedge-shaped. What are these three categories? Aren't they all pillows? Today, all three types are used interchangeably; it's the stuffing or the form that determines the use. At one time the rule for each pillow, cushion, and bolster was clearly defined. Pillows were used to support the head during sleep or rest, cushions were used to sit, kneel, or lie on, and bolsters were used as an ornament on a bed or as support along the back of a couch. Today's decorators refuse to accept such limitations. Pillows and cushions are used at the back of couches for support, and bolster shapes are made into soft throw pillows. So now you can be as creative as you like and choose the type that will serve your needs.

Pillows are the quickest and easiest to make because they are thick in the center, tapering to the outer edge, requiring only one seam. This is called a knife-edge. Cushions and bolsters are the same thickness from center to outer edges, just like a box, and have two major seams. A box-edge cushion requires only a little more time to cut and sew; a bolster, because it is larger, will naturally require more handling. Instructions are given for knife-edge pillows and box-edge cushions and bolsters with some interesting variations.

FORMS AND FILLERS

Forms can be purchased in almost any size or shape. Polyurethane forms are available for pillows, cushions, and bolsters and some places will cut shapes to order. Fabric-covered forms may be purchased with feather, foam chip, or polyester fiberfill stuffings. Other ready-made forms may have a solid foam covering with chips as a filler, or the polyester fiberfill may be preshaped into pillow forms.

However, you may wish to make your own forms and stuff them with foam chips, polyester fiberfill, kapok, or even old nylons. For pillow furniture you may want to use styrofoam pellets. Then too, you will find it easier to put on the cases if you cover the polyurethane foam forms with lightweight fabric. When making a form, it's best to draw a pattern on paper. First, determine the size, then add a ½" seam allowance on all edges.

To make a round pattern, use a pencil, string, and a push-pin. Cut a groove in the pencil near the point; tie one end of the string along the groove. Place a magazine on a flat surface and lay a piece of paper over it. Tape paper in place or weight it down at the corners. Tie string to pin, making distance between pencil point and pin one-half the desired diameter. Insert pin into magazine and draw circle. Example: For a finished 12″ form the diameter would be 13″ (including seam allowances) so the distance between the pin and point should be 6½″ (figure III-1).

III-1

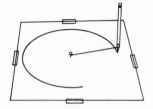

Knife-Edge Forms

Cut two fabric pieces the desired shape. Squares, rectangles, and triangles can be drawn on the wrong side of the fabric with pencil and ruler. Be sure to put one or more straight edges along the lengthwise and crosswise grain. Pin the two pieces together (figure III-2), matching grain lines; stitch ½″ from edge, leaving an opening for stuffing. Trim away any corners. Turn right side out. Stuff as desired. Turn in opening edges ½″; pin. Pin folded edges together and sew

opening securely shut, using slip-stitch method 2 in Chapter VIII.

Box-Edge Forms (figure III–3)

Cut two fabric pieces the desired shape for the top and bottom and a strip the desired height, the length of the perimeter or circumference plus 3″. Example: For a finished rectangle form 10″ × 15″ × 3″ cut two 11″ × 16″ rectangles and a 4″ strip 56″ long.

1. For a cushion with corners, leave 2″ free, stitch top to strip, right sides together, keeping edges even and stitching ½″ from edges. At each corner, stitch to within ½″ of next side; with needle in fabric, raise presser foot and clip strip to needle. Pivot fabric on needle until next side is lined up with presser foot. Make sure strips and top are flat so fabric won't pucker. Drop presser foot and sew remainder of strip in place, stopping about 1″ from opposite end.

2. For a round cushion, make reinforcement stitches (see Chapter VIII) along both edges of boxing strips a scant ½″ from the long edge. Clip to stitching at even intervals. Stitch strip to top just inside the reinforcement stitches, leaving 2″ free. Keep raw edges even and spread clips as you stitch, stopping about 1″ from opposite end.

III-2

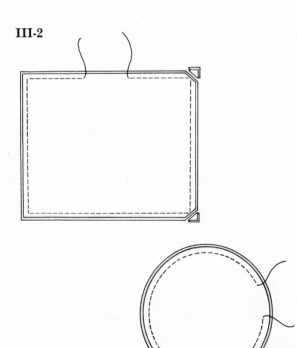

III-3

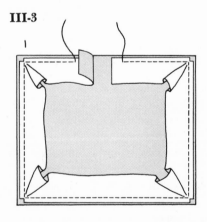

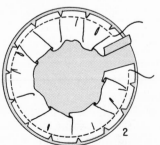

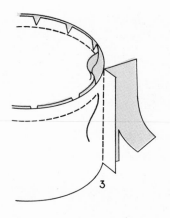

3

3. For both types, join strip ends in a ½"
seam, keeping top free; trim away excess.

4. Finger-press seam open and complete
stitching.

5. Now stitch bottoms to strips in the same
manner, lining up edges with top and leaving
an opening for stuffing.

Turn right side out. Stuff as desired. Turn in
opening edges ½"; pin. Pin folded edges together and sew opening securely shut, using slip-
stitch method 2 in Chapter VIII.

Polyurethane Foam Forms

To cover, cut fabric the same measurements as
the form. Do not add seam allowances. Foam
should be compressed slightly so the cover will
be snug. Stitch covers together in a ½" seam,
following the directions given for making your
own forms. Be sure to leave an opening large
enough to insert the foam.

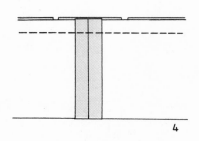

4

BASIC KNIFE-EDGE PILLOW COVERS

These easy-to-make pillows can be as simple or as
elaborate as you wish—great for the beginner
and the experienced alike—just two pieces of
fabric are needed, one for the top and another
for the bottom. A beautiful or hard-to-handle
fabric may need a plain cover; others will take a
decorative seam in stride. To add cording, ruffles,
or fringe to match the decor, see *decorative seams*
in Chapter VIII or make a sunburst top, using
cording or ruffles for added interest.

Needlework pillow tops are great accent color
accessories as they can be made to match your
color scheme. Crewel embroidery, bargello, and
needlepoint tops often need to be blocked so the
pillow will hold its shape without pulling or
puckering. If your needlework needs blocking,
turn to Chapter VIII for instructions. Be sure
to use runproof threads or yarn so your needlework can be blocked quickly. When constructing
a pillow with a needlework top, back it with a
layer of durable fabric to prevent undue stress
on the stitches, canvas, or fabric. Simply cut a
piece the same size or shape as needed for the pillow and baste it to the wrong side of the needlework. Handle the two layers as one during
construction.

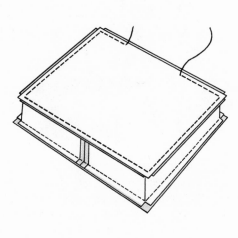

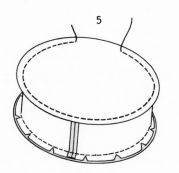

5

There may be times when you want to make
a knife-edge pillow cover and stuff it instead of
using a form. Make from washable fabric; pillows stuffed with foam chips or polyester fiberfill can be washed with care.

Every teen-ager needs a room of his/her own with ample storage space. Designer Shirley Regendahl creates a charming bed–sitting room that any craftsperson can duplicate. One wall contains a sofa bed with a tailored cover, round bolsters, throw pillows, and cushions all made from Waverly Fabrics' red-and-white ticking. Matching window shades made with "Lam-Eze" by Joanna Western Mills Co. pull down over storage shelves, and the platform with drawers provides stack-away space for sport gear and bulky equipment. The chair seats are reupholstered with matching fabric, too.

RIGHT: *Ruffled throw pillows and a cushioned old church pew are used by designer Bobbi Stuart to help create a cozy dining area in a kitchen. At the window are a ruffled valance with side panel, sill-length curtains, and a "Barbados" window shade by Stauffer Chemical Co. A floor-length table cover with matching reupholstered chair seats and a high chair for the little one complete the corner that will be used for any meal of the day.*

III-4

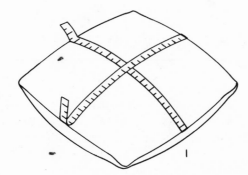

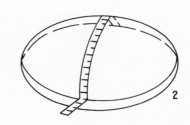

MEASUREMENTS: When using ready-made forms (figure III-4):

1. Measure the length and width for squares and rectangles.

2. Measure the diameter for circles.

Then add 1″ to each measurement for seam allowances. Use the same pattern you made for the forms when covering your own.

There are several ways that closures can be made for knife-edge pillows.

SLIP-STITCHED CLOSURES: Plain edges without trim may be slip-stitched together using method 2 in Chapter VIII. When using trim (figure III-5):

1. Be sure to machine-stitch the trim in place ½″ from the opening edge. Turn right side out. Turn in seam allowances of trim, and pillow top along stitching; pin. Turn in bottom edges ½″; pin.

2. Pin folded edge of bottom over stitching on top. Slip-stitch to trim.

ZIPPER IN A SEAM: Use for a knife-edge pillow (figure III-6). If using trim in the seam, baste it to one section for the top.

1. Open zipper, place face down on right side of top with zipper teeth along the basting for the trim (or ½″ from raw edge on a plain top); pin. Stitch close to the teeth through all thicknesses, making sure pull can slide easily.

2. Close zipper. Turn seam allowance and zipper tape under top. On the matching edge of the bottom, turn it in ½″; press. Pin pressed edge over zipper, keeping ends of top and bottom even; stitch ¼″ from pressed edge.

ZIPPER IN CENTER OF PILLOW (figure III-7): Use for round or ornamental pillows. Insert zipper in an opening created at the center of the bottom. Cut out top as needed. Then fold pattern in half and add ⅝″ for seam allowance (along the straight edge for shaped tops). Cut two sections for bottom. Turn in one section ½″; pin.

III-5

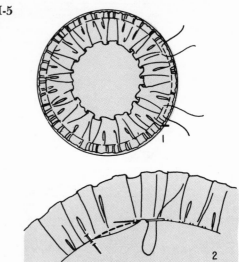

III-6

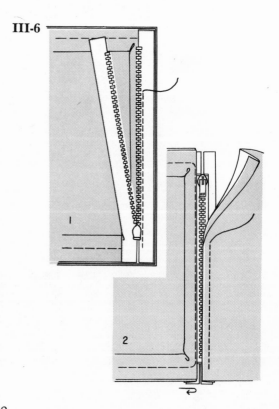

78

III-7

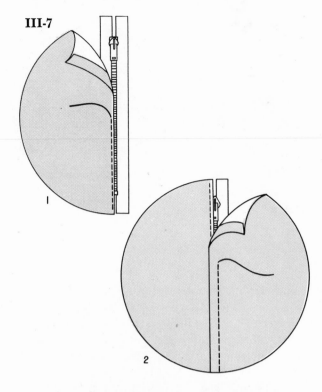

1. Place folded edge over zipper tape, leaving just enough room for the pull to slide easily; pin to zipper tape. Using a zipper foot, stitch close to pressed edge.

2. Next turn in remaining section ⅝"; pin. Place this section over zipper with folded edge along stitching on opposite side; pin to zipper tape, keeping shaped edges of both bottom sections even. Stitch zipper in place through all thicknesses.

Decorative Edges

These adornments are what make a ho-hum fabric into an outstanding pillow. There are many beautiful ready-mades available, but the classic favorites are cording and ruffles made with self- or contrasting fabric.

Fabric plays an important role when making your own edgings. When purchasing fabric be sure to allow extra yardage for self-trim or buy enough contrasting fabric. To make cording, narrow bias or straight strips are needed, and ruffles are made from a double thickness when used on pillows, so wider and much longer strips are needed. Be sure to select a light- to medium-weight fabric so ruffles will gather easily. To apply cording, ruffles, or purchased edgings to pillow tops see *decorative seams* in Chapter VIII.

CONSTRUCTION: Cut out pillow top and bottom as required for your choice of closure. If making self- or contrasting trim, cut out as many strips as needed. Then make cording or ruffles, if that type of edging is being used. Machine-baste trim to top before proceeding (figure III-8).

For a slip-stitched closure:

1. Pin top to bottom; stitch together in a ½" seam or just inside the basting line used to hold trim in place, leaving an opening large enough to insert form.

Trim away excess fabric at corners or points. Turn pillow cover right side out. Complete closure as directed in figure III-5.

When using a zipper in a seam, apply zipper as shown in figure III-6, steps 1 and 2. Open zipper, *now*; you don't want to stitch the remaining edges together and not be able to turn the cover right side out.

2. Fold top over bottom along zipper, with right sides together and raw edges even. Make sure zipper tapes are even at opening end, too. Stitch in a ½" seam or just inside the line of basting used to hold trim in place. Trim away excess fabric at corners or points. Turn pillow right side out.

For a zipper in the bottom half of the pillow, insert zipper as shown in figure III-7, steps 1 and 2. Open zipper.

3. With right sides together, raw edges even, and zipper tapes touching at opening edge, stitch top to bottom in a ½" seam or just inside the line of basting used to hold trim in place. Turn cover right side out through zipper.

III-8

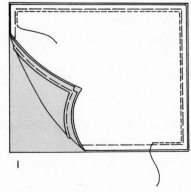

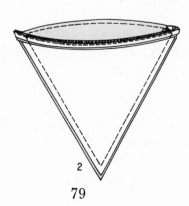

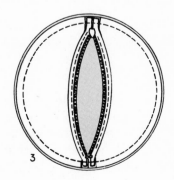

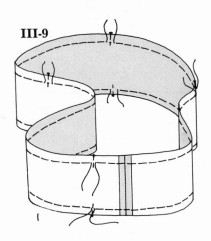
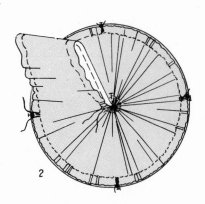
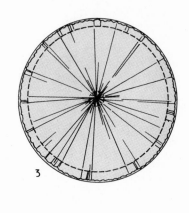

NOVELTY KNIFE-EDGE PILLOW COVERS

What good is a pillow story without some variations? Here are some alternatives that should pique your creative instincts.

Sunburst Top

Make pattern for a circle as directed in figure III-1.

MATERIALS NEEDED:

A strip of fabric 1½ times the length of the circumference plus 1″ and as wide as ½ the diameter plus 1″

A circle of lightweight fabric for backing

A circle of pillow fabric for the bottom (a slip-stitched closure must be used)

Self-cording the length of the diameter, plus 1″

Two large button forms

Button and carpet thread

Long darning needle

CONSTRUCTION (figure III-9):

1. Stitch strip ends in a ½″ seam; press open. Divide strip into quarters; mark both edges with pins. Gather both edges between pins.

2. Divide backing into quarters; pin. Place wrong side of strip over backing along the outer edge, matching pins, and repin. Pull up gathers; secure thread ends and distribute evenly. Baste.

3. Pull up gathers at center of pillow. Sew securely to backing. NOTE: Some fabrics may be too bulky at the center to gather flat. Ease in the excess as you baste the center gathered area to the backing.

Add cording to pillow top, joining ends as shown in *corded seam*, Chapter VIII. Sew top to bottom as instructed in figure III-8, step 1. Insert pillow form and slip-stitch opening shut (see figure III-5). Complete pillow with tufted buttons, using the following instructions.

BUTTON TUFTING (figure III-10): Cover buttons with self-fabric following package instructions. Using button and carpet thread, thread a long needle. Double the thread and tie ends to one button shank, leaving about a 3″ tail.

1. Insert needle through pillow, then through remaining button's shank. About ¼″ from emerging threads, insert needle back through pillow to the first side, then through button shank. Repeat procedure one more time.

2. Pull thread taut, forming dimples on both sides of pillow. Knot thread ends securely; cut off thread ends.

III-10

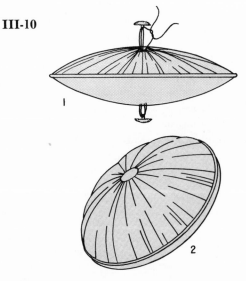

Fast and Washable

Pillow covers should be made of firm, washable fabric; stuffing should be foam chips or polyester

80

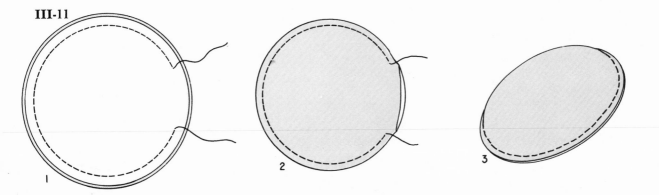

fiberfill. When soiled, simply machine-wash in warm or cold water and dry at medium to cool temperature.

Top-stitched Edges (figure III-11): Make a pattern the desired size or shape, adding ¾″ on all edges. Cut two fabric pieces.

1. With right sides together, stitch in a ½″ seam, leaving an opening for turning. Turn right side out; press.

2. Topstitch ¼″ from finished edges between opening edges. Stuff pillow; turn in opening edges ½″; press.

3. Pin pressed opening edges together. Complete topstitching.

Flange Edges (figure III-12): Make only square or rectangular pillows by this method. First decide on pillow size and width of the flange. Example: For a 12″-square pillow with a 2″ flange, two 17″ fabric squares are needed (12″ for pillow, 4″ for flange on all edges, and 1″ for seam allowances on the same edges).

1. With right sides together, stitch top to bottom in a ½″ seam, leaving an opening for stuffing. Trim corners. Turn right side out; press edge.

2. Stitch close to finished edges between open-

ing edges and again 2″ away, forming the flange. Stuff pillow. Pin opening edges together and again 2″ away to hold stuffing in place.

3. Stitch opening edges together and remaining flange edge in place, connecting both rows of previous stitching.

PILLOW SHAMS

This type of pillow cover has knife-edges and is usually loose fitting, with a lapped closure for easy removal. Quite often the sham is used as a decorative cover for bed pillows, so think of them as a second pillowcase that is removed every night. Each morning the pillow is reinserted when the bed is made. Today, however, pillow shams are used everywhere and they can be as snug or as loose as desired. Ruffles are the favorite trim, with a flange the second choice.

Construction (figure III-13): Determine finished length and width, adding 1″ for seam allowances (add an additional 1″ to each measurement for easy removal). Make a pattern, then cut out the front. Divide pattern in half crosswise. Add 6″ to this line. The larger section is

III-12

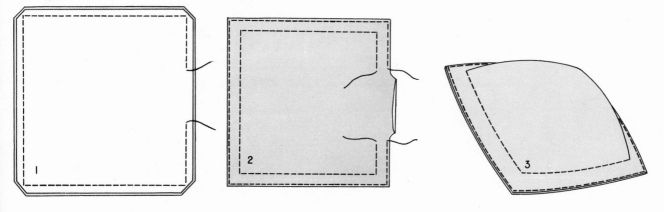

the size needed to make a back closure. Cut two fabric pieces this size for the back.

1. Turn in opening edge of each back piece 1″; press. Turn in raw edges forming a hem; pin. Stitch hem edge in place.

Baste a ruffle to the front as instructed in Chapter VIII.

2. With right sides together, pin one back section to the front, keeping raw edges even. Pin remaining back section in place; hemmed edges will overlap, forming closure. Stitch back to front in a ½″ seam.

3. Turn right side out through lapped opening; press.

4. For a flange edge, add 2″ to 4″ on all edges. Prepare back same as for the preceding construction, steps 1 and 2. Stitch front to back in a ½″ seam. Trim corners. Turn, press edges. Stitch desired width away to form flange.

III-14

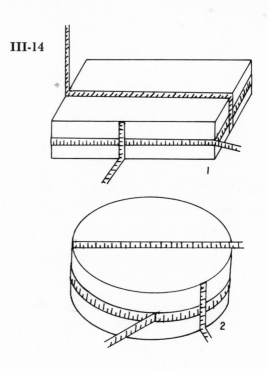

III-13

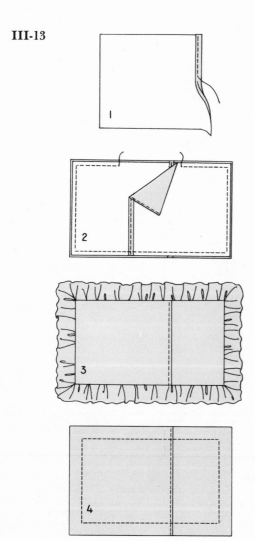

BASIC BOX-EDGE CUSHION COVERS

This type of cushion is used on upholstered furniture, slipcovers, and outdoor furniture, in recreational vehicles, and for church pew kneeling pads. Usually it has self-corded seams.

MEASUREMENTS (figure III-14):

1. For squares and rectangular forms, measure length, width, height, and then around the form for boxing strip length.

2. For round forms, measure diameter, height, and then around the form for boxing strip length. Add 1″ to all measurements for seam allowances.

CLOSURE (figure III-15): A nearly invisible zipper application is used for these cushions. For squares and rectangles, use a zipper 2″ to 4″ longer than one edge. For round forms, use a zipper at least ⅓ the length of the boxing strip measurement. Cut a strip as long as the zipper tapes and 1½″ wider than the boxing strip (including seam allowance). Cut strip in half lengthwise. With right sides together, machine-baste strips in a ¾″ seam; press open. Center zipper, face down, over basted seam. Using zipper foot, stitch along center of each zipper tape. Remove basting.

III-15

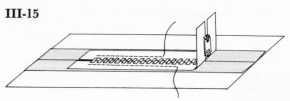

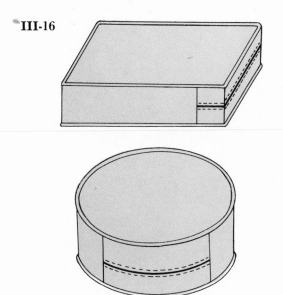

III-16

CONSTRUCTION (figure III-17): To the length and width measurement, add the height plus 1″ for seam allowances. Example: For a 12″-square cushion that is 3″ deep, cut two 16″ squares. Cut two fabric sections the size needed for the top and bottom. The opening may be slip-stitched shut, or use a zipper 1″ shorter than the cushion width.

1. To join the two fabric sections, place right sides together along the corresponding edge; mark zipper length. Stitch in ½″ from each end to markings. Machine-baste remainder of seam. Press seam open.

III-17

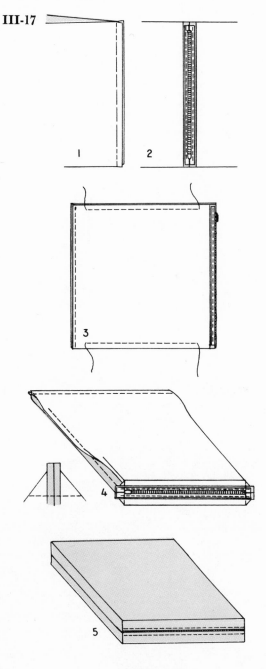

For stiff, heavy, or vinyl fabric, use the exposed-zipper method for cushioned lounges in Chapter VI.

CONSTRUCTION (figure III-16): Cut out pillow top and bottom. Cut strips for zipper and remainder of boxing strip after subtracting the length of the zipper (do not include tape ends), plus 4″ for seams. Example: For a 12″-square cushion 3″ deep, cut two 13″ squares for top and bottom. Use a 14″ zipper and cut a strip 5½″ wide and 15½″ long for closure. Cut boxing strip 4″ wide and 38″ long. Cut strips for self-cording using twice the length of the entire boxing strip as a guide, as instructed in *decorative seams,* Chapter VIII.

Make self-cording first so cushion will go together quickly. Make zipper closure as directed in figure III-15.

Stitch one end of zipper strip to boxing strip in a ½″ seam. Press seam toward boxing strip. Baste cording to tops and bottoms. (NOTE: Center zipper over one end of a square or rectangular cushion top.) Start stitching 1″ from end of zipper strip; stitch boxing strip to top same as for form (figure III-3, steps 1, 2, 3, and 4).

Open zipper. Stitch boxing strip to bottom in the same manner. Turn right side out; insert form.

QUICK BOX-EDGE CUSHION COVERS

This method can be used only for squares and rectangles. Use the measurement as given in figure III-14, step 1.

Needlework-covered throw pillows help to create a charming provincial mood designed to control light and camouflage some awkward elements. Gray-and-white ticking is used for the padded cornice, the window struts that are enhanced with fabric-covered plywood panels, and the laminated shades. Crisp white panel curtains soften the effect at each side, while plain scalloped white café curtains hide the radiator and air conditioning unit.

A pillow-covered trundle bed–sofa slipcovered in Bloomcraft's "Red Tulip" fabric with matching pillow shams is used by designer Abbey Darer to help create a grown-up room for a preteen. Matching Priscilla curtains and valances, a coffee table with a floor-length cover, and tie-cushion pads for wicker chairs form a lovely focal point. Surround the print with polka-dot fabric from Hannet Morrow Fischer, Inc., for the walls and the Stauffer Chemical Co. "Trim-Lam" window shades and you have a room to please a tomboy or a little lady.

2. Center zipper, face down, over basted seam; pin. Stitch zipper in place close to teeth, leaving enough room for the pull to slide easily.

Remove basting. Open zipper.

3. Stitch sides and remaining end in a ½″ seam beginning and ending ¾″ from edges. Press side seams open.

4. Bring zipper and side seams together forming a point; pin. Mark seams where base of triangle is same measurement as the cushion height. Stitch between pins to form corner; trim to ½″. Stitch remaining seam to form corners in same manner.

5. Turn right side out; insert form.

BOLSTER COVERS

The most common use of the bolster is as a backrest for an armless and backless couch. Bolsters, too, are box-edge, so the cover construction varies only slightly from box-edge cushions.

Wedge Bolsters (figure III–18)
This is by far the most widely used bolster and is not complicated to make. When combined with matching covers, wedge bolsters help transform a high-riser, a Hollywood, or a daybed into a couch. Directions for making those covers appear in Chapter IV.

MEASUREMENTS: Measure length; then measure up one side, across top, down the other side, and

III-18

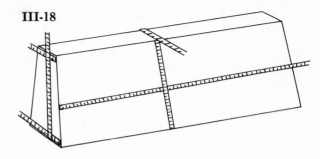

across bottom for width. For ends, measure height and both top and bottom width. Add 1″ to all measurements for seam allowances. Be sure to make a pattern for the ends.

CLOSURE: The bottom opening may be slip-stitched shut or closed with a zipper. If you can't find a zipper long enough (usually 36″), use two, each 18″ long. The area will be confined when inserting zippers, as the fabric will form a tube (figure III-19).

1. To insert zipper, stitch bottom edges together at each end for ⅝″ in a ½″ seam. Press seams open.

2. Continuing across opening edge, turn in these edges ½″; press. Do not stretch fabric.

3. Open zippers. Center face down, over one opening edge, with stops ½″ from each end. (Pull tabs will meet at the center of opening when zippers are closed.) Pin one tape of each zipper in place with teeth along opening edge;

III-19

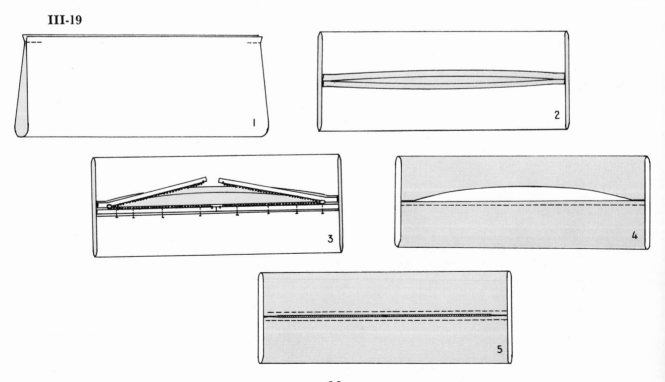

overlap ends where they meet at the center and pull down to clear stops.

4. Use a zipper foot and work through opening. Stitch along the center of zipper tape (about ¼″ from pressed opening edge) from one end of the opening to the other. Close zippers. Pin remaining opening edge in place over zipper with pressed edges meeting.

5. Open zippers and stitch pinned zipper tapes in place. NOTE: When making a pair of bolsters, do same steps for each as you work.

CONSTRUCTION (figure III-20): Cut out long cover section and both end pieces. Cut strips for self-cording to be used on each end (see Chapter VIII). Make self-cording first, then stitch to ends. Insert zippers in long cover section following figure III-19, steps 1–5. Open zippers.

1. Using a zipper foot, stitch ends to large section in a ½″ seam.

2. Turn covers right side out, pushing corner at each end in place so cording extends smoothly; insert form.

III-20

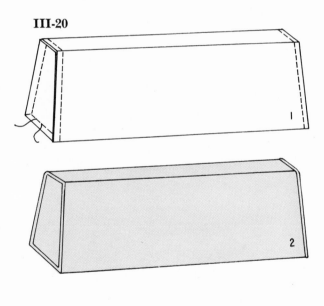

Round Bolster

This round shape is often used by decorators in a smaller, softer version as a throw pillow. The ends may be more decorative than those of the wedge bolster—fringe, ruffles, and decorative trims may be used instead of cording. Ends may be gathered like the sunburst pillow (figure III-9). Add a button or a tassel to the center.

MEASUREMENTS (figure III-21): Measure the length and then around the form. Measure diameter of ends. Add 1″ to all measurements for seam allowances.

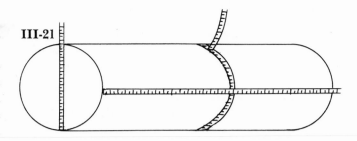

III-21

CONSTRUCTION (figure III-22): Cut out long cover section and both end pieces. Cut bias or straight strips for self-cording, if being used. When making a pair, do the same step for each as you work. The simplest closure is the slip-stitched method. To insert zipper, follow the method used for the wedge bolster, figure III-19, steps 1–5. Make cording first, if being used, to save time. Insert zipper. Baste cording or trim to end circles.

1. Add reinforcement stitches a scant ½″ from both ends of the tube. Clip, at even intervals, to the stitching.

2. Open zipper. With right sides together pin ends to tube, spreading clipped seam allowances as you pin, keeping outer raw edges even. Stitch from the tube side, just inside the reinforcement stitches.

3. Turn right side out through zipper opening. Shape ends smoothly and insert form.

III-22

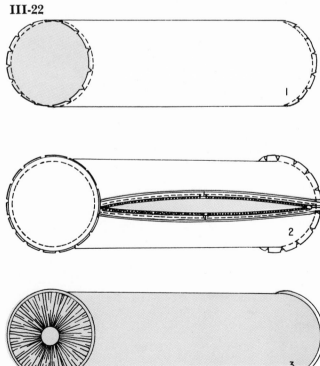

Bon Bon Bolster

MATERIALS NEEDED:

A round polyurethane form 14″ long with an 8″ diameter

A rectangle of fabric 25½″ wide and 34″ long for the cover

Two strips 2″ wide and 8″ long for bands

18″ zipper

1½ yards of fringe

CONSTRUCTION (figure III-23): Insert zipper same as figure III-19, steps 1–5. Add trim to ends as instructed in *extended trim as an edge finish* in Chapter VIII. Add two rows of gathering

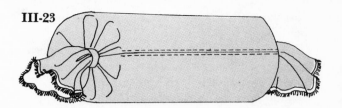

III-23

threads 1″ apart 4½″ beyond trim. Pull up gathers as tight as possible; fasten ends securely. Turn in long edges of strips to meet; press. Slip-stitch a strip over the gathers at each end, turning in raw ends where they meet. Slip-stitch ends together.

IV
Bed Fashions for
Every Life-Style

Today's bedroom has become one of the most versatile rooms in the home—there is little space that does not serve a dual purpose. We all need a place to call our own—where we can relax, pursue a hobby, or just dream—and the bedroom is the most logical place!

A bed is usually the largest and most important piece of furniture in the room, and it may be covered to suit the life-style of its inhabitants—formal with luxurious or classic fabrics for the traditional bedroom, contemporary to serve multiple needs with up-to-the-minute fabrics, or way-out treatments for members of the family with strong, bold tastes.

There are two basic styles of bedspreads—flat and fitted—with many variations. Even the covers used to transform a bed into a couch for daytime use are a variation of the flat and fitted styles.

BEDS TO COVER

The style of your bed must be considered when selecting a bedcover (figure IV-1):

1. The Hollywood bed with or without a headboard and always without a footboard

2. The classic bed with matching head- and footboards

3. The traditional bed with a canopy

4. The high-riser or twin-size Hollywood bed covered to become a couch

5. The simple lines of a platform bed with a traditional mattress or one of polyurethane foam cut to size

6. The loft bed for the daring who also have the good fortune to have a room with a high ceiling

IV-1

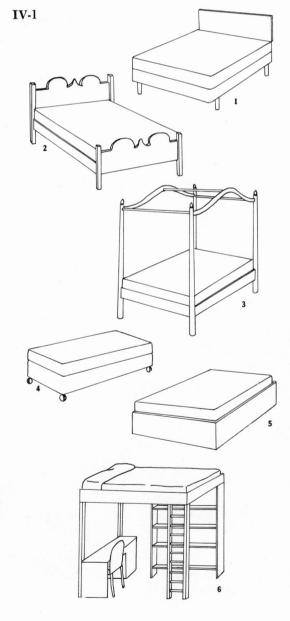

ABOVE: *Bloomcraft fabric in a light and dark version is used for this simple throw bedspread with a contrasting ruffle and a heading, topping a gathered dust ruffle with a matching pillow sham. The beautiful carved wooden headboard is pointed up with a contrasting panel, gathered canopy valance, and tieback curtains designed by Olga Gordon. The matching gathered valance, tieback curtains, and café curtains frame a contrasting fabric window shade made with a kit from Joanna Western Mills Co.*

LEFT: *Any do-it-yourselfer can create a bedroom like this one designed and constructed by the author. West Point Pepperell sheets and matching quilted bedspread are used for the framed fabric walls, the canopy, and the fitted bedspread. A ready-made bedspread is used to make an elasticized fitted coverlet that fits snugly over the blankets. Extra fabric is used to cover the box-edge pillows. The bed-sized pillows are covered with the three matching "Galleria Rose," "Stripe," and "Water-Color" pillowcases. Throughout this book you will find vignettes of other areas of this room showing a slipcovered boudoir chair, a fabric-covered lampshade, and a striped fabric-covered desk with matching curtains. How-to instructions are given for all of these items.*

93

The impact of one fabric is used by designer Shirley Regendahl in creating this charming under-the-eaves bedroom. Waverly Fabrics' "Village Stripe," from their Old Sturbridge Village Crafts Collection, makes the gathered canopy valance, tieback curtains, and covered headboard that match a Waverly ready-made fitted bedspread. A table cover, a chair cushion, and walls covered with matching fabric complete this provincial bedroom.

The round-the-room treatment by ASID designer Ray Kindell updates a one-room apartment in an old town house. The fitted band cover for the studio couch and the slipcover of the love seat match the valance and laminated window shade from Window Shade Manufacturers Association. Painted shutters add charm to this classic room and hide an air conditioning unit. Conso trim adds a touch of contrast to the crewelwork fabric.

FABRIC AT WORK

Careful consideration must be given when selecting fabrics—any bedspread that is used during the day for lounging or relaxing should be made of a more durable fabric than a bedspread in a formal room where it is removed each night to eliminate any unnecessary wear.

Bedspreads may be as simple or as elaborate as you wish—fabric, color, texture, or printed and woven designs along with the addition of decorative bands, edge trimmings, cording, pleats, bands, ruffles, or godets will help make your bedspread a masterpiece. The traditional fabrics such as chintz, satin, gingham, cotton sateen, velvet, linen, faille, organdy, and dotted swiss are now joined by new decorator fabrics in the most fantastic print designs and textures, as well as by corduroy, denim, fake fur and suede, kettle cloth, quilted cottons and satins, and the new synthetic sheers.

Many of the fabrics lend themselves to plain, unfinished seams or self-finishing seams. Others, given their qualities, would work best with a lining. Seams and linings must be considered, as most bedspreads must be pieced to make even the most simple style large enough.

Bedspreads may be long enough to cover the pillows or they may end at the headboard, using ruffled or flanged pillow sham covers, bolsters, or an attached pillow cover.

BEDSPREAD STYLES

The two types of bedspreads (flat and fitted) have many variations that may cause some confusion. The following breakdown should help make the whole bedcover story easier to understand.

Flat Bedspreads

A rectangle of fabric with rounded or square corners for the foot of the bed will make a bedspread that will enhance a casual, contemporary, or formal room. The Hollywood bed and the high-riser are naturals for this type; beds with footboards do not look well with this bedspread.

THROW: A floor-length rectangle that may cover the pillows or not. Make it plain and simple or decorate seams and edges. Just about any fabric is suitable—light and airy or medium and heavy.

COVERLET: A smaller version of the throw, the coverlet is used with a dust ruffle. Make of medium- to heavyweight fabric.

COMFORTER: A utilitarian bedcover that has become a glamorous bedspread. It, too, is a smaller version of the throw and is most often used with a dust ruffle. Made of two lightweight fabric layers with several sheets of polyester batting that are tied in place through all thicknesses with cord or yarn, it is a great coverup for platform or loft beds.

Fitted Bedspreads

There is no end to the variations that start with this basic shape—tailored and neat or frilly and airy. The top is one large rectangle that goes to the edges of the bed. The side and foot edges (called the drop) may be smooth, pleated, ruffled, or trimmed with any of innumerable decorating details. Fabric combinations are often used as well.

FITTED BOX: A fitted top with smooth sides and ends may be split for a footboard. Medium- to heavyweight fabrics such as faille, velvet, denim, or quilted fabrics are used for traditional and contemporary bedrooms.

TAILORED: A fitted top with a self- or contrasting corded edge and inverted pleats at the corners. This classic may be made of any medium- to heavyweight fabric. The choice will set the mood—decorator prints, linen, velvet, tapestry, corduroy, brocade, denim, or ticking.

GATHERED FLOUNCE: A fitted top with a corded or trimmed edge and a gathered floor-length flounce. Use light- to medium-weight fabric or combine a heavier weight for the top with a fabric that will gather more easily for the flounce. A quilted gingham top with an unquilted matching flounce makes a durable spread. It may be split for a footboard or canopy bed.

PLEATED FLOUNCE: This fitted top with a corded edge and a floor-length pleated flounce may have several styles of pleats—inverted, box, a combination of inverted and box, or knife pleats. Fabric requirements are the same as for the gathered flounce.

RUFFLED TIERS: The shell of this bedspread is really a fitted box with ruffles applied to the drop. Use two or three tiers of self- or contrasting ruffles with a heading. Fabric requirements are the same as for a gathered flounce. Eyelet, organdy, or dotted swiss with a lining, as well as gingham, are excellent choices.

FITTED BAND: This style has a fitted top with a fitted band 4″–6″ wide completed with a pleated flounce. Both edges of the band are usually trimmed with self- or contrasting cording. Fabrics suggested for any of the fitted bedspreads are suitable.

FITTED COVERLETS: These short beauties have a fitted top with an 8″–12″-wide fitted band that may be scalloped or shaped. Corners may be stitched or pleated. Fitted coverlets are used with a dust ruffle. Use medium to heavy fabric. Uncut corduroy and quilted fabric make great coverlets.

Dust Ruffles

These utilitarian creations are exactly what their name implies. The flounce extends from the box springs to the floor, hiding those little dust balls that collect under a bed between cleanings. They may be gathered, knife-pleated, or tailored with an inverted pleat at each foot corner. The gathered or knife-pleated ruffle may be made with a continuous drop or split for a footboard. Use lightweight, easy-care fabrics such as sateen, percale, sheets, or any fabrics with cotton and polyester fibers for the flounce. Muslin and discolored sheeting or any other inexpensive but durable fabric may be used as a foundation to cover the springs. A fitted sheet will make an excellent foundation too.

Couch Covers

Any style flat or fitted bedspread, with slight modifications, may be used to cover a couch. All four sides are covered to the floor. Both ends and one side are stylized and the back is made perfectly plain because it is placed against the wall. Fabric selection is most important—choose a type that will withstand the wear required of a couch. Any durable medium- to heavyweight fabric such as ticking, sailcloth, corduroy, decorator fabrics, velveteen, and tapestry will be appropriate.

COUCH THROWS: Make this cover with four rounded corners. Anchor it with an edge of extra-large cording.

FITTED BOX FOR A COUCH: A smooth drop on the front corners with a split for the back corners. Use an outstanding fabric for pizzazz.

TAILORED COUCH: A corded edge all around with an inverted pleat at each corner. Prints, textured weaves, or napped fabrics are all used for this cover.

GATHERED OR PLEATED FLOUNCE FOR COUCH: Couch covers with these edges, when made of fabric on the light side of the medium range, should be used in a room that does not get roughhouse treatment.

FITTED-BAND COUCH: This classic couch cover has a 4″–6″-wide band with a pleated or gathered flounce—an inverted pleat at each corner with one at the center is the favorite. Fabric selection is just about unlimited.

MEASURE BED ACCURATELY

Be sure to make up the bed with sheets, pillows, and any blankets you may use under the bedspread. The bulk will affect most measurements. Use a firm, unstretchable tape measure that is not worn. Accuracy is important. Insert a pin into the blanket where the tape ends; move tape and continue measuring.

Bed with Pillows

These are the standard ways to measure a bed (figure IV-2). The variations will follow.

1. TOP LENGTH (measurement #1): Measure from back of pillows at mattress edge, up over pillows, and down to blanket, continuing to foot of bed at mattress edge. Add 12″–15″ to this measurement for a tuck-in allowance to go under the pillows.

2. TOP WIDTH (measurement #2): Measure across bed from one side to the other side of mattress (over made-up bed).

3. DROP LENGTH TO FLOOR (measurement #3): The overhanging fabric that extends from top edge of bed to floor along the two sides and foot edges. Measure from top edge of mattress (over made-up bed) to within ½″ of floor or rug.

IV-2

Bed without Pillows

Measure width and drop (measurements #2 and 3) same as for bed with pillows.

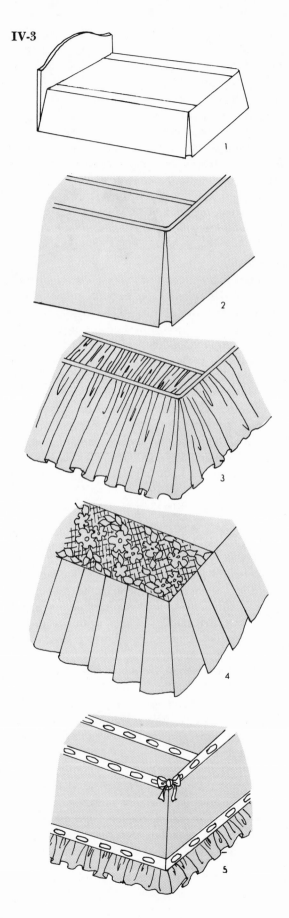

4. TOP LENGTH (measurement #4): Measure from head edge of mattress (over made-up bed) to foot at mattress edge.

5. COVERLET: Measure length with pillows (measurement #1) or without pillows (measurement #4) and width (measurement #3), then measure drop. Measure the drop length from top edge of mattress (over made-up bed) to 2″–6″ below bottom edge of mattress (measurement #5).

6. DUST RUFFLE: Remove the mattress and measure the springs. Use length (measurement #4) and width (measurement #3) to measure the springs. Measure the ruffle drop length from top edge of springs to within ½″ of floor or rug (measurement #6).

COUCH: Measure width and drop (measurements #2 and 3) same as for bed with pillows. Measure the top length (measurement #4) same as for bed without pillows.

MAKE AN ESTIMATED YARDAGE LAYOUT

Now that you have picked out a bedspread style that you want to make, the next step is to purchase the fabric.

Using the measurements as a guide, make a diagram on paper that will help you be more accurate when estimating the yardage. The layout need not be fancy or drawn with a ruler, as it is meant to tell how many lengths of fabric will be needed. Seam allowances, hems, style variations, and fabric design repeats must be added.

Fabric widths may be anywhere from 44″ to 70″, so you must think in terms of seams to make the bedspread wide enough for any bed. Standard purchased bedspread sizes are as follows:

• Twin—82″ by 112″
• Double—96″ by 112″
• Queen—105″ by 120″
• King—120″ by 120″

A spread made to the exact measurements that

will just touch the floor on all sides will vary IV-4 slightly in most cases as each person may use different thicknesses of bedding.

Check the items carefully on the following pages, adding the measurements to each fabric length as required.

Piecing (figure IV-3)

The greatest selection of fabric is available in 44"–48" widths; for certain sizes of fitted bedspreads, fabric must be pieced together to make one bedspread section.

1. When piecing, *always* use one width at the center of the bed with a narrower strip at each side.

2. If the seam is quite visible and detracts from the beauty, treat it as a planned addition and insert cording, or whatever other trim you are using, where the drop joins the top.

3. For satin or other suitable fabrics, you may wish to cover the narrow pieced sections with a gathered strip

4. or lace.

5. Use eyelet

6. or other band trim and then use the trim to decorate the edges of the drop or pillow sham, if desired.

Fabrics with nap, one-way designs, or design repeats require special consideration when making fitted bedspreads or dust ruffles (figure IV-4). Have the nap run down from the head to the foot; for the drop, have the nap run down from the seam edge to the floor. Flat bedspreads will not present a problem when cutting; *be sure* the nap is going in the same direction on all sections when piecing or you will have some dull and some bright strips.

For one-way designs, stripes, and fabric with design repeats, the fabric should be cut in the

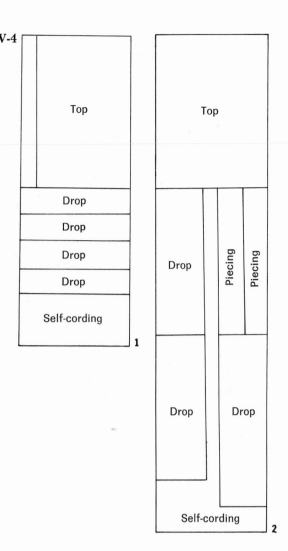

same manner as for the nap fabrics—distinct floral or scenic prints will detract from your carefully sewn project if they hang sideways or upside down from the bed.

1. Cut and piece the top from lengthwise strips, but cut from selvage to selvage along the crosswise grain for the drops.

Fabrics without nap that have a solid color, an allover design, or a texture:

2. Cut along the lengthwise grain for the drops on fitted bedspreads if it will save fabric.

Self-Trims

Any trim such as cording or ruffles will require additional fabric, unless there is leftover fabric due to the measurements required.

Lining a Bedspread

This is quite simple and will add body to the more delicate or sheer fabrics. Use any lightweight fabric that has the same cleaning require-

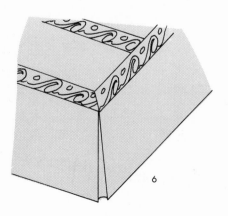

ments as the bedspread fabric. Cotton sateen is a good choice as a lining for lightweight fabrics to help prevent the color of your blankets from showing through. A throw or coverlet is lined to the edge. A fitted style usually has only the top lined, but for some fabrics and trims it would be just as easy to line each drop section as to hem it.

Seam Allowance
Use ½" seam allowances for all plain seams and those with cording, ruffles, or pleats. Use ⅝" seam allowances for French and flat-felled seams. See how to make these seams in Chapter VIII.

Hem Allowances
The head edge is hemmed with a ½" hem; allow 1". Use a 1" hem on all other edges; allow 1½". When lining, add a ½" seam allowance on all edges. For dust ruffles, use a ¼" hem: allow ½".

CORDED HEM: This finish adds weight that will help hold the spread in place (figure IV-5). Use large cording about 1" in diameter or several rows of ½" cord. Cut bias or straight strips as directed in Chapter VIII. Strips must be wide enough to accommodate the cord plus 2½" for seam and hem allowances.

1. For one row of large cord, wrap fabric around cord; pin.

2. Mark both fabric layers and measure. Add this measurement to the 2½" allowance.

3. For several rows of cording, fold fabric over

IV-5

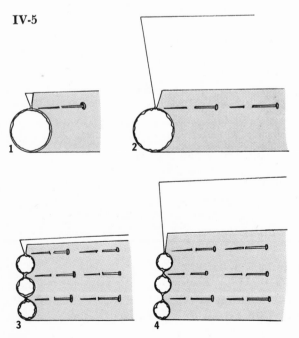

the cord. Pin between the rows and pin the raw edges together.

4. Mark both fabric layers: remove pins and cord and measure. Add this measurement to the 2½" allowance. Adjust bedspread measurement to accommodate the cording as instructed for extended trim requirements in the following paragraph.

EXTENDED TRIM REQUIREMENTS: Ruffles, fringe, cording, or other trimmings that extend beyond the edge of the drop will affect the total length and must be calculated for correct yardage (see *extended trim as an edge finish* in Chapter VIII). Subtract the finished width of trim that extends beyond the hem edge, then add ½" seam allowance or the width suggested to attach trim as a hem finish.

Extra Fabric Needed for Fitted Bedspreads
To accommodate the style variations of fitted bedspreads, additional fabric is required for the following types.

FITTED BOX: The drop may be made of one continuous fabric strip or it may be split for a footboard. The drop must not look skimpy when it encircles the bed. Allow a small amount of fabric to be eased to the top when stitching. Add 2" to each side drop measurement and 1" to the foot drop measurement.

For a footboard, allow an additional 7½" to each side drop measurement for an extension and hem, and 3" to the foot drop measurement for hems (figure IV-6).

TAILORED: The drop is usually cut and pieced to make three sections and two pleat underlays. The drop should not look skimpy, forcing the pleats to hang unevenly, when it encircles the bed. Add the same amount of fabric to be eased

IV-6

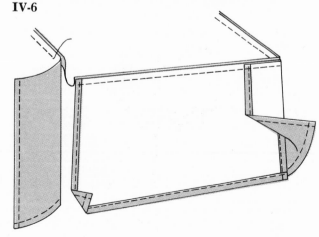

to the top as recommended for the fitted box.

To make an 8″-deep inverted pleat, add 6½″ (2″ for ease and 4½″ for pleat fold) to each side drop measurement, and 10″ (1″ for ease and 9″ for pleat fold) to foot drop measurement. Cut a 9″-wide section the length of the drop for each pleat underlay.

GATHERED FLOUNCE: For heavier fabrics make flounce 1½ times the straight-edge measurements; for light- to medium-weight, double it; for sheers or semisheers, triple the measurement.

For a footboard, flounce should be made in three main sections, with hemmed edges ending at the corners for the foot drop and the side edges extending 6″ beyond the corner. Allow 1½″ for each side edge (figure IV-7).

IV-7

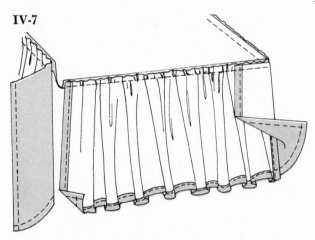

RUFFLED TIERS: The shell of this bedspread (top and drop) is made exactly like the fitted box bedspread explained above for a continuous or footboard drop. *Ruffles with a heading* (see Chapter VIII) are applied to the drop with one tier's hem edge even with the drop hem edge. Other tiers lap ½″ over the heading of the ruffle below it with the top ruffle heading extending above the edge of the top. Select the desired ruffle finish and make it 1½–3 times the fullness of the drop.

Sheer, semisheer, or lightweight fabrics that allow the color of the blankets to show through *must* be backed. Use a solid color opaque fabric with the same cleaning requirements for the top backing and the drop.

For other fabrics, make shell same as for a fitted box bedspread, then make ruffles of matching or contrasting fabric.

PLEATED FLOUNCE: Make a pattern to establish the fullness (figure IV-8). Tape together 6″-wide strips of newspaper or other scrap paper.

Pleats may be 1″–4″ deep. Plan for a pleat to fall at each corner if possible. The drop may be entirely pleated or at even intervals.

1. When inverted or
2. box pleats are used singly, make each fold 3″–4″ deep.
3. For a combination of the two, make pleats 1″–2″ deep.
4. Knife pleats are usually 1″ deep.

For a very heavy, thick, or napped fabric, make a *mock inverted pleat*.

5. The drop at both sides and foot end at corners forming a slit and a layer of fabric hangs free underneath. Add 1½″ for a hem on slit and underlay edges.

IV-8

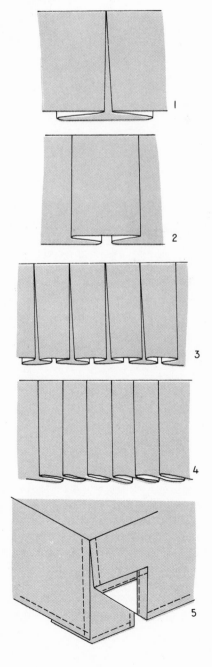

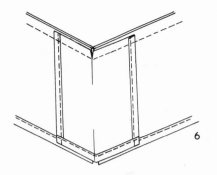

6

6. Underlay should be at least 8″ wide when hemmed.

For a footboard, a pleat should fall at each corner. Make an opening at the inner fold. Add 1½″ to the fold that lies next to the outer pleat layer of the foot drop. Add enough to the side drop extension of the pleat so it will measure 7½″ (6″ for an extension plus 1½″ for the hem). For knife pleats, on one side of the corner make a 5½″ turn-back instead of another pleat and allow the 7½″ for the extension (figure IV-9).

fabric before cutting out spread. Straighten ends and draw cutting lines on wrong side of fabric. If selvages are pulled or uneven, draw a straight line and cut away. To save time, cut out any self-strips needed for cording, ruffles, or other trim.

HEMS (figure IV-10): Use your ironing board, an iron, and a 6″ metal ruler to save time.

1. For the head hem, turn in raw edge 1″, wrong sides together; press. Turn under raw edge ½″; pin. Stitch inner fold in place.

2. For the drop hem(s), turn in raw edge 1½″; press. Turn under raw edge ½″; pin. Stitch hem in place.

3. For a curved corner, make a row of long machine stitches ½″ from raw edge to ease hem to fit.

4. Turn up 1½″ hem allowance as directed in step 2. At the curve, pull up thread from both ends, easing in fullness until it lies flat. Tie thread ends securely. As you turn under the raw edge, turn in curve along stitching; pin. Stitch eased area in place when stitching entire drop hem.

IV-9

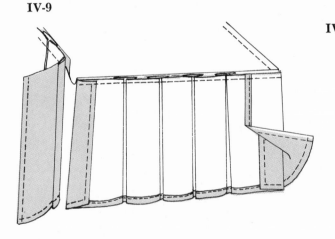

SEWING PROCEDURES FOR ALL BEDSPREADS

It's a pleasure to make a simple bedspread of beautiful fabric with straight seams and hems—the novice will be thrilled with the results and the more skilled will want to add other decorative touches. Don't limit yourself to the styles as they are presented on the following pages—combine any of the techniques that will help create a one-of-a-kind original.

PREPARATION: Bedspreads are washed frequently in a busy room, so when in doubt, shrink

IV-10

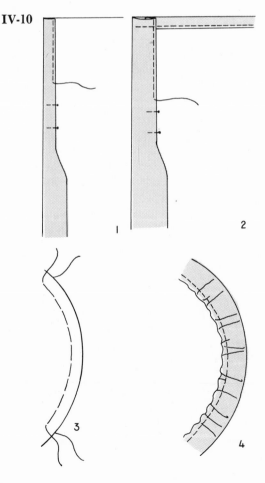

1

2

3

4

Flat Bedspreads

Simple or elegant, these great bed covers are used for every life-style. Make perfectly plain or decorate to your heart's content. Hem all edges or line it. Make it of all one fabric or of pieces. Use a solid color or a print.

THROW:

1. This classic bedspread (figure IV-11) is the quickest and easiest style to make. Cut out spread as planned. To round corners, use a yardstick. To mark point for drop corner, use the measurement of the drop plus the hem allowance. Measure from each side of corner using the established amount; pin. Now measure up the drop from each pin to establish corner; mark with pencil on wrong side of fabric.

2. Pivot from this point, measure an inch at a time, and mark a cutting line for rounded corner. Pin piecing sections to center panel; stitch. Make the hem at the head edge and hem the drop in one continuous stitching.

PATCHWORK THROW: Use large, 12"–20" squares and cover seams and hem edges with wide bias tape, decorative band trim, or contrasting fabric strips with the raw edges turned in and pressed. Center a row of squares in the middle of the bed and use narrower strips at each side and foot end if necessary. Allow 4"–6"

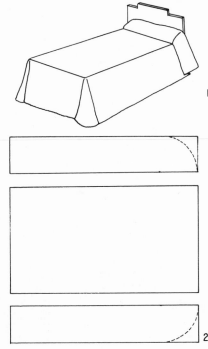

for "shrinkage"—when piecing and stitching a number of seams, the fabric will become smaller and the bedspread may be too short on all edges. Add ⅜" seam allowances to all edges of the squares. Arrange patches in rows as they will appear on bed (figure IV-12).

1. Join each long row, one at a time, by pinning squares wrong sides together; stitch in a ⅜" seam; press seam allowances open.

2. Lap trim over seam allowances, starting and ending ½" from each edge; stitch in place close to both edges.

3. When all long strips are completed, join these strips together in a ⅜" seam, matching intersecting seams. Press seams open.

4. Trim away underneath seam allowances as shown.

5. Stitch trim over seam allowances in same manner. Turn up hem edges ⅜"; press. Lap trim over pressed head edge and stitch in place.

IV-12

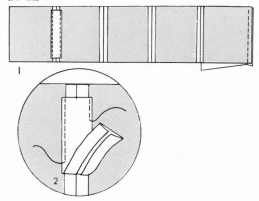

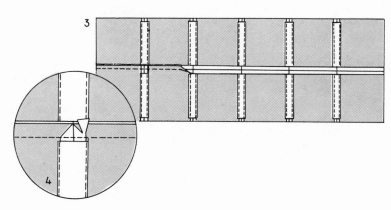

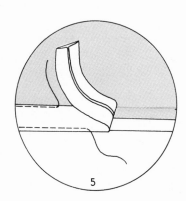

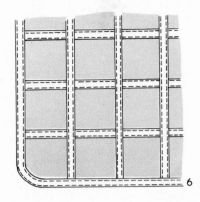

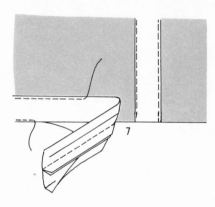

2. Trim square corners.

3. Cut out wedges on rounded corners to eliminate bulk.

4. Turn right side out; press. Turn in opening edges ½″; press. Pin pressed edges together and stitch close to the folds, closing the opening.

COVERLET (figure IV-14): A narrower version of the throw.

1. Make coverlet the same as the throw (figure IV-11),

2. cutting and piecing coverlet as planned.

IV-14

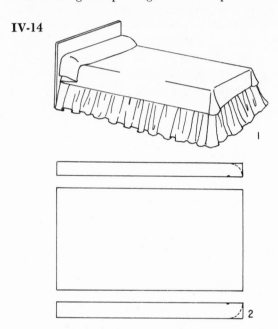

6. Stitch to side and foot edges, turning in ends at head and easing inner edge to fit at rounded corners. If you didn't allow enough for shrinkage, don't apply trim over the pressed back edge.

7. Encase the raw edge with two strips of trim stitched together along one edge. Sandwich the raw edge between the trim layers for ⅜″. Stitch in place through all thicknesses.

Lining a throw (figure IV-13). Cut lining same as spread.

1. Join piecings to center panel. Press all seams open. Pin right sides together; stitch lining to throw in a ½″ seam, leaving an opening on the head edge to turn throw right side out.

COMFORTER: When used as a bedspread, its only requirement is to be decorative and complement the room decor. Add cording, ruffles, or fringe to the drop edges for a special touch. Comforters do not cover the pillows owing to their bulk. Make matching or contrasting pillow shams and dust ruffle to complete the bed ensemble.

IV-13

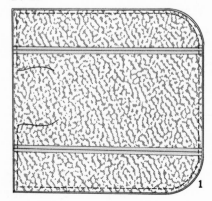

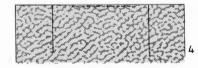

104

This is a great way to use up fabric scraps. Make a patchwork top and use a sheet as the back or make a patchwork top and back for a reversible comforter. Use fabrics that all require the same care. All double-knits of the same weight; satin, velvet, and other delicate fabrics; or the favorite cotton-and-synthetic blends. Sheets are great for both top and back. The back may be made of a solid color for reversibility. Cotton, sateen, flannel, and chintz are longtime favorites.

The knots that create the puffiness in a comforter should be spaced evenly 6"–10" apart. For patchwork, place a knot at each corner of a 6"– 8" square. For larger squares, knot center of patch; for extra-large squares, knot the center of the patch and at the center of each seam. It may be possible to make diamond or square patterns with the knots, using the fabric design. For plain colors or allover prints, mark off positions for knots on the right side of the top before sewing it to the back. Marks will be covered by knots.

MATERIAL NEEDED:

Two fabric sections (2½" larger on all edges to allow for shrinkage when comforter is knotted) the desired size

Three layers of polyester batting (cotton batting is not recommended as it pulls apart)

Thread for seams

Crochet cotton or synthetic knitting worsted yarn

A large-eyed, long darning needle for knotting

T-pins to hold batting

NOTE: Faded lightweight blankets may be used in place of batting. Make sure their color will not show through the fabric. Remove binding and cut to size, if necessary.

CONSTRUCTION (figure IV-15):

1. Machine-baste trim (if used) to all edges of the top. Stitch along one end over the basting to attach trim permanently to the opening edge. Pin the back to the top, with right sides together.

2. Starting and ending 6" from the corners on one end, stitch sides and other end in a ½" seam. Do not turn right side out.

To position batting, work on a large, flat surface (the floor is usually best). Spread out the comforter covering with the back uppermost. Place one layer of batting over the fabric, with its edges along the stitching. Trim along stitching if necessary. To piece batting, lap edges 1"; sew together with long, loose basting stitches. When piecing more than one layer, arrange batting so the pieced edges do not fall on top of

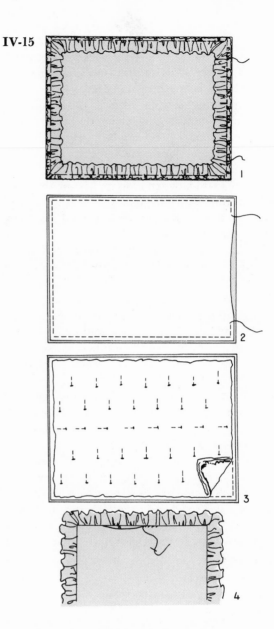

IV-15

each other. Otherwise, a ridge will be visible when light strikes the comforter a certain way. Position additional layers in the same manner.

3. With T-pins, pin batting (or blankets) to back *only*, along the outer edges near the stitching, keeping top free of pins. Pin batting to back along the center by placing one hand into the opening. Pin in between the first pin rows.

With the batting pinned in place, carefully turn cover right side out through opening. Transfer T-pins to the outside and repin batting to back. Spread out the comforter smoothly; pin all layers together through all thicknesses, using more T-pins if needed.

4. Turn in each opening edge ½" or along the trim stitching; pin. Now pin opening edges to-

gether, removing extra pins as you work. Slip-stitch opening edges together, using method 2 from Chapter VIII. NOTE: Opening may be stitched shut by machine if desired.

Still working on a flat surface, knot comforter layers together, working along the outer edges first, then through the center both lengthwise and crosswise. Then finish one quarter at a time. Keep the top and back wrinkle-free at all times. To knot extra-large comforters, sit on the floor and carefully pull the comforter over your legs, keeping it flat. Slide yourself around the comforter instead of moving it.

To knot comforter (figure IV-16), thread a darning needle with about 50″ of thread or yarn and double it. Make ¼″ stitches at patch corners or marks.

1. Insert needle ⅛″ from mark down through all thicknesses; reinsert needle and bring it back up through comforter ⅛″ on other side of mark. Pull thread or yarn until the end is about 2″ long.

2. Tie into a square knot by lapping the short ends over the long threads with the needle. Tuck short ends under the loop formed between fabric and crossed threads.

3. Pull knot up tightly, pulling all layers of fabric and batting to form an indentation on both sides of the comforter. To complete the knot, lap short ends over the long threads. Tuck short ends under loop formed by the threads and pull knot tight. Cut threads to a 1″ length above the knot.

IV-16

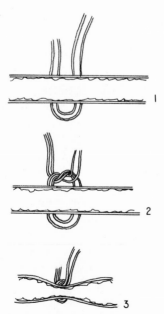

Fitted Bedspreads

These decorator's delights may seem complicated, but they require only straight seams and hems for most styles. Since the top is always a separate fabric section, experiment with contrasting colors, textures, and prints when selecting fabric for the drop. This is also a great way to experiment with matching quilting—quilt the top in your own design or around a motif in your fabric. Then make the drop in matching un-quilted fabric.

Corners at the foot of the bed with a fitted top look best when slightly rounded so they will hang correctly over the made-up bed and mattress. Corners that are too square will cause the bedspread to droop, breaking the line of the smooth top.

IV-17

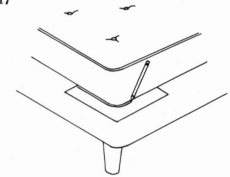

To make the corners that match the mattress (figure IV-17), place a heavy piece of paper or cardboard between the mattress and the springs. Trace the shape of the corner onto the paper, supporting it with one hand as you draw. Cut out shape and use as a pattern for fitted bedspread and dust ruffle corners.

FITTED BOX (figure IV-18):

1. This style bedspread takes a minimum of fabric because of its smooth, straight lines. Choose an exquisite fabric that will make its own impact without needing any trim.

2. Measure, plan (using figures IV-2, IV-4, and IV-6), and cut out spread for the continuous drop, piecing as necessary.

3. Do the same for the three sections needed for a split. Be sure to allow for ease as explained in the section on estimated yardage, page 98.

4. For a continuous drop, stitch hem in place on one long edge. Pin drop to top, easing in fullness. Make ¼″-deep clip about ¼″ apart at

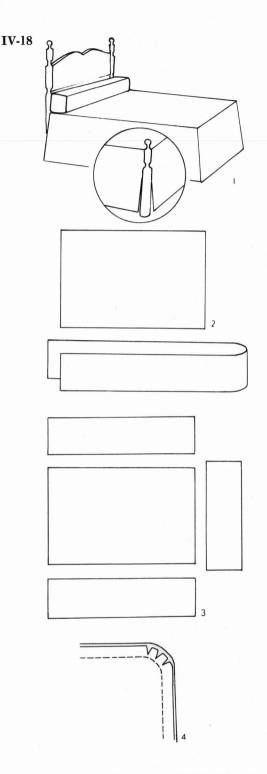

IV-18

foot drop to end of top, easing in fullness. Pin side drops to top in same manner, lapping hemmed ends over foot drop (see figure IV-6). Stitch in one continuous seam. Make hem at head edge.

Lining a fitted bedspread (figure IV-19):

Cut lining (figure IV-19) same as for the bedspread top, piecing if necessary. Make hem(s) on the long edges of the drop, then hem the head edges of the drop.

1. Place the hemmed ends of the drop ½″ from the head edge of the top. Baste drop to top. Fold drop in over top with seam exposed.

2. Pin lining over drop. Stitch ends and sides in a ½″ seam, leaving an opening on the head end to turn spread right side out.

3. Turn spread right side out; press. Turn in opening edges ½″; press. Pin pressed edges together. Stitch opening shut close to pressed edges.

IV-19

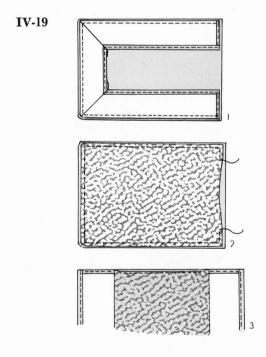

corners so seam allowance will lie flat. Do not clip deeper or the fabric may fray and you won't be able to make a ½″ seam. Stitch drop to top. Make hem at head edge.

For a footboard, stitch hems in place along ends and one long edge of the foot drop. Hem one end of each side drop (end that will extend under the foot section) and one long edge. Pin

TAILORED (figure IV-20):

1. With the addition of cording around the top side and foot edges, this favorite is used for every mood—casual, traditional, or contemporary—on beds without footboards.

2. Measure, plan (see figures IV-2, IV-4, and IV-8, steps 1, 5, and 6), and cut out spread, piecing as needed. Cut out strips for self-cording and

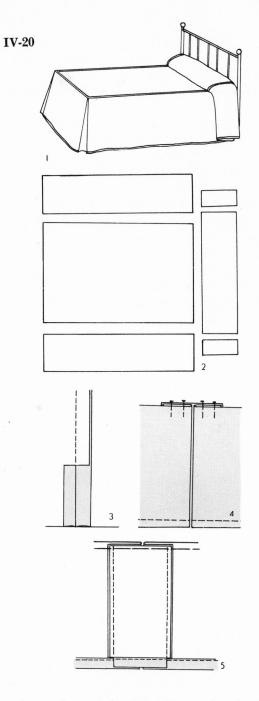

IV-20

place. Machine-baste cording to top. Pin drop to top, easing in fullness; center pleat folds at corners; stitch. Make hem at head edge.

If desired, line top same as fitted box, figure IV-19.

GATHERED FLOUNCE (figure IV-21):

1. The top looks best with some type of trim around its edge—cording or trim inserted in the seam or band trim stitched around the edge after flounce is stitched in place.

2. Measure, plan (see figures IV-2, IV-4, and IV-7), and cut out spread, piecing as needed for a continuous flounce.

3. Do the same for a footboard.

If self-cording is being used, cut out strips and make cording and machine-baste to top to save time when assembling bedspread. Refer to Chapter VIII if you need help with gathering.

4. For a continuous drop, stitch hem in place along one long edge. Add gathering threads to the other. Pin flounce to top, dividing extra fabric equally. Adjust gathers; pin and stitch flounce to top. Make hem at head edge.

5. For a footboard, stitch hems in place along ends and one long edge of the foot drop. Hem one end of each side drop (end that will extend under the foot section) and one long edge. Add gathering threads to the long unhemmed edges, ending gathering threads 6″ from hem side edges. Pin foot flounce to top ½″ from each corner, dividing extra fabric equally. Adjust gathers; add more pins and stitch in place. Pin side flounce to top; adjust gathers. Pin and stitch sides and extensions to foot edge over the previously stitched foot seam.

If you would like to use a sheer or lightweight fabric, it must have a backing so the color of the blankets won't show through. There are two ways to use backing: First, the bedspread fabric for the top and drop may be backed with an opaque fabric, cut the same size. The second method is to use matching top layers of fabric and backing, and then make a smooth opaque drop (same as for a fitted bedspread) with the gathered flounce sandwiched between the backed top and the smooth opaque drop.

For either method, place the wrong side of the bedspread fabric over the right side of the matching backing fabric sections and machine-baste the two layers together ¼″ from the cut edges. Handle as one layer throughout construction. For a pieced top, baste the backing to the bedspread fabric and then stitch the seams.

make cording to save time when sewing the bedspread together.

3. Stitch pleat underlays to side and foot drops in a ½″ seam. Clip seam allowances 2½″ above hem edges; press open below clip. Do not press seam open above clip.

4. Stitch hem in place along this long edge of the drop. Mark center of pleat underlay with pin. Fold side and foot drop so they meet at center of pleat underlay, forming an inverted pleat.

5. From the wrong side, baste pleat folds in

108

IV-21

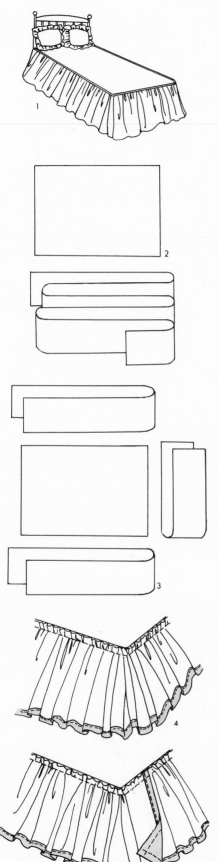

PLEATED FLOUNCE (figure IV-22):

1. For a custom finish, insert cording or other trim in the seam around the top or stitch band trim around the edges after the flounce is attached.

2. Measure, plan (see figures IV-2, IV-4, IV-8, and IV-9), and cut out spread, piecing as needed for a continuous flounce.

3. Do the same for a footboard. Use pattern you made as a guide for cutting to pin flounce to top.

For a continuous drop, stitch hem in place along one long edge. Start at one edge of the top and form pleats. Measure and pin pleats in place, ending at opposite head edge. Any excess fabric may be trimmed away or more added if necessary. Stitch flounce to top. Make hem at head edge.

IV-22

For a footboard, stitch hems in place along ends and one long edge of the foot drop. Hem one end of each side drop (end that will extend under the foot section) and one long edge. Pin foot flounce to top, turning back pleat fold for each end, and place fold ½″ from each corner. Measure pleat in place. Stitch foot flounce to top. Starting at the foot, pin side drops to top, extending hemmed edges over foot pleat fold (see figure IV-9). Measure and pin pleats in place; stitch to top. Make hem in head edge.

RUFFLED TIERS (figure IV-23): This frilly and airy ruffled bedspread looks best when the top ruffle is applied so the heading extends above the edge of the top. There are many straight strips that require extra handling, but the resulting look is worth the time spent.

1. Just make a fitted box bedspread (figure IV-18) and add the tiers.

2. Measure, plan (see figures IV-2, IV-4, IV-6, and IV-7), and cut out, piecing as necessary for a continuous drop.

3. Do the same for a footboard drop.

Prepare ruffles as planned, narrow-hemming the short ends before adding gathering threads. Refer to Chapter VIII for ruffles and for gathers to review the recommended techniques.

Make bedspread shell exactly as directed for fitted box, figure IV-18.

4. For a continuous drop, pin one ruffle strip to the lower edge with hems even, distributing ruffles equally, with ends even with head edge. Adjust gather; pin and stitch to drop alongside both rows of gathering threads. Do the same for all other rows except the top, lapping the ruffle ½″ over the heading of the tier below. Pin and stitch top ruffle strip in place with the heading extending above the seam used to join the drop to the top in the same manner.

5. For a footboard, narrow-hem the ends of all ruffle strips for the sides and foot. Stitch all tiers to the foot drop in the same manner as for the continuous drop, placing hemmed ends even with ends of foot drop. Stitch tiers to each side, placing hemmed ends even with the head edge and where the extension meets the foot drop.

For sheer or lightweight fabric, use an opaque fabric for a backing so the blanket colors won't show through. Machine-baste the backing to the bedspread top ¼″ from the cut edges. Then complete the opaque drop and stitch in place. Add tiers as instructed in steps 4 and 5. For a pieced top, baste the layers together and then stitch the seams.

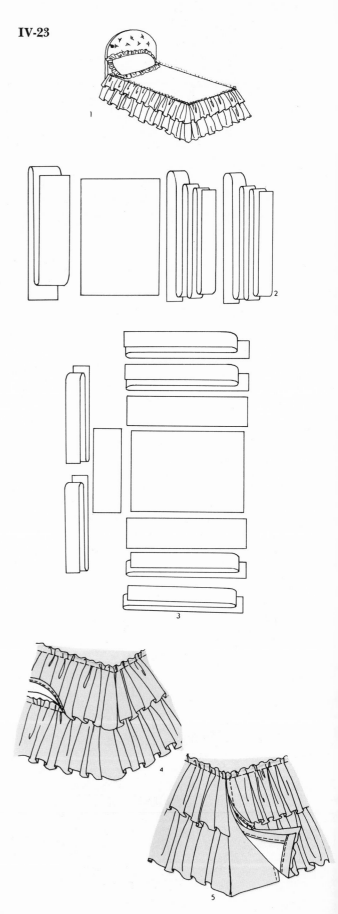

IV-23

110

FITTED BAND (figure IV-24):

1. The tailored look of this bedspread has long been a favorite and cording adds just the right decorator touch.

2. Measure, plan (see figures IV-2, IV-4, IV-7, IV-8, and IV-9), and cut out spread, piecing as necessary for a continuous drop.

3. Do the same for a footboard.

Cut out bias or straight strips and make cording as directed in Chapter VIII. To save time when assembling the bedspread, remember to make enough cording for both edges of the band.

Machine-baste cording to both long edges of the band. Pin and stitch band to top. Stitch hem in place along one long edge of the flounce. Use pattern you make as a guide for pinning flounce to band. Measure and pin pleats in place, starting at one head edge and ending at opposite side. Any excess fabric may be trimmed away or more may be added if necessary. Stitch flounce to band. Make hem at head edge.

FITTED COVERLET (figure IV-25): These bed covers may be as tailored or as grand as you like —and the dust ruffle should be planned to complement the style. For a platform or loft bed use the elasticized version for an easy-to-make bed.

1. Use a plain band, decorate its edges with trims or ruffles, or shape the edges. Or tuck in the edges with elasticized corners as shown in the photograph in this chapter with a platform bed

IV-24

IV-25

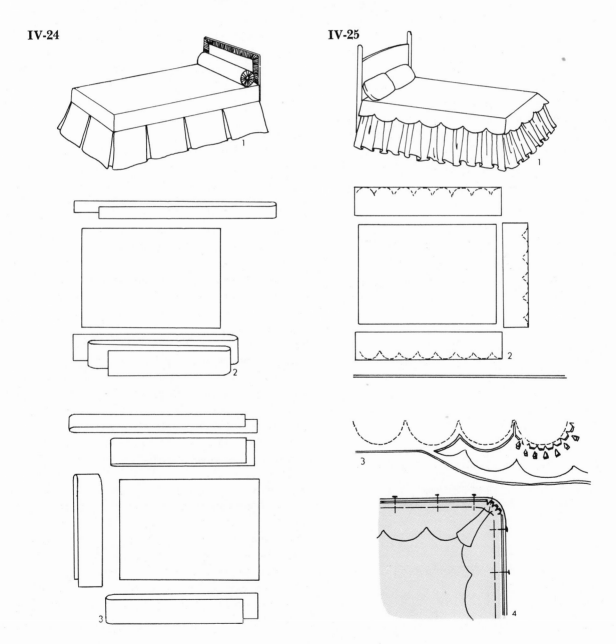

and featuring a quilted coverlet, contrasting framed fabric walls, a canopy, and lots of pillows.

Shaped edges and those with extended trim should be lined. For medium to heavy fabrics, use lightweight fabric for lining, selecting fabric that requires the same laundry care as the bedspread.

2. Measure, plan (see figures IV-2 and IV-4), and cut out spread; piece as necessary. On the wrong side of fabric, draw shapes on the drop, making sure the center of the design falls at each corner.

3. Stitch lining to the band fabric along the shaped design. Trim seam, clip inner curves and corners, and cut out wedges to eliminate bulk on outer curves. Turn band right side out; press. Machine-baste long raw edges together.

4. Pin band to top, centering design on each corner. Make ¼"-deep clips at corners, if necessary, so seam allowance will lie flat. Stitch band to top. Make hem in head edge.

ELASTICIZED FITTED COVERLET (figure IV-26): Make a drop section for the head end, too (just like a fitted sheet). Make drop as wide as needed to reach the springs (over the made-up bed) plus

IV-26

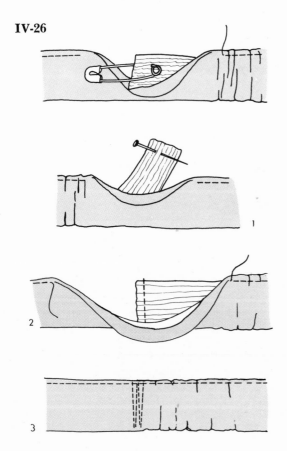

2"–4" for a tuck-in with the regulation 1½" hem allowance. Use four 12" strips of ¾"-wide elastic for the corners. Join drop in a continuous strip. Stitch hem in place along one long edge, leaving 2" openings about 12" from each side of each corner (24") to insert elastic.

Pin drop to the coverlet top, centering openings so they are the same distance from each corner. Make ¼"-deep clips at corners, if necessary, so seam allowances will lie flat. Stitch drop to top.

1. With a safety pin attached, insert elastic into one opening at a corner and slide elastic through hem. Pin free end so it won't slip into hem.

2. Pull elastic out the other opening, making the hem cup in so it will fit under the mattress. Stitch ends of elastic to drop, keeping hem free.

3. Stitch openings shut and stitch across elastic several times through all thicknesses to hold elastic securely in place. Apply elastic to the remaining three corners in the same manner.

Machine-Quilting

Add a special decorator's touch to your bedspread—quilt the top of any fitted bedspread. A quilted gingham top with a gathered flounce has been a longtime favorite. A satin bedspread with a quilted top and a pleated flounce would make a handsome covering in a formal bedroom. For the ambitious, a quilted throw may be just the right challenge.

Fabric selection is most important. Use tightly woven light or medium fabric: calico, sheets, or any cotton blend make great quilt tops. A less expensive solid color fabric may be used for the back of the quilting if it has the same cleaning requirements as the bedspread fabric.

Use polyester batting (cotton batting is not recommended unless the quilting is no more than 2" apart). A quilting foot attachment is essential for a smooth finish. Cut the two fabric layers at least 3" to 6" larger on all edges than needed for unquilted top. Buy a sheet of batting that is as large or larger than the top measurements. Fabric "shrinks" as it is quilted because the fabric draws in over the batting. Be sure any fabric motifs are centered both lengthwise and crosswise when cutting out the top. Piece if necessary and press the seams open, making the seams at the sides as recommended for all bedspread piecing. Use a center seam for the backing so that all the seams do not fall at the same place, as it would make the quilting lumpy.

QUILTING DESIGNS: Decide how the fabric will be quilted (figure IV-27). It may be quilted in 1) large squares, 2) diamonds, 3) lengthwise lines, or 4) around a motif in your fabric, using the stripes, checks, plaids, florals, geometrics, or figures as a quilting pattern. To quilt in long, straight lines, mark fabric with chalk or a soft lead pencil before assembling. For squares, draw a line through the center of the fabric lengthwise and crosswise. For diamonds, draw a diagonal line from the corners of the fabric. For lengthwise lines, draw a line through the center of the fabric lengthwise. When a motif is used on the fabric, no lines are needed.

ASSEMBLE QUILT: Work on a large flat surface (usually the floor is the best place). Spread out the back fabric with the wrong side up. Place the batting over the back, keeping both layers smooth. Cover the batting with the top, right side up (figure IV-28).

1. Smooth all three layers; work from the center out, keeping the back and top fabric edges even, and pin the layers together with T-pins. Pin every 10"–12" down through the center, then work toward the edges. It is important to baste the layers together as instructed to prevent the layers from slipping.

2. Baste along the center lengthwise and then 10"–12" away, smoothing the fabric as you work so no wrinkles are formed in any of the fabric layers. End the last basting rows near the raw edges. Next, baste crosswise 10"–12" apart in the same manner. Remove pins as the basting is completed.

IV-27

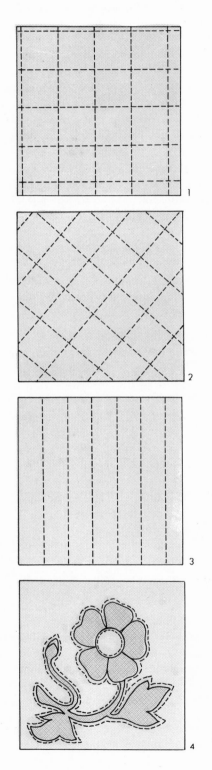

IV-28

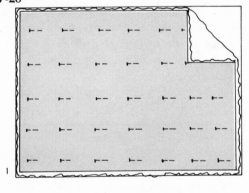

Before quilting, make a test using 8–10 stitches to the inch. Test presser foot pressure and thread tension. Adjust if necessary, following sewing machine manual. For straight lines, place the guide bar on either side of the needle. Stitch along the drawn lines and then make rows 3″–4″ apart, placing guide along the previous row of stitching. To quilt fabric motifs, remove guide and stitch along the design as desired. Spaces between the rows of stitching should be no larger than 6″–10″.

To make a larger work surface around your machine, use a card table or chair backs to support the fabric so it won't pull and distort. Roll up quilting in a tight roll to place under the machine head.

When entire section is quilted, cut to the required measurements.

Dust Ruffles

A custom-made dust ruffle that will enhance your new coverlet or comforter is a much speedier project—the lightweight fabrics are so easy to sew (figure IV-29). The ruffle may be gathered or knife-pleated or have an inverted pleat at the corner. Make just like a fitted bedspread; see illustration below. The gathered or knife-pleated ruffle (on the left) may be adapted for a footboard; a dust ruffle may be attached to a fitted sheet (on the right) for a quickly made variation.

You may make a ruffle and then fasten it to the box spring with nylon hook and loop or snap tape. The tape must be sewn to the springs by hand with a curved needle or glued in place with fabric glue.

The two methods described below—a flat foundation and a fitted sheet foundation—are quicker and easier to make because everything is machine-sewn.

FLAT FOUNDATION: Any of three types of ruffle may be used. Cut out and piece the flounce and the foundation as planned.

For a gathered ruffle, follow the instructions for a fitted bedspread with a gathered flounce, figure IV-21, for the continuous or footboard drop. Stitch ruffles to foundation in the same manner.

For a pleated ruffle, follow the instructions for a fitted bedspread with a pleated flounce, figure IV-22, for the continuous or footboard drop. Stitch ruffle to foundation in the same manner.

For an inverted pleat at the corners, follow the instructions for a tailored bedspread, figure IV-20. Stitch ruffle to foundation in the same manner.

FITTED SHEET FOUNDATION: Any of the three types of ruffle may be used (figure IV-30). To establish a stitching line for the dust ruffle, place fitted sheet on box springs and draw a line around the side and foot edges along the top edge of the springs. Remove sheet.

These ruffles are made like the gathered or pleated flounce or tailored bedspreads with slight modifications: When cutting out the ruffle allow 1″ for the top seam allowance instead of the recommended ½″. Turn in the top long edge 1″ and press.

For a gathered ruffle in one continuous strip, cut, piece, and press down the 1″ top seam allowance.

1. Stitch hems in place along ends and the remaining long raw edge. To the top edge of the ruffle, add two rows of gathering threads, placing one row ¼″ from the pressed-in seam allowance and the other row ¼″ away. Turn to Chapter VIII if you need help with the gathering techniques.

2. Pin ruffle to sheet with the pressed edges along the marked line, dividing extra fabric equally and placing the hemmed edges at the corner seams of the sheet at the head. Adjust gathers; pin and stitch to sheet along both rows of gathering threads.

3. For a gathered ruffle to accommodate a footboard, cut, piece, and press down the 1″ seam allowance as planned. Stitch hems in place along

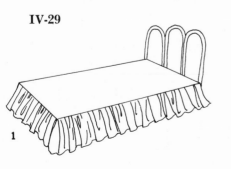

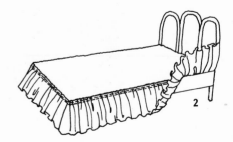

1

2

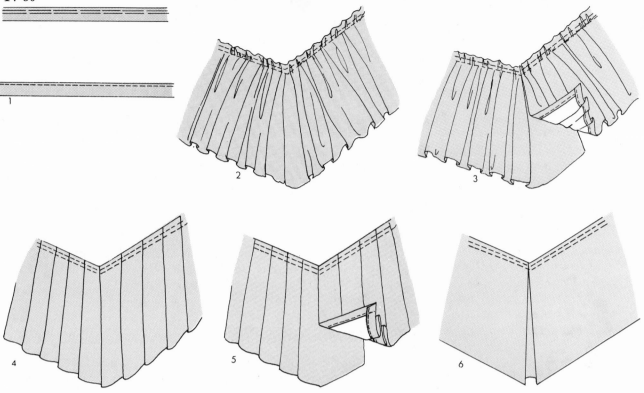

ends and remaining long edge of the three ruffle sections. Add gathering threads same as step 1 above, ending the threads 6″ from the foot hems on the sides. Pin side ruffle to sheet with the pressed edge along the marked line of the long side edges, with the ungathered extensions pinned to the foot edges. Divide extra fabric evenly and place opposite hemmed edges at the sheet's corner seams. Adjust gathers; pin. Pin foot ruffle to sheet in the same manner, placing side hems at the sheet's corner seams over the extensions. Stitch ruffle to sheet along both rows of gathering threads.

4. For a pleated ruffle in one continuous strip, cut, piece, and press down the 1″ top seam allowance as planned. Stitch hems in place along ends and remaining long raw edge. Use pattern you made as a guide for cutting to pin ruffle to sheet (see figure IV-9). Place one hemmed side edge on the sheet's corner seam at the head with the pressed edge along the marked line. Measure and pin pleats in place, ending at opposite head seam. Stitch ruffle to sheet ¼″ from pressed edge and again ¼″ away.

5. For a pleated ruffle to accommodate a footboard, cut, piece, and press down the 1″ seam allowance as planned. Stitch hems in place along

ends and remaining long raw edges of the three ruffle sections. Use pattern you make as a guide for cutting and to pin ruffle to sheet (see figures IV-8 and IV-9). Pin side ruffles to sheet, placing one hemmed end at the sheet's corner seam at the head with the pressed edge along the marked line. Measure and pin pleats in place, ending at sheet's corner seam at the foot. Pin extensions to foot along marked line.

Pin foot ruffle to sheet in the same manner, placing side hems at the sheet's corner seams over the extensions. Stitch ruffle to sheet ¼″ from pressed edge and again ¼″ away.

6. For an inverted pleat at corners, cut, piece, and press down the 1″ seam allowance as planned. Make inverted pleats at corners same as for a tailored bedspread (see figure IV-20). Stitch hems in place along ends and remaining long raw edges. Stitch ruffle to sheet ¼″ from the pressed edge and again ¼″ away, aligning pleats with corners.

Couch Covers

Use these easy-to-make styles to convert a bed into a couch for the multipurpose bedroom.

The styles are quite similar to the bedspreads

of the same name; only slight changes are needed to make a practical and fashionable couch cover-up. All four sides of a couch are covered. Since the one long edge is against a wall, it is not necessary to pleat or gather it—use a plain rectangle of fabric for the back drop of the couch cover.

THROW (figure IV-31): This loosely draped cover is the easiest to make.

1. To help keep the cover in place, use cording around the entire edge.

2. Measure, plan (see figures IV-2, IV-4, and IV-5), cut out, and piece fabric as planned, rounding corners as directed for the throw bedspread, figure IV-11. Cut out and piece corded hem strips, if used.

CORDED HEM (figure IV-32): The same techniques are used as for bias and straight-grain strips, cording, and corded seam described in Chapter VIII. Wrap fabric over cord, wrong sides together, with one long edge extending 1½″ above the other.

1. To make large cording, using a zipper foot, stitch as close to cord as possible to form the narrow side.

2. To make several corded rows, fold fabric, wrong sides together, with one long edge extending 1½″ above the other. Crease fold slightly, then lay one strip of cord along the crease and fold back into position; using a zipper foot, stitch close to fold.

3. Open fabric and stitch remaining rows of cord in the same manner.

Turn in the long wide edge ½″ and press. This will be the hem edge. Pin cording in place with the ½″ seam allowance along the raw edge of the bedspread, easing cording around the corners so it will lie flat when extended.

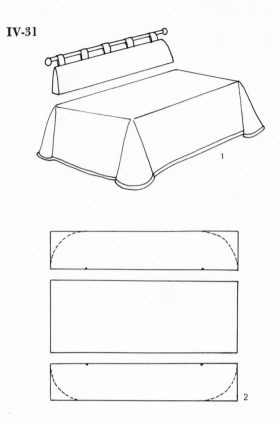

IV-31

4. Stitch cording to bedspread, starting and ending 2″ from each end of the cord.

5. Finish large cording as explained in the corded seam section in Chapter VIII.

6. For the rows of cord it would be easier to clip out the cord and stitch the ends in a seam that will fall on an inner corner fold, sewing the seam allowances flat on the underside of the hem.

7. Turn cording down and hem allowance up to cover seam. Stitch pressed edge in place, making tiny pleats at corners to ease in fullness.

IV-32

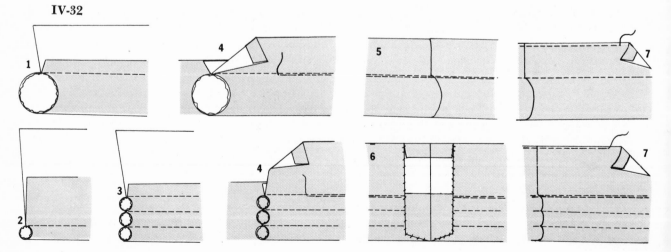

116

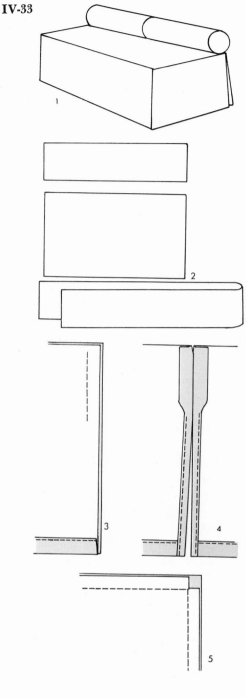

IV-33

3. Stitch hems in place along one long edge of each drop section. Stitch back to longer drop section in a 1″ seam, starting ½″ from the raw edges and ending about 6″ away.

4. Press seams open, turning in slit 1″. Turn in raw slit edges and stitch in place.

5. Pin drop to the top, placing the slits at two corners, easing in the fullness. Stitch drop in place. To stitch a square corner, if necessary, stitch seam to within ½″ of opposite edge at corner. With needle in fabric, raise presser foot. Clip seam allowance of the drop to needle. Pivot fabric on the needle so you can stitch other side of corner. Be sure all layers of fabric are smooth and fold the drop out of the way at corner. Drop presser foot and complete stitching.

TAILORED COUCH (figure IV-34):

1. Cording may match or be contrasting. Use it on all four edges of the top. Make an inverted pleat at each front corner of the couch.

2. Cut out and piece as directed for tailored couch when making an estimated yardage layout. Make pleats same as for the tailored bedspread, figure IV-20, steps 3, 4, and 5. Stitch back drop to the section after the pleats are made. Stitch hems in place along the entire lower edge of the drop. Machine-baste cording to top as directed for a corded seam in Chapter VIII. If the corners are square, stitch and clip as instructed for the fitted box for a couch, figure IV-33, step 5.

IV-34

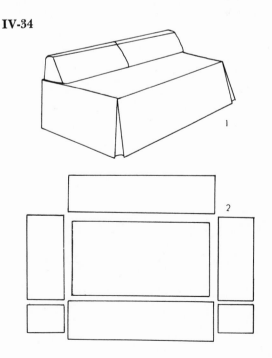

FITTED BOX FOR A COUCH (figure IV-33):

1. This style has a fitted drop that encircles the entire couch. For easier removal, the back corners have slits. Allow 1″ for these two seams allowances so they may be narrow-hemmed. Be sure to allow for ease as explained in the estimated yardage layout section for a fitted box bedspread.

2. Cut out and piece as planned.

117

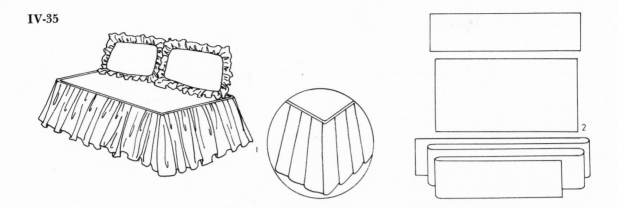

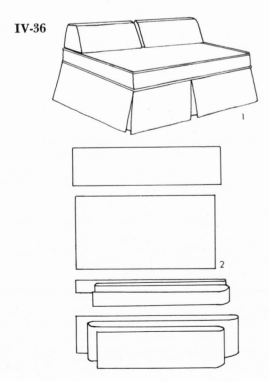

Gathered or Pleated Flounce for a Couch (figure IV-35):

1. Trim all four edges of the top with cording for a better-wearing cover and match the fullness of the flounce to the fabric weight.

2. Cut out flounce and top as instructed in the estimated yardage layout section for a gathered or pleated flounce.

Stitch all fabric for the flounce in one continuous strip and stitch the hem in place along one long edge. Machine-baste cording to top as directed for cording in Chapter VIII.

For a gathered flounce, follow the instructions for figure IV-21 for the continuous drop, making the backdrop flat and gathering the ends and front edges. Stitch flounce in place in the same manner.

For a pleated flounce, follow the instructions for figure IV-22 for the continuous drop, making the back smooth and pleating the ends and front edge.

Fitted Band Couch (figure IV-36): Emphasize both edges of the band with cording for durability.

1. The cover is made like the fitted band bedspread with a few exceptions.

2. Cut out cover as planned; piece as necessary. Cut out strips for cording and make as directed in Chapter VIII. To save time, make enough cording to go around all four edges of the top and the three lower edges of the band.

Machine-baste the cording to the top and one long edge of the band. Carefully measure and mark where the corners will fall on the band. Use pattern you make as a guide when estimating the yardage for the shorter drop. Pin flounce to band, measuring and pinning pleats in place. Stitch flounce to band. Stitch back drop to the band and flounce. Now, stitch hem in place on entire lower edge of the drop. As the last step, stitch drop to the corded top, matching corners.

Bed and Couch Accessories

A custom-made bedspread or couch cover, created by you, may need a few accessories to give it real emphasis. Pillow shams, pillows, cushions, bolsters, attached pillow covers, headboards, and canopies are some of the items you can make to add decorator touches.

Pillow shams are the easiest to make for a spread that does not cover the pillows. They will serve two purposes—to finish the spread in style and to cover the pillows used for sleeping. Bits of contrasting colors in the form of throw pillows

118

will add pizzazz to the spread that covers the pillows. Bolsters are tailored cushions that will be at home in a casual or formal room when made of fabric that matches your bed or couch. These classic accessories are explained in detail in Chapter III. There you will find complete step-by-step instructions for every type of pillow, cushion, and bolster shown throughout the book.

ATTACHED PILLOW COVER (figure IV-37): Perhaps you have chosen a bedspread with a gathered or pleated flounce and do not wish to cover the pillows—there's a simple way to cover the bed pillows with matching fabric.

1. Cut a piece of fabric 35″ long and as wide as the bed plus 4″ for the hems. (Be sure to check length measurement if you have oversized pillows.)

2. Turn in the ends and one long edge 2″; press. Turn in the raw edges ½″; pin and stitch hems in place. Turn remaining long raw edge to the outside ½″; press. Place this pressed edge ⅝″ from head edge; pin and stitch close to pressed edge and ½″ away. Tuck free edge under pillows. NOTE: If spread was pieced, make same piecing seams to match when cutting out pillow cover.

IV-38

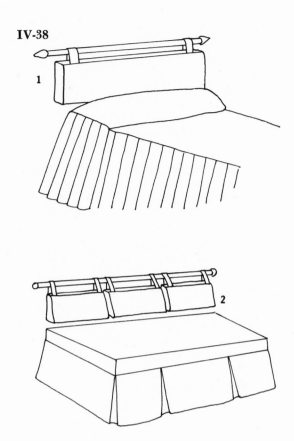

HEADBOARDS: In the traditional setting, headboards are made of wood, metal, brass, or rattan. Today, headboards or backrests may be in the form of free-hanging cushions, a decorated wall, a canopy attached to the bed in the usual way and covered with fabric, or a combination of several treatments.

FREE-HANGING CUSHIONS (figure IV-38): Attached to a wooden or metal pole with fabric tabs, this type of 1) headboard or 2) backrest is usually made with polyurethane box-edge foam cushion forms and covered with fabric matching the bedspread or couch. Mount pole so the cushions hang free on the rod several inches above the bed pillows or couch edge. Pillow headboards may be 14″–24″ wide, the full length of the bed, or composed of two or three pillows of the same dimensions. They may be 2″–3″ thick.

Make the tabs the same as those used for the draperies with tab hangers in Chapter II, page 51. Cut out and attach cording to cushion top and bottom, then baste the tabs to the boxing strips before completing the cushion as instructed in Chapter III, page 83.

IV-37

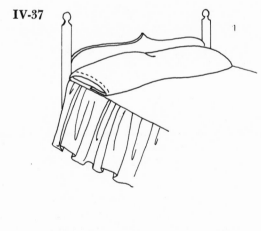

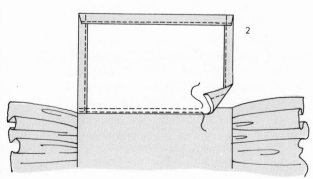

Decorated Walls

Make a fabric-covered panel the width of the bed, reaching to the ceiling, or make a casement curtain backdrop suspended between wooden strips as shown in the first photograph in this chapter.

To make a panel, cover a thin piece of plywood or masonite with flannel or batting and a layer of fabric as instructed to make a flat cornice in Chapter II, page 54. Nail covered panel to wall and then glue trim around the edges to cover the nailheads if you are not using a canopy valance and tieback curtains.

To make a casement curtain backdrop, use 1½ x 1½ wooden strips painted to match fabric or woodwork and fastened together with corrugated nails and white glue as instructed for the framed walls in Chapter VII, page 168. Use sash or café curtain rods to attach curtains to insert.

CANOPIES: Traditionally, canopies encircled the bed; today it may be a narrow canopy with side draperies or a valance that follows the contour of a sloped ceiling.

To attach a canopy to the ceiling, make a frame the dimensions of the bed of 1 x 2 pine strips and anchor it to the ceiling with toggle bolts or molly screws, as directed in the installation tips of Chapter II, page 27. Hang valance with nylon hook and loop or snap tape by making a ruffle with a heading and stitching it to one tape section. Staple or tack the remaining tape section to the frame.

To make a draped canopy to go with the casement curtain backdrop, turn to Chapter VII, page 168.

Fabric-Covered Headboards (figure IV–39)

Are you tired of your headboard? Would you like something different? It's easier to do than you think. Restyle it with polyurethane foam or a padded slipcover. First remove any knobs or gingerbread so you have fairly smooth lines. Use ½″-thick polyurethane foam, double-faced tape, matching or contrasting fabric, nylon hook and loop tape or snap tape.

Remove headboard and trace the shape (figure IV-39). Cut two foam sections ½″ larger than the top and side edges, using the pattern and a strip as wide as the headboard edges to fit between the two large sections.

Tape foam to the front and back of the headboard and then tape the narrow strips in place.

IV-39

Don't worry if the edges aren't exactly even; the cover will pull them into place.

Now make a cover ¼″ smaller on all top edges then you made the foam, allowing ½″ for seams. Make it long enough to wrap down under headboard. (For a custom finish, cord both seams.)

1. At the posts, cut a facing so it will fit around it down to the edge of the cover. Stitch facing in place in a ½″ seam; clip stitching at corners. Turn facing to inside; press. Turn in raw edges and stitch in place.

2. Adjust free edges so they overlap at the bottom of the headboard and stitch fastening tape to the edges. Pull cover over headboard and close.

Slip Cover

This is a simplified cover that can be made in a small amount of time. Make a flat envelope of fabric (figure IV-40) with a corded seam around three edges and a hem at the lower edge. Use heavyweight interfacing, an old blanket or quilted mattress cover, or stiffening. Measure the circumference of the headboard for the width, and up over one side and down over the other for the length. Divide each measurement in half. Add about 2″ to the width measurement

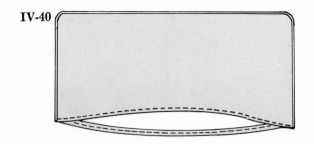

IV-40

(1″ for two side seam allowances and 1″ for ease). Add 4″ to the length (½″ for the top seam allowance, 1½″ for the hem at the lower edge, and 2″ for ease). If using a blanket or quilted pad, you may need more ease to slip the cover over the headboard. Pin stiffening around headboard to see just how much larger it must be.

Make a pattern for the top if it is shaped. Cut two sections of fabric and two sections of stiffening. Machine-baste the stiffening to the wrong side of the fabric and handle the two layers as one during construction. Cord the seam to help hold the shape. Stitch the two sections together along the side and top edges. Turn up the opening edges 1½″; press. Turn in the raw edge ½″; pin and stitch hem in place, slip the cover over the headboard—it should fit snugly but not be so tight that it pulls and collapses the corded edge.

V
Slipcovers and Simple Reupholstery— The Ultimate in Decorating

Slipcovers are preferred by many professionals —the personality of a room may be changed completely with new coverings for good upholstered furniture. Slipcovers are an inexpensive way to renew the life of your favorite pieces, pieces that have become faded or soiled long before they begin to show wear. When moving to a new home you may discover that your furniture colors clash with the carpet and walls, or you may simply want a seasonal change. Whatever your needs, slipcovers are the answer.

The simple reupholstering of chair seats used in the dining room, kitchen, and elsewhere is another decorating trick designers use to add touches of color in a room. A stapler is often the only tool needed when covering these chair seats.

Throughout this book you will find many classic styles that have been slipcovered or reupholstered or given loose or tie-on seat cushions for a totally new look. The styles illustrated on the following pages were selected to show the basic steps needed to complete each project. Be sure to examine your furniture carefully to see where the styles differ and make the appropriate additions or deletions.

SLIPCOVERS

The many styles of overstuffed furniture are limitless—some of the basic types (figure V-1) are:

1. sofas
2. love seats
3. lounge chairs with or without an ottoman
4. occasional chairs
5. boudoir chairs
6. chaise longues.

V-1

These two photographs show a chair before and after it was re-covered. First, the hand-me down, soiled, and faded, but very durable and comfortable velvet boudoir chair. Next, the transformed beauty with a slipcover designed and constructed by the author. West Point Pepperell's "Galleria Rose" quilted bedspread is used to make the slipcover that matches the platform bed and other features of a bedroom decorated with their sheets and pillowcases shown throughout the book. The pillow and lampshade are made from a matching solid color sheet and trimmed with the lace and satin ribbon removed from the hems of sheets used on the walls.

BOTTOM LEFT: *A young, eclectic mood is created by designer Shirley Regendahl with the favorite classic—red-and-white checks. The reupholstered chair seats and the place mats are made from the same fabric used on the walls to decorate the bay window. A "Lam-Eze" kit by Joanna Western Mills Co. is used for the shades that complement the pinch-pleated café curtains. Matching window seat cushion, bolsters, and throw pillows with blue accents create a focal point for this contemporary dining room.*

BOTTOM RIGHT: *Creating a serene background for hospitality is the goal of interior designer Ann Heller, ASID, in this three-windowed dining alcove. In the making are needlework tie-on chair cushions emblazoned with eagles for the ladderback chairs. Since only two are done, they are used at the head and foot of the table. Waverly Fabrics' blue plaid fabric is used for the place mats, gathered valance, and sash curtains. Breneman's "Heirloom" vinyl shades complete the window unit of this traditional dining area.*

FABRIC TO COVER THEM ALL

Slipcovers should be made of tightly woven, durable fabric such as barkcloth, denim, corduroy, ticking, Indian head, decorator fabrics, quilted cotton fabrics, linen, sheets or sheeting by the yard—anything that is washable and preshrunk. For a formal room you may wish to use damask, brocade, cotton-backed satin, or other medium-weight upholstery fabric that is dry-cleanable. Several years ago the Celanese Fibers Marketing Company introduced knitted fabrics specifically designed for slipcovers. The demand for this product was not great, however, and the fabric was discontinued. Some double-knits may make satisfactory slipcovers, but neither the manufacturer nor the fiber producer will take any responsibility for durability or results. So take heed—knits are not recommended for slipcovers at this time.

When a fabric is not preshrunk, be sure to shrink it before making your slipcover or the cover may be too small after laundering. Do the same for any purchased trim that is not preshrunk. To shrink, see *shrinking fabric* in Chapter VIII.

Fabric designs are an important consideration. An allover print or an even stripe does not require additional fabric for placement, but a fabric with a predominant design motif or clusters of stripes must have these designs centered on the front of the backrest, on each arm, and on the cushions.

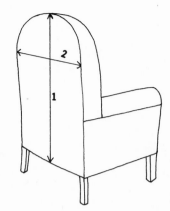

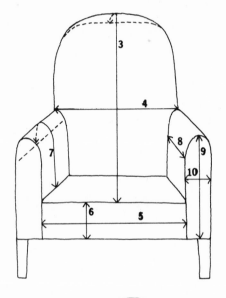

MEASURING FOR A SLIPCOVER

Before you start, remove any cushions. Use the seams of furniture as the starting and ending points when measuring. Each chair or sofa should be measured separately, even if they all seem to be identical—slight variations in width or length may require additional fabric. Decide on the style of slipcover you wish to make— glance through this book and examine the types of slipcovers. Do you want a slipcover with or without a flounce? Measuring for a chair or sofa requires the same procedure, but you must remember to allow for all cushions and pieces for the front and back of the backrest. Add 2″ to all measurements, as 1″ seam allowances are recommended for fitting. Add 4″ for a tuck-in at the side and back edges of the seat and where the arm joins the front. This allows the cover to give with the body weight. Slip your hand into

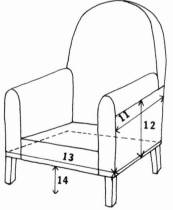

the creases to see how far you can reach into the fold. This will give you an idea of how the excess fabric is tucked into the crease for a smooth fit.

MEASUREMENTS: Measure each chair or sofa, using these step-by-step procedures (figure V-2):

Back.

1. Measure the length from the highest point to the lower edge of the fabric (measurement #1). Add 2″ for seam allowances.

2. Measure the width at the widest point (measurement #2). Add 2″ for seam allowances. NOTE: For a sofa or loveseat, piece back as required, allowing for one or two additional fabric widths in the required back length needed for your style. The back does not need to be seamed exactly like the front when it is separated with a strip of cording.

Front.

3. Measure from the seam on the back up over the top edge (measurement #3). Add 10″ (8″ for two 4″-deep tuck-ins and 2″ for two 1″ seam allowances).

4. Measure the width at the widest point (measurement #4). Add 10″ (8″ for a 4″-deep tuck-in on each side and two 1″ seam allowances). For a chair with a T-cushion and an extension to accommodate it, measure across the front at widest point and add 10″. NOTE: For a sofa or loveseat, use as many seams as the upholstery does, allowing one or two additional fabric widths in the required front length needed for your style.

Front Edge.

5. Measure the length of the front edge (measurement #5). Add 2″ for seam allowances.

6. Measure width of the front edge from seam to seam (measurement #6). Add 2″ for seam allowances.

Arm. Two are needed.

7. Measure the arm from the seam where it joins the side to the seat (measurement #7). Add 5″ (4″ for one-half the tuck-in and 1″ for seam allowances).

8. Measure the width at the widest point (measurement #8). Add 5″ (4″ for one-half the tuck-in and 1″ for seam allowances).

Arm Fronts. Two are needed.

9. Measure length from seam to seam at highest point (measurement #9). Add 2″ for seam allowances.

10. Measure width at widest point (measurement #10). Add 2″ for seam allowances.

Sides. Two are needed.

11. Measure length from seam to edge of upholstery fabric at highest point (measurement #11). Add 2″ for seam allowances.

12. Measure width at widest point (measurement #12). Add 2″ for seam allowances.

Flounce.

13. Measure around the bottom where the upholstery fabric ends to determine the flounce length (measurement #13).

14. Measure width from fabric edge to floor (measurement #14).

To the flounce length measurement, add 2″ for the opening for all styles (figure V-3).

a. For a gathered flounce, double the length measurements.

b. For a flounce with an inverted pleat at each corner, add 48″ (12″ for each pleat).

c. For a box-pleated flounce, triple the length measurement.

To the flounce width measurement, add 2½″ (1″ for a seam allowance and 1½″ for a hem).

V-3

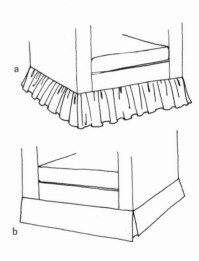

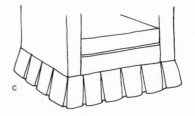

V-4

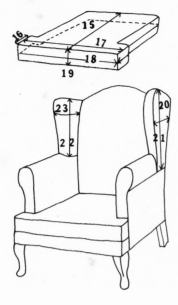

MAKE AN ESTIMATED YARDAGE GUIDE

To make a beautifully tailored slipcover, this important step must be calculated accurately—errors could be costly. First, make a chart to find out the rectangular measurement of each section required, and then make a layout with the pieces to determine how much yardage is needed and how many fabric design repeat lengths may be needed.

Back
  1. Length .... + 2″ = _____
  2. Width .... + 2″ = _____

Front
  3. Length .... + 10″ = _____
  4. Regular width .... + 10″ = _____
      T-extension width .... + 10″ = _____

Front edges
  5. Length .... + 2″ = _____
  6. Width .... + 2″ = _____

Arm (allow for 2)
  7. Length .... + 5″ = _____
  8. Width .... + 5″ = _____

Arm fronts (allow for 2)
  9. Length .... + 2″ = _____
 10. Width .... + 2″ = _____

Sides (allow for 2)
 11. Length .... + 2″ = _____
 12. Width .... + 2″ = _____

Flounce
 13. Length .... = _____
      Gathered: 2 x #13 .... + 2″ = _____
      Inverted pleats: #13 .... + 50″ = _____
      Box pleats: 3 x #13 ...... + 2″ = _____
 14. Width .... +2½″ = _____

Cushion (cut as many as needed)
 15. Length .... + 2″ = _____
 16. Extension length .... + 2″ = _____
 17. Width .... + 2″ = _____
 18. Boxing strip length .... + 1″ = _____
 19. Boxing strip width .... + 1″ = _____

Wings (allow for 2 of each)
 20. Back length .... + 2″ = _____
 21. Back width .... + 2″ = _____
 22. Front length .... + 2″ = _____
 23. Front width .... + 5″ = _____

Cushions (figure V-4). Be sure to allow for extra cushions when measuring for a sofa or loveseat.

15. Measure the length at the deepest point (measurement #15). Add 2″ for seam allowances.

16. Measure extension length (measurement #16). Add 2″ for seam allowances.

17. Measure the width at the widest point (measurement #17). Add 2″ for seam allowance.

18. Measure around the top edge of the cushion to determine the length of the boxing strip (measurement #18). Add 1″ for seam allowance; a ½″ seam allowance is used on cushions.

19. Measure the thickness of the cushion to find the boxing strip width (measurement #19). Add 1″ for seam allowances.

Wings. Two are needed.

20. Measure the back length from the top seam at the highest point to the seam that joins it to the side (measurement #20). Add 2″ for seam allowances.

21. Measure the back width at the widest point between the seams (measurement #21). Add 2″ for seam allowances.

22. Measure the front length from the seam where it joins the arm (measurement #22). Add 2″ for seam allowances.

23. Measure the front width at the widest point (measurement #23). Add 5″ (4″ for a tuck-in and a 1″ seam allowance).

NOTE: Be sure to allow for the necessary additional fabric widths that will be required for a sofa or loveseat when calculating the yardage for the slipcover front, back, and cushions.

Using the figures calculated from the measurements, make a diagram (figure V-5) representing the pieces needed to make your slipcover. Fabric widths are usually 45″, 48″, 50″, 54″. The width may be 72″ if you use sheeting or much greater if you use bedspreads. The width will help determine the placement of the pieces. When the total length has been determined, divide the amount by 36 for the estimated yardage. To this amount add as many design repeats as needed. If you plan to make self-cording and you do not expect to have much leftover fabric, add at least 1 yard extra. Each cushion will require two cording strips; a cording strip should be used between the flounce and the cover; both arm fronts should be corded—and the front edges of the wings are usually corded, too.

NOTE: If you want to use a napped fabric or a one-way design, it will be necessary to cut the flounce from selvage to selvage. Rearrange the pieces as shown in the layout to save fabric, if possible.

FITTING AND CUTTING YOUR SLIPCOVER

This step is the most time-consuming, but the results are well worth the effort. Since there are so many styles of chairs and sofas, each one will have special fitting and cutting procedures. The classic is the wing-backed chair with the T-shaped cushion; this style was selected to show the step-by-step procedure needed to complete a slipcover.

To save wear and tear on your back, place your upholstered piece on a table or on saw-trestles (sawhorses) of appropriate height.

Step 1—Start with the Chair Front (figure V–6)
Place the fabric on the chair with the right side facing you, as few upholstered pieces are symmetrical. Be sure to straighten one end of the fabric. For fabric with a predominant motif or a cluster of stripes, center the design on the front; then determine the final position, allowing 1″ to extend beyond the back seam.

1. Pin fabric in place along top edge with at least 5″ extending beyond both side creases.

V-5

131

V-6

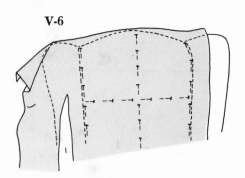

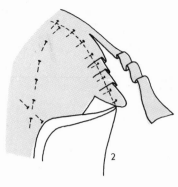

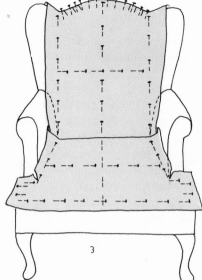

Mark a 1″ seam allowance at the highest point and pin fabric to the chair. Smooth fabric to fit the contour of the chair. Pin along the center of the chair lengthwise and across the center crosswise, keeping fabric grain straight. Now pin along each crease. Trim away excess fabric so each side measures about 5″ beyond the pins at the creases, ending near the back of the seat.

2. Smooth fabric upward toward top of chair and shape top edge to fit the contour. Pin securely, making tiny pleats so fabric will lie flat. Be sure to use the same number of pleats on each side. Trim away excess fabric to within 1″ of the back seam.

3. Continue cutting away the fabric the same width; form a 4″-deep tuck-in (it will measure 8″ long when opened); pin. Smooth fabric across the seat, pinning as indicated. Pin fabric in place across the seat, pinning as indicated. Pin fabric in place along the front edge and trim to within 1″ of the chair edge.

Pin fabric in place along the front edges. Trim to within 1″ of chair edges. Make a ½″ clip at a 45° angle at the corners. Complete this cutting and fitting step by trimming away the remaining side edge of the seat. Do not cut into the strips allowed for flounce and cushion boxing.

Step 2—Fit and Cut Piece for the Front Edge (figure V–7)

Center fabric on front with raw edge extending at least 1″ above the chair seam. Pin fabric to chair along the center of both lengthwise and crosswise grain, smoothing fabric to fit and keeping the grain balanced. Next, pin along front edges. Trim all edges to 1″ beyond the chair edge. Do not cut into the strips allowed for flounce and boxing. NOTE: For a sofa or loveseat, fit the fabric first on the left side and then on the right side, allowing a 4″ tuck-in at the left and right edges only, and a tuck-in at the seat for

each fabric panel. Next add the center panel, if necessary, allowing for a tuck-in at the seat. Pin the panels together and trim the seam allowance to 1″. Shape the back to fit the contour, if necessary, and pin in place.

V-7

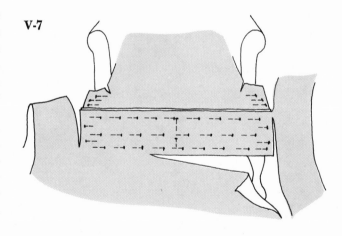

Step 3—Fit and Cut the Arm Pieces (figure V–8)

The sketch shows only one side completed, but do both arms at this time. Center a predominant design on the arms, also. To make sure you will place the fabric on straight grain, make a big + with pins along a lengthwise and a crosswise thread, as there are more contours on the arm to be fitted.

Position fabric on the arm and pin to the upholstery fabric along both grains with the front edge extending 1″ beyond the widest point of the arm front and 1″ beyond the seam where the arm piece joins the side. Fit the fabric smoothly over the arm; pin in place along the front and side edges. Use a flat, blunt object or your thumbnail to form a small groove in the fabric along the creases where it will join the back, wing, front, and seat; pin to upholstery along the creases. Trim the front, side, and wing or back edge to 1″ beyond the seams. Fit front edge by making tiny pleats if necessary. Trim the seat and back edges to 5″ from the crease for the other half of the tuck-in. If your chair has arms of a different shape, fit the pieces in the same manner using the seams of the upholstery as a guide. Be sure to use 1″ seam allowances on all edges that do not require a tuck-in. Do not cut into the flounce or boxing strips.

V-8

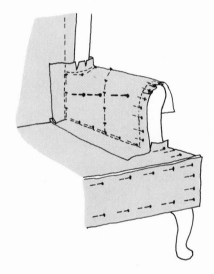

Step 4—Fit and Cut the Sides (figure V–9)
This piece has a 1″ seam allowance on all edges. Mark the lengthwise and crosswise grains same as for the arm. Position fabric on the side. Pin to the upholstery along both grains with the front edge 1″ beyond the widest point and 1″ above the highest point where the side piece joins the arm. Fit the fabric smoothly over the side; pin in place along the front, arm, back, and bottom edges. Make a ½″ clip at a 45° angle at the corner of any T-extension. Trim all edges to 1″ beyond the upholstery edges for a chair without a flounce. For a chair with a flounce, it may be necessary to level the bottom edge, as the flounce should be the same width around the chair. To do this, make the side and back bottom edges the same distance from the floor as the front edge. Mark the distance along the sides and

trim away the bottom edge along the marks, if necessary. Do not cut into the strips allowed for the flounce and boxing.

V-9

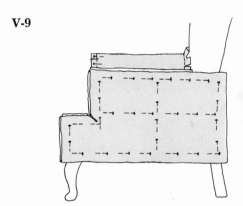

Step 5—Fit and Cut the Arm Front (figure V–10)
Mark the lengthwise and crosswise grain same as for the arm and sides. Pin to the upholstery along both grains with one side extending 1″ above the highest point where the arm front joins the arm piece. Fit the fabric smoothly over the arm front. Pin in place along all edges and trim the edges to 1″ beyond the upholstery.

V-10

Step 6—Fit and Cut Wings (figure V–11)
Your chair may just have a boxing strip for this step, or the arm piece may join the front as it would for a barrel or boudoir chair. In any case, a 1″ seam allowance should be used

133

V-11

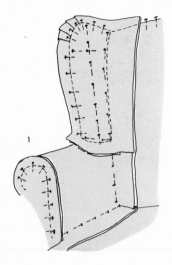

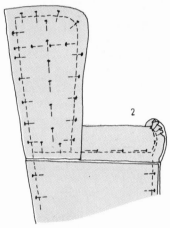

on all the edges except where it joins the front. This edge must have a 5″ tuck-in allowance.

1. Position fabric on the wing front; pin in place along both grains, making sure any part of the design is the same for both sides. Have the top and bottom edges extend 1″ beyond the seam where it joins wing back. Pin the three edges to the upholstery, forming tiny pleats at the top if necessary. Use a flat, blunt object or your thumbnail to form a small groove in the fabric along the crease where it will join the front; pin to upholstery along crease. Trim the three edges to within 1″ of the upholstery. Trim the front edge to 5″ from the crease for the other half of the tuck-in.

2. Position fabric on the wing back; pin in place along both grains, making sure any part of the design complements the sides. A 1″ seam allowance is used on all edges. Have the top and back edge extend 1″ beyond the seam where the wing pieces are stitched together on the upholstery. Pin along all edges and the trim to within 1″ of the edges and seam.

Step 7—Fit and Cut Back (figure V-12)

Position fabric on back, centering any design. A 1″ seam allowance is used on all edges. Pin in place along both grains with the top and side edges extending fabric at least 1″ beyond the back edges and top seams. Trim all edges to within 1″ beyond the back edges and top seams. Trim all edges to within 1″ of the back edges and seam for a chair without a flounce. For a chair with a flounce, make the bottom edge the same distance from the floor as you did for the sides. NOTE: For a sofa or loveseat, center fabric designs as required for extra panels and pin the wrong sides together. Trim these seam allowances to 1″.

V-12

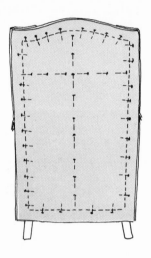

STITCHING THE SLIPCOVER TOGETHER

When you have completed all the fitting and cutting steps, the worst is over. These steps simply cannot be done quickly if you want a well-fitted slipcover. Decide which seams will be trimmed with your choice of self- or contrasting cording, fringe, or any purchased trim that will enhance your slipcover. Measure the seams that are to be trimmed. Make self-cording before you start if that is the type of trim you plan to use, using the amount established when measuring, plus at least a yard extra for seam allowances.

Step 1—Pin All the Edges Together for Stitching

Remove the pins used to hold the grains in place. With wrong sides together, pin all the 1″ seam allowances together, placing the pins parallel to the edges and seams of the upholstery. Be sure to retain the pins used to form the pleats for shaping and make sure the cover still has a snug fit. Pin the tuck-in edges together along the creases.

On the chair back, leave an opening at one edge, starting 2″–4″ below the top seam. If your chair has a tapered back, it's a good idea to leave both back edges open. Mark the opening edges where they meet with a row of pins on each edge.

Step 2—Remove the Cover Carefully
On the wrong side, crease fabric along the pins, folding it over the seam, back opening edges, and tuck-in allowances. On the wrong side of the fabric, mark creases with chalk or a soft lead pencil by rubbing the side of the point along the crease. Do not remove pins until you are ready to stitch.

Step 3—Stitch Seams
The order in which the seams are stitched together depends on the style. In most cases, slip-covers are stitched in this manner. The numbers on the sketch (figure V-13) indicate the order used to stitch the classic wing-chair slipcover together. Remove pins. Pin sections along markings, right sides together. Stitch the seams where the wings join the arm, as this seam is not corded.

Add cording to the front and top edge of wing back pieces, to the arm front pieces, and then to the top and side edges of the narrow front and extension pieces.

With right sides together, stitch wing sections together and stitch wing back to arm pieces. Then stitch the arm pieces and wing back pieces to the side pieces.

With right sides together, stitch the arm front pieces to the arm and side pieces. Then stitch the arm front to the back edge of the seat extension.

With right sides together, stitch the front piece to the sides and to the front edge of the seat and extension.

With the tuck-in edges pinned right sides together along the marks, stitch the raw edges of the tuck-in together, tapering the top edge to fit the back edge. Make sure you leave just enough fabric at the very top to form an ample crease. If the tuck-in does not fit exactly where it meets at the seat and arm, fold in the excess as you stitch. This will be hidden when the fabric is tucked into the crease. The sketch shows the seam as it would look from the wrong side before it is tucked in (figure V-14). NOTE: At this time stitch

V-13

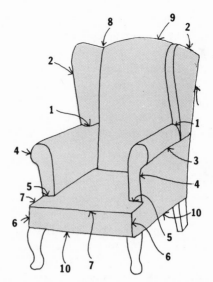

any additional panels in place that are needed to cover the front and back of a sofa or loveseat.

Cord the top and side edges of the back, if desired. Stitch the back to the front, wing back, and side pieces, leaving one or both edges open 2″–4″ below the top.

At this point, put the cover on the chair and check the fit. Make any changes necessary before proceeding. Do not make bottom edge too tight. The cording and flounce seam will create bulk and make the fabric smaller along the seam.

Step 4—Back Opening
At this time, the back opening edges should be pressed into position so the tape fasteners may be stitched in place after the bottom edge of the slipcover is added. Use snap tape or Velcro® strips.

To prepare opening, turn in only the back edge along marks; press. Measure the width of the tape fastener and make the back edge this

V-14

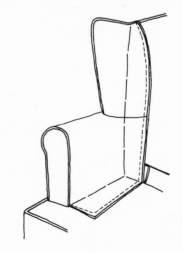

135

width by folding the raw edge under, wrong sides together; press. The wing back and side edges will form the extension for the underneath layer of the opening. Make this extension as wide as the tape by turning back the raw edges, right sides together, and press.

When the bottom edge is finished, stitch the ball strip of the snap tape (or the loop strip of the Velcro®) over the extension, and the socket strip of the snap tape (or the hook strip of the Velcro®) to the back edge, ending with a snap above the bottom edge seam and make the Velcro® even with the seam. Be sure the balls and sockets of the snap tape are aligned. Stitch across the top of the opening for reinforcement.

Step 5—Bottom Edge Finishes

Complete the bottom edge with your choice of finish. Since most slipcover styles are finished with cording, stitch it in place at this time, making the back edge even with the fold. (See *corded seam* in Chapter VIII.)

For a slipcover without a flounce, make a casing with a drawstring with or without cording. Use twill tape for the drawstring. Cut four fabric strips the length of the bottom edge between each pair of legs, adding 2" to each for narrow hems. Make strip twice the width of the thickest legs plus 1½". Turn in the narrow ends of all strips 1"; press. Then turn in the raw edges and stitch hems in place. Mark position on bottom edge of slipcover for the strips. Pin strips in place. Narrow-hem the edges without strips that go over the legs on the outside, making sure you do not

V-15

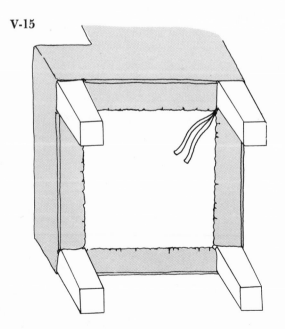

use the entire 1" seam allowance. Stitch strips to slipcover using the outer edge of the narrow-hemmed spaces for the legs as a guide for the seam depth. Trim seam allowances to ¼". Turn in remaining long strip edges ¼" and place fold a scant ⅛" over the previous stitching. Stitch in place, forming casings. Add tape fastener to back opening edges. Insert drawstrings through casing with a large safety pin, starting and ending at opening edges. Fit cover on chair. Turn in the edges over the legs so the hem does not show. Pull up drawstring to bring bottom edges to the underside of the chair. Tie drawstring securely and tuck ends out of sight (figure V-15).

For all types of flounces, cut strip as planned in measurement #13, piecing if necessary. Make a hem at both narrow ends. Turn in ends 1"; press. Turn in raw ends ½" and stitch hems in place. Now hem the bottom long edge of strip by turning it up 1½"; press. Turn in raw edge and stitch hem in place (figure V-16).

V-16

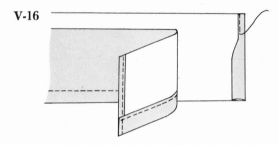

For a gathered flounce, prepare strip as instructed in figure V-16. Measure each side of the bottom edge. Mark each corner on the cover. Double each measurement as a guide for the gathering threads. Leave 1" free at each end and mark the four corner positions with pins on the flounce. Add gathering threads, breaking stitches at the pins. Pin flounce to cover at each corner, with the narrow hem even with the underlap of the opening, and extend the flounce 1" beyond the overlap opening edge. Pull up gathers to fit; distribute evenly. Turn extended flounce end over the back opening edge to the underside of gathers and slipcover; pin. Stitch flounce in place. Turn flounce down; press. Add tape fastener to back opening edges (figure V-17).

For a flounce with an inverted pleat at each corner of the chair, prepare the flounce strip as directed in figure V-16. Mark each corner on the cover. Pin flounce to cover with one narrow hem even with the underlap of the opening. Make one

V-17

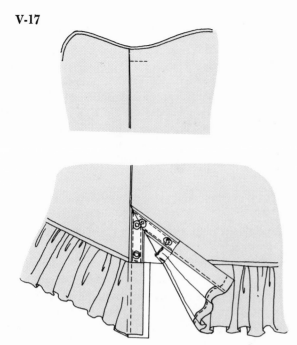

V-18

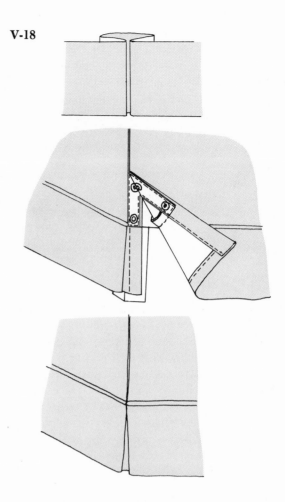

half of the pleat (2″ deep) at this same opening edge, having the fold aligned with the back edge when closed. Make an inverted pleat at each corner, making each fold 2″ deep with a 4″ space across the folds, pinning flounce to cover. At the back opening edge, make the other half of the pleat with the fold aligned with the finished edge. Turn the remaining flounce end over the back opening edge to the underside of the pleat and slipcover; pin. Stitch flounce in place. Turn flounce down; press. Add tape fastener to back opening edges (figure V-18).

For a box-pleated flounce, prepare the flounce strip as directed in figure V-16. Mark each corner of the chair on the cover. Next divide the flounce strip into the four sections; allow 3 times each measurement and 1″ for each of the back opening edges. Start with the front edge and make an

uneven number of pleats 5, 7, 9, or 11. Form pleats as shown in figure V-19. On the side and back edges make an even or uneven amount of pleats, the top layer as near the measurement for the front as possible. (The shape of your chair will help determine the number of pleats.)

1. The sketch shows how the pleats would look if they were not stitched in place. Place the free end at the edge of the underlap of the opening. Make one half of the pleat having the fold

V-19

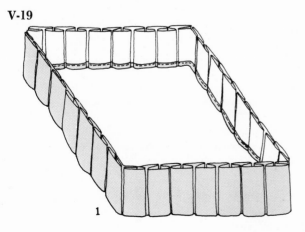

1

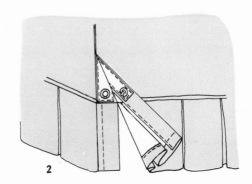

2

137

aligned with the back edge when closed. Pin all pleats in place. Make the other half of the pleat at the back opening edge with the pleat fold aligned with the finished edge. Turn in the remaining flounce end over the back opening edge to the underside of the pleat and slipcover; pin. Stitch flounce in place. Turn flounce down; press.

2. Add tape fastener to back opening edges.

Step 6—Cover Matching Cushion

To make the style of cushion that is appropriate for your chair, see the basic box-edge cushion cover and the quick box-edge cushion cover in Chapter III.

SIMPLE REUPHOLSTERY

Here is a great way to show off your needle art. Many needlecrafters down through the ages have made chair covers that are now expensive antiques. Simply follow the direction for measuring and making a pattern and then transfer it to your embroidery foundation.

In many cases these chairs do not require sewing. For those that have a seam along the top edge, with or without cording, the method used is the same as for the basic box-edge cushion in Chapter III.

There are some interesting examples of reupholstered chair seats shown in photographs throughout this book.

FABRIC FOR DURABILITY

The first and most important decision is fabric selection. A chair seat receives more use than any other part of the chair. Here is a chance to use some of the great synthetic leather-looks or extra-heavy upholstery fabric that is impossible to sew on some domestic sewing machines. For the classic look, use tightly woven, durable fabrics such as denim, linen, barkcloth, decorator fabrics, ticking, corduroy, or quilted cotton fabrics.

MEASURING FOR A NEW CHAIR SEAT

Each chair should be measured separately even when all of them seem to be identical—slight variations in the length or width may require additional fabric (figure V-20).

1. For a plain, unseamed seat, measure the length at the deepest point (measurement #1).

2. Measure the width at the widest point (measurement #2).

V-20

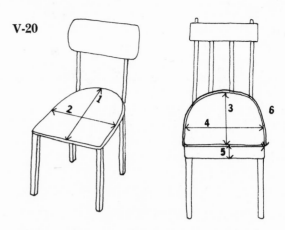

Add 6″ to each measurement so you will have 3″ on each edge to pull to the underside over padding and the wooden base.

3. For a seamed seat, measure the length at the deepest point (measurement #3).

4. Measure the width at the widest point (measurement #4).

5. Measure the boxing strip width from the seam to the chair edge (measurement #5); add 3″ to this measurement so you can fasten the fabric to the underside over the padding and wooden base.

6. For the boxing strip length, measure around the top edge of the pad (measurement #6); add 1″ for ½″ seam allowances. Use the measurement for self-cording, too.

MAKE AN ESTIMATED YARDAGE GUIDE

To calculate the yardage needed there are several items to consider. If you want to use a predominant motif or a cluster of stripes at the center of each seat, make a pattern using the measurements. This will aid you tremendously at the store. For most cases, however, make a diagram that represents the pieces needed to cover more than one chair (figure V-21). Fabric widths are usually 44″, 48″, 50″, or 54″. The fabric width will determine whether you get two seat covers across the fabric.

1. For a plain, unseamed cover, arrange pieces as economically as possible.

V-21

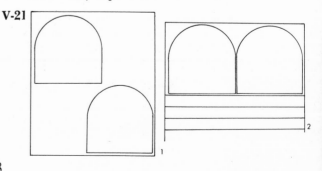

2. For a seamed cover, allow for the boxing strips as well.

When the total length has been determined, divide the amount by 36 for the estimated yardage. To the amount add as many design repeats as needed. If you plan to use self-cording, add at least ¼ yard extra for each chair. NOTE: If using a napped fabric, be sure to cut the covers so the nap runs in the same direction on all matching chairs.

REUPHOLSTER CHAIR SEATS

Follow these simple steps to replace chair seat covers.

Step 1—Remove Seat

Place chair upside down on a table (figure V-22). When reupholstering more than one chair, mark both the chair and the seat with corresponding numbers so the screw holes will line up quickly.

1. Take out the screws and securely tape them to the chair bottom near the point of removal.

2. Remove the covering by pulling out all staples or tacks with a chisel or screwdriver. Be careful not to tear the fabric so it may be used for a pattern.

V-22

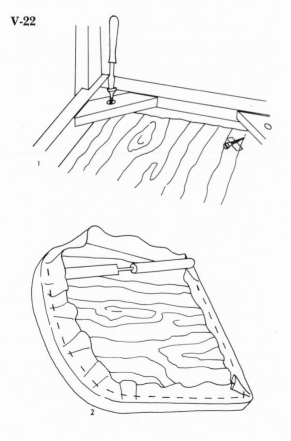

Step 2—Repad Seat

Replace the padding, if necessary, with a foam sheet twice the thickness of the original padding at its highest point. Make a pattern using the wooden base and have foam cut to shape or draw the shape on the foam and cut out. For a chair without a seam, one edge of the foam should be rounded with shears so the cover will fit smoothly. Glue the foam padding to the wooden base with white glue along the outer edges.

Step 3—Cut Fabric

Use the old upholstery fabric as a pattern. Place right side of fabric pattern on the wrong side of the new fabric, making sure the design motif on the new fabric is centered under the pattern. Pin in place along the outer edge and cut out the new seat cover (figure V-23).

V-23

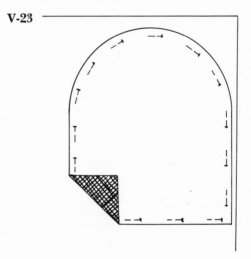

Step 4—Fabric Replacement

Center seat over the wrong side of the new upholstery fabric with the padded side down (figure V-24).

1. Starting with the front edge, pull fabric up over the padding to the wooden base and staple or tack at the center about ½″ from the fabric edge. Next, gently pull the fabric taut at the back edge; staple. Now secure the center of each side edge in the same manner.

2. Check right side of the seat to make sure any design motif is centered. Staple the front edge every 1½″–2½″, keeping the edge smooth. Then staple the back edge in the same manner, keeping the fabric taut. Make tiny pleats to make the fabric lie flat along a curved edge. Do the side edges in the same manner, pleating in the excess fabric on the wooden seat. At the corners, pull

fabric taut at the longest edge; staple. Then make pleated folds to ensure a smooth corner on the right side of the seat. Be careful not to cause puckers at the corners.

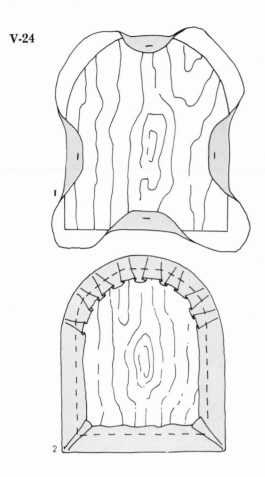

V-24

Step 5—Replace Seat

Now that the seat is reupholstered, fasten it in place with the screws. If the holes have been covered, locate them with your fingertips and then pierce the fabric before fastening. NOTE: If your chair has a simple upholstered padded back, remove the back by unscrewing it and reupholster in the same manner as recommended for the seat.

LOOSE CHAIR-SEAT COVERS

There are quite a few styles shown throughout this book that are either loose pillows or cushions that may be tied in place. Make a pattern, following the outer edges of the chair seat to be cushioned. Use polyurethane foam forms or make your own.

When making your own form, make a pattern the same size as the chair seat. Then add ½" to

the pattern on all edges. If you are making a knife-edge pillow, add an additional ½" on all edges to allow for the "shrinkage" caused when the flat fabric pieces are stuffed—it will make the pillow slightly smaller.

To make tie-on seat cushions, simply insert self-fabric ties in the seam at points that match the chair backs before stitching the seam. Follow instructions for making pillows and cushions in Chapter III (page 75), using an opening that is slip-stitched shut.

To make ties (figure V-25), cut two strips 1½" wide for each tie and long enough to tie in a small bow.

1. Fold strip lengthwise, stitch ends and long edge in a ¼" seam, leaving an opening for turning. Turn right side out; press. Stitch opening shut.

2. Pin the two strips at the required spot on the pillow or cushion after the trim, if used, has been basted in place.

3. Complete as instructed and tie in place.

V-25

VI
Leisure-Time Furniture—
Redecorate Your Own

The trend toward a more casual life-style is prevalent throughout our nation as we gain more leisure time. Americans who live in the sun belt stretching across the South and Southwest spend much of their free time outdoors on their patios or lawns. Others inhabiting the northern zone may have glassed-in porches, recreation rooms, vehicles, seasonal homes, or camps. Whatever your life-style you can apply your sewing skill to create comfortable, casual furnishings that can "take it," using bright, fade-resistant colors and durable fabrics.

Look over your present outdoor or leisure furniture. The frames are probably still sturdy, but the covers may be worn or faded. Or maybe the "sale" furniture you purchased on impulse clashes with some of the good pieces you have. Evaluate your situation and then use ideas found on these pages and throughout the book to decorate a smart, relaxing leisure-time living area.

Casual furniture may serve two areas: outdoors during the warm months and indoors during the colder season. Or it can be used exclusively indoors for contemporary decorating. Director's chairs and rattan, bamboo, or redwood furniture are excellent choices for these dual purposes.

Update pool and patio aluminum- or wood-framed furniture with new covers, or make slipcovers for recliners that have vinyl webbing. For your next barbecue, picnic, or pool party, dress up your outdoor table and benches with brightly colored covers. When you want to get away from it all, make a hammock and hang it in a quiet corner of the backyard.

FABRIC FOR FUN AND SUN

With so many fabrics available, there are few limitations. For chairs, hammock, recliner, or any type of furniture that must support the weight of an adult, choose medium- to heavyweight tightly woven fabric that will not stretch. Canvas or duck should be the first consideration, with denim corduroy, ticking, decorator fabrics, or sailcloth the next choices. A single thickness of canvas or duck is sufficient, but for other fabrics it is best to use a double thickness. If you must use a designer sheet or other lighter-weight fabric, use a double thickness or underline each layer with heavy muslin or one of the other medium-weight fabrics. If you prefer to use fake fur or suedelike vinyl for director chairs, these fabrics must be underlined with a medium-weight fabric to prevent stretching.

For outdoor tablecloths and bench covers, you can choose any tightly woven easy-care cotton-and-blend fabric or a lightweight vinyl that is easy to sew.

Cushions and pillows meant for leisure-time activities should be made of medium- to heavyweight fabrics such as those previously mentioned.

Be sure to select fabric that is fade-proof, has soil release properties, and is resistant to mildew. Finished items may be sprayed with special chemicals, such as those used to waterproof raincoats and shoes, that will make them more waterproof, thus helping to eliminate some of the problems stated above. Test a fabric scrap with the spray to be certain the chemicals will not change the colors or damage the fabric.

See how to straighten ends on heavyweight fabric in Chapter VIII.

Be sure to make a test seam for unfamiliar fabrics or when using several layers of fabrics as one. Machine tension may need to be balanced, and large-size needles (size 16 or 18) will be needed to prevent splitting of heavy threads. For vinyl or other leatherlike fabric, baste with pins and paper clips, placing pins in seam allowances only, as the pin marks will not disappear.

NEW COVERS FOR DIRECTOR'S CHAIRS

These versatile chairs have a long life and are equally adaptable indoors and out. As indoor dining and occasional chairs, they may be expensively constructed of heavy chrome or hard-finished wood with leather or fur seat and back or be the traditional natural wood with decorator fabrics color-keyed as accents.

Here is a fine opportunity to show off your needlework skills. Use your old covers as a pattern and insert a needlework piece at the center of the back and seat sections or use the fabric design to make an interesting patchwork block. For the director's chairs pictured in this chapter, a striped canvas was used to form the geometric design that measures 11¾" by 7" for the back and 11¾" by 16" for the seat, plus a ¾" seam allowance on all edges. Adjust the size of the foundation fabric or needlepoint canvas so your handiwork will be the correct size for your chair when completed.

Choose the double-thickness cover in order to protect the wrong side of your needlework and hide the unsightly seams and thread endings. The single-thickness cover is more suitable for most other fabrics without a decorative insert.

To make the double-thickness cover using ¾"-wide striped Sunbrella® canvas (cut lengthwise), about 1⅜ yards are needed. Adjust this yardage when substituting needlework done on other material.

To make a single-thickness cover, use about ¾ yard of canvas or duck (cut crosswise).

Re-cover versatile director's chairs for use as great double-duty furniture—they're used indoors as well as out. The author made new covers from Sunbrella® canvas from Glen Raven Mills, Inc., using the stripe to form geometric patchwork on the back and seat.

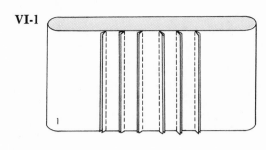

VI-1

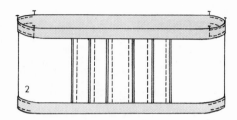

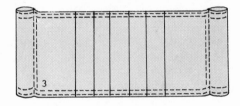

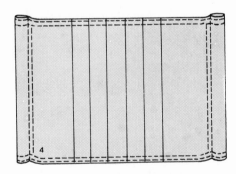

1. Assemble patchwork blocks or use your own needlework block. Stitch block to strip for the back, using ¾" seam allowances, and form a tube. Slip tube over the chair back dowels to make sure it is snug enough.

2. Turn in both long raw edges ¾"; press. Center needlework block and fold the two layers flat. Place a pin in each layer about 3" from the folds. To hold these raw edges in place (after the casing is made for the back dowels), stitch ¼" from the top and bottom pressed edges (between the pins), and again ¼" away.

3. Turn right side out and fold flat, centering the needlework block. Pin remaining unstitched edges together. To form a casing at each end of the cover for the dowels, stitch about 2¼" from each narrow end and ¼" from the long pressed edges, stitching the two layers of the tube together. Stitch again ¼" away, inside the first row of stitches.

4. Assemble seat cover in the same manner as for back cover, making the casing for the seat dowels narrower. Be sure to test seat tube before finishing the edges. The seat has a tendency to stretch more than the back as it supports the bulk of a person's weight. Make sure it is taut before completing.

Single-Thickness Covers

Make these from one layer of heavy fabric, using the old covers for a pattern. Allow 1" on each long edge for a ½"-wide hem and be sure to allow enough fabric on the ends to hem the casings. Use the same number of rows of stitches as for the original cover.

For fake fur, suede, vinyl, other stretchy fabrics, or lightweight fabrics, cut a layer of tightly woven medium-weight fabric and machine-baste it to the wrong side of the outer fabric. Handle as one layer during construction. If fur is too bulky, trim it away close to foundation fabric before turning it under. It may be necessary to trim fur at casing edge so dowels for the seat may be inserted into slot. NOTE: These covers for the back and seat are made just like a casement curtain. Narrow-hem the front and back edges and make plain casing at each side to insert the wooden dowels on the back above the arms and the metal dowel for the seat slot.

CUSHIONED LOUNGES

There are many types of lounging furniture—settees, chairs, ottomans, and chaise longues—

Double-Thickness Cover

Straighten ends. For this style cover, you will need a tube of fabric for the back and seat the required width and length for your chair, plus a ¾" seam allowance on all edges. For the striped covers shown on the director's chairs, additional pieces were needed (8½" by 34" for the back, 17½" by 27½" for the seat), plus the patchwork blocks.

CONSTRUCTION (figure VI-1): Use the longest stitch on your sewing machine, size 18 needles, and nylon thread size D/E.

Wooden patio furniture made by the Shinnecock Indians from the Long Island Reservation is enhanced by cushions of Sunbrella® canvas from Glen Raven Mills, Inc., designed and made by the author.

and each is designed for your comfort. Why not add a spark to your outdoor living room by re-covering the cushions in new, bright colors, or by making cushions for that not-so-comfortable chair, chaise longue, or settee.

The wooden settee and lounge chairs shown in the photo were made by the Shinnecock Indians from the Long Island Reservation. The furniture did not have cushions, so patterns were needed. If you are confronted with the same situation, use newspaper and masking tape and make patterns to fit the outer measurement of both the back and the seat, then add ½″ to all edges. Have foam cushion forms cut to the pattern size or buy foam and cut it to your needs with a large serrated knife or an electric double-bladed carving knife with serrated edges. The foam forms for these chairs were then covered with Sunbrella® canvas. For the total pillow and cushion story see Chapter III. Any of the fabrics

suggested may be used, with the proper precautions. Smooth vinyl with a knit back may also be used.

Review the information about forms in Chapter III. Should you decide to make your own forms, use the same pattern to cut out fabric. Follow the instructions for basic box-edge cushion covers. Cut fabric strips on straight grain for cording; see *bias* and *straight strips* in Chapter VIII.

CONSTRUCTION (figure VI-2): Use the longest stitch on your sewing machine. Make cording first to save time, following instructions in Chapter VIII.

1. Machine-baste cording along sides and front of shaped edges. Do not use cording on the strip that does not show when cushions are in place; clip corners.

2. Clip curves if cushion has this shape. Taper ends as instructed for *corded seams* in Chapter

146

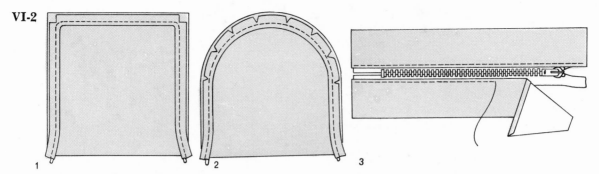

VIII. Complete cushions as directed for the basic box-edge cushion covers.

Exposed Zipper Closure

For stiff, heavy fabrics such as canvas or vinyl, it is best not to cover the zipper teeth with fabric. After you have determined the boxing strip width, cut a strip the length of the zipper including tapes. Fold strip in half lengthwise; cut along fold. Turn in one long edge on each strip ¼"; press.

3. Place pressed edge of strips over zipper tapes (at least a ¼" overlap), making unit as wide as the boxing strip measurement. Stitch each pressed edge to zipper tape. NOTE: If you are using two zippers in place of one long zipper, have zipper pulls meet at center of strip; overlap tape ends and pull to the underside so the raw ends do not show on the outside.

RECLINE IN STYLE

Recliners are favorites of all sunbathers and are most comfortable for solid relaxation. Replace a cover when the frame is still in good condition, or if vinyl webbing isn't to your liking, make a terry cloth slipcover for sheer delight. It will absorb moisture if you plop down straight from

A sturdy aluminum frame with a torn plastic cover was about to be discarded. It is given new life with a coat of paint and a new cover made of Sunbrella® canvas from Glen Raven Mills, Inc., and is ready for sunbathing. Cover designed and made by the author.

the pool or perspire from sunbathing, and you can slip the cover off and wash it easily.

The following directions may be used for either a replacement cover or a slipcover. For the latter, simply eliminate the elastic support needed for the seat.

MATERIALS NEEDED TO MAKE COVER:

3 yards of 31"-wide Sunbrella® canvas or terry cloth

12 yards of 1"-wide twill tape

Nylon thread size D/E (for canvas)

Machine needles size 18 (for canvas)

Heavy-duty thread (for terry cloth)

Machine needles size 16 (for terry cloth)

For replacement cover: 3¾ yards of 1"-wide elastic

6 flat hooks, 1" wide

Straighten ends. Cut a top about 92" long and 23½" wide. (NOTE: You should have at least an 8" turn-back at each end; adjust length if necessary.) The seat area determines the width. Fabric should be wide enough to fit between the hinges plus 1½" for seam allowances. From the remaining long strip, cut two sections (about 21½" long and 7¾" wide) for seat extensions and four sections (about 15" long and 7¾" wide) for back and foot extensions.

CONSTRUCTION (figure VI-3): Use longest stitch on your sewing machine.

1. Hem seat extensions by turning in the short raw ends ½" and then form a ¾"-wide hem; stitch in place.

2. To form a casing, turn up long selvage edge 1⅝"; stitch ¼" from selvage and again ¼" away, backstitching at beginning and ending. NOTE: If your fabric does not have a selvage edge, turn in raw edge ¼" and stitch close to fold.

3. Narrow-hem the short raw ends of the back and foot sections; turn in ends ¼" and then turn in again about ⅜"; stitch in place. Make casing with long selvage edges the same as for seat sections.

VI-3

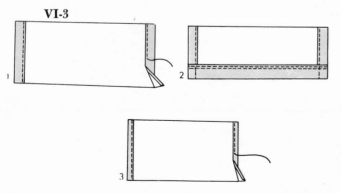

VI-4

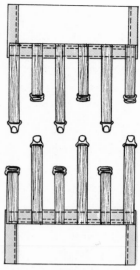

Note: This step is required for the replacement cover only.

To make elastic supports for replacement cover, cut six 15" strips and six 7½" strips of 1"-wide elastic. Using three long and three short strips of elastic, insert through opening on hooks with hooking section out; pin ends together. Insert remaining elastic through opening on eyes with narrowest bar out; pin ends together. NOTE: If hooks have three holes instead of a bar, fold elastic in half and sew hooks and eyes to folded end.

On the wrong side of the seat sections, pin elastic with hooks and eyes over casing with raw ends of elastic even with selvage edge, alternating long and short elastic strips with hooks on one section and corresponding eye strips on other sections. Stitch each elastic strip in place ¼" from raw ends and again along outer edge of casing as shown (figure VI-4).

To attach seat, back, and foot sections (figure VI-5), pin seat section to each side of the center of the cover. Leaving about a 7" space (wide enough to clear hinges), pin back and foot sections to the long edges of cover. Stitch all six sections to cover in a ¾" seam.

Shape cover ends to fit narrower recliner ends (figure VI-6).

1. On one side, draw a seam line above last casing section. For the recliner shown in the photo, the ends were 17¼" wide between seam lines. Make a straight line for about 7" above the back- and footrests. At the end, draw a line 4" in from long cut or selvage edge to within several inches of the first line. Make a gradual curve from one line to the other. Next, add a ¾" seam

148

VI-5

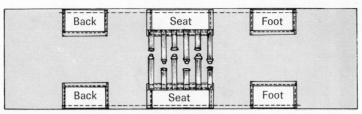

Note: When making a terry cloth slipcover, disregard the elastic and hooks on the illustrations.

VI-6

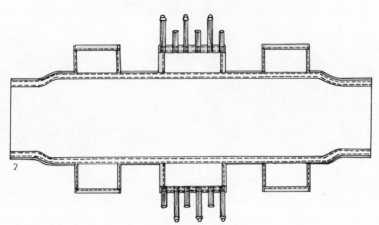

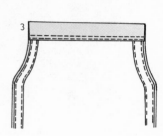

VI-7

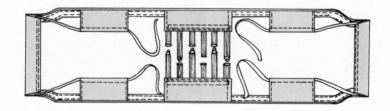

allowance. Cut along the outer line. Fold canvas in half lengthwise and pin. Cut away same amount on opposite side. Next, fold canvas in half crosswise and cut remaining end in same manner.

2. To finish long edges, turn in straight ends along machine stitching; pin, pulling casing sections out. Turn in remainder of edge ¾″, clipping curve with about ⅜″-deep clips so seam allowance will lie flat; pin. Lap twill tape over seam allowances with outer edges even. Stitch along this edge, first making little pleats on curve so tape will lie flat on inner edge. To make these pleats, use a pin and shove folds of tape toward machine needle as you stitch. Stitch inner edge of twill tape in place.

3. Make casing in ends. Turn up ends 2″. Turn in raw edge ½″; pin. Stitch close to fold and again ¼″ away.

To install cover (figure VI-7), cut two pieces of twill tape 2 yards long for the back and foot and two pieces 1½ yards long for a terry cloth cover. Insert one long strip through the three casings on the headrest and the other on the footrest, using a large safety pin. Insert shorter strips into casing for seat for the terry cloth cover.

Lay cover on a flat area and insert recliner frame into casing extensions. Hook elastic supports together if making a replacement cover and tie twill tape ends together at each side of seat, pulling tape taut for smooth-fitting back- and footrest.

A calico print by Spring Mills, Inc., for an umbrella table and benches is the perfect touch for patio–poolside entertaining. The zippered tablecloth, with a ruffle that hides an elasticized anchor band, and the fitted elasticized bench covers were designed and made by the author.

TABLE TOPICS FOR THE OUT-OF-DOORS

Add sparkle to your next picnic, patio, or pool party with a colorful tablecloth and bench covers to match. Just about any washable fabric will do —you may even wish to use a vinyl fabric.

Think "wind" when creating your own design; devise ways to anchor your tablecloth and bench covers with elastic or twill tape ties to hold it down. Make contrasting pocket or fabric loops on tablecloths to hold napkins. Trim the edges at will with ruffles, fringe, lace, or any other ready-made or self-fabric trims that are washable.

Your guests will bless you for covering the benches. Expensive swimsuits or knitted sportswear have been ruined by snags or pulls from unseen rough edges on wooden benches.

The tablecloth and bench covers shown here were made of Springmaid permanent-press fabric. The tablecloth has a corded ruffle with an elasticized anchor band to prevent the cloth from blowing away. The bench covers have the same anchor band. These anchor bands can be adapted for any shape table or bench.

MATERIALS FOR TABLECLOTH AND FOUR BENCHES:

6½ yards of 44/45"-wide fabric
15 yards of ¼"-wide elastic
4 yards of ½" twill tape
32" separating zipper (one 22" and one 10" separating zipper may be substituted)
Heavy crochet cotton and 1 snap for ruffle
Polyester thread #50 for general sewing
Button and carpet thread for gathering
Size 14 machine needle

Tablecloth

This round tablecloth needs a seam at the center. A separating zipper will be inserted in one half of the seam so cloth will fit around the umbrella pole. An elasticized band anchors the cloth securely to the table.

Cut out two equal half-circles. For the fabric shown, a 1" seam allowance was needed to have the seam fall at the center of each square design. Use at least a 1" seam allowance for all fabrics. The diameter of the table is 60"; to this measurement add 1" for seam allowances and 1" for a drop around the table edge. Divide this measurement (62″) in half (31″).

Fold fabric right sides together along the crosswise grain at least 31″ deep, matching selvages and centering a design on the fold. Measure in 1″ from the selvage, down along the fold, and make a dot at this point. (This will establish where the 1″ seam line will fall when the tablecloth sections are joined together.) With a yardstick, use the dot on the fold as a pivot point, and make a quarter-circle measuring 31″. Move the yardstick only an inch at a time, marking fabric with every move (figure VI-8). Pin the fabric layers together along the markings, keeping the selvages even; cut out. Open half-circle and place on remaining fabric, right sides together, matching selvages and fabric design along the seam line; pin. Cut out remaining half-circle.

VI-8

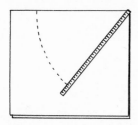

For the elasticized anchor band, cut a strip 4½″ wide and as long as the table circumference, plus 12″ for ease. Piece where necessary. (Band strip will be at least 6 yards long.) Adjust band width if your table is more than 1″ thick. Cut a strip 6″ wide and 9 yards long for ruffle, piecing where necessary (1½″ fullness makes a lovely applied ruffle with a heading when using this type of fabric).

On a fabric scrap, draw a 6½″ circle with a 3″ circle at the center. See figure III-1 in Chapter III. Cut out along line of larger circle. This circle will be a facing for the pole hole.

CONSTRUCTION: Pin long straight edges of half-circles, right sides together, matching designs at 1″ seam line. If you find pins unsatisfactory, slip-baste seam (see *basting* in Chapter VIII). Using a 1″ seam allowance, stitch to center of seam; break stitches and machine-baste remainder of seam (figure VI-9). Press seam open.

VI-9

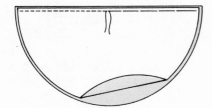

1. Now fold the pole hole facing (figure VI-10) in half, right sides together, and slash to the center. Cut out a hole at the center of the circle, leaving a ½″ seam allowance beyond the 3″ circle line.

2. On the wrong side of the tablecloth make a large dot at the exact center of the seam for the umbrella pole hole. Now center the facing, wrong sides together, over dot with cut edges along basted seam.

3. Pin one-half of the facing to tablecloth. Fold facing along the seam; pin free end of facing to basted tablecloth seam allowance in about a ½″ seam.

4. Do the same for the other facing end, making sure the facing will lie flat.

5. Remove basting. Stitch each facing end to the tablecloth seam allowance along the pinned seams, keeping tablecloth free. Clip each tablecloth seam allowance to crease halfway between dot and inner facing edge.

6. Trim tablecloth even with facing and along crease below clip.

VI-10

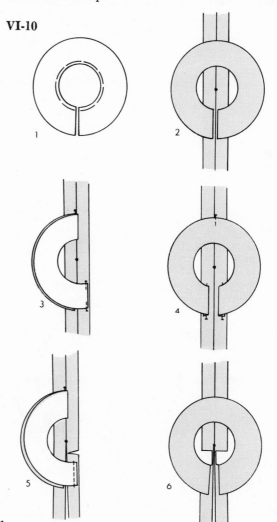

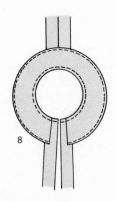

7. Turn facing to outside along creased seam line. With right sides together, pin facing to tablecloth making sure everything is flat. Stitch facing to tablecloth along the 3″ circle marking between opening edges. Cut a hole in tablecloth, trimming hole seam allowance to ¼″. Clip to stitching at about ¼″ intervals.

8. Turn facing to the wrong side; press. Stitch ¼″ from finished edge and outer raw edge.

To make a casing on one long edge of the anchor band (figure VI-11), turn up raw edge ⅝″; pin close to fold. Trim to ⅛″ any seam allowances that will be covered by casing so safety pin will slide through easily.

1. Turn in raw edge ¼″ and remove pins as you work while stitching casing in place along inner fold.

2. Divide raw band edge into eighths; mark with pins. Do the same for the tablecloth. With right sides together, pin band to cloth, matching pins. Pin band securely to cloth, placing pins at 2″–3″ intervals, easing band to fit. Stitch in a ½″ seam.

3. Turn seam allowance toward band; press. Stitch seam allowance to band ¼″ from seam.

VI-11

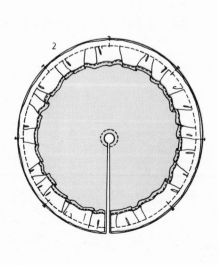

4. Cut a 4-yard strip of elastic and insert through casing with a safety pin attached to one end. Pin free end to band (above casing) so elastic won't snap into casing. Stitch across each end of casing to hold elastic in place. Distribute fullness evenly.

Place zipper under one pressed tablecloth edge, face up, with separating end at umbrella hole (figure VI-12). Pin cloth to zipper tape with pressed edge along center of teeth. Tuck raw tape end between the band and its seam allowance at casing edge.

VI-12

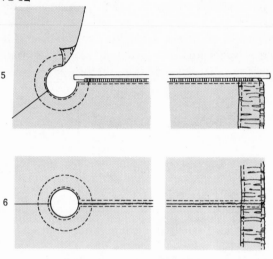

5. Using zipper foot, stitch zipper in place through center of tape.

6. Pin remaining edge to zipper tape with pressed edges meeting at center of zipper. Tuck in tape end and stitch in place.

The ruffle is finished with a corded hem, but it may also be finished with a narrow hem. To

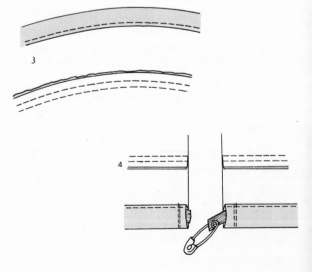

make a ruffle with a heading and a corded hem, see Chapter VIII.

Ruffle should be about 5½" wide when hemmed (figure VI-13).

7. Narrow-hem one end of ruffle and make a 1" hem in the opposite end.

8. Divide ruffle strip in eighths; mark with pin. Gather ruffle ½" from one finished edge, following special instructions for applied ruffle (Chapter VIII), breaking stitches at pins. Divide tablecloth in eighths. Pin ruffle to band at markings, pinning over the gathering threads; place corded edge along seam. Pin narrow-hemmed end even with zipper stitching. Extend wide-hemmed end over zipper so it will cover narrow end at least ¼". Pin this end at zipper stitching. Adjust gathers to fit evenly. Pin ruffle in place at 1¼" intervals along gathering threads, keeping corded edge even with seam. Stitch ruffle to band just above and below gathering threads so they can be removed. Keep band flat as you stitch.

9. Sew a snap to ruffle extension over zipper to hold in place.

Bench Covers

Contour benches are easy to cover if you make a pattern. Use this technique for any size or shape bench. The anchor band will hold the covers firmly in place.

Make a pattern the shape of the bench top, using newspaper and masking tape. For rectangular benches, simply take the measurements and add 1" to each measurement for seam allowances.

Pin bench pattern to wrong side of fabric, drawing in a ½" seam allowance on all edges. Cut out bench top along marking. Use this fabric section to cut out the other three bench tops. Cut four 3½"-wide strips the perimeter of the bench plus 12". (Adjust band width if your benches are thicker than ¾".) Piece where necessary.

CONSTRUCTION (figure VI-14): Stitch band in a ½" seam; press open.

1. Make a ⅜" casing on one long edge same as for table, figure VI-11, step 1, leaving 1" opening to insert elastic.

VI-13

7

8

9

VI-14

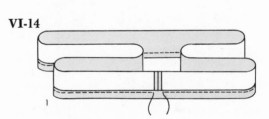

2. Divide band into quarters and mark center of long edges and short ends of bench top. With right sides together, pin band to top, matching pins. Starting ½" from corner, stitch band to top along long edges and short end, keeping excess corner fabric free.

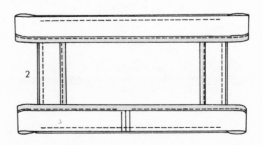

3. Next stitch corners. Divide excess fabric in half and form a pleat on each side of corner.

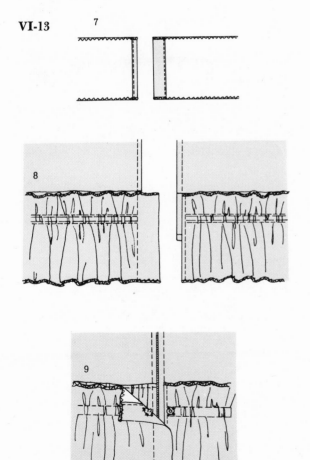

153

Stitch first pleat in place to corner. With needle in fabric, raise presser foot; clip top layer to needle.

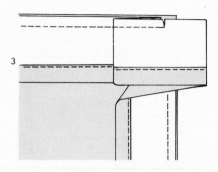

4. Pivot fabric on needle, spread clip, and stitch remaining pleat in place. Repeat for remaining corners.

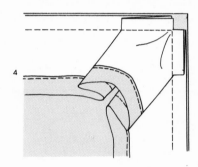

5. Insert a 2¾-yard strip of elastic through opening in casing with safety pin (figure VI-15). Pin opposite end to band so it won't pull into opening. Lap ends, and stitch securely.

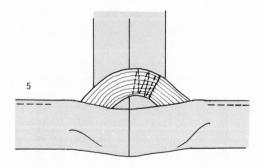

6. Stretch elastic and stitch opening shut, overlapping stitches.

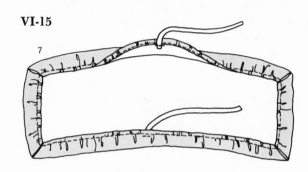

7. To hold the inner curved edge of casing tightly to bench, turn in raw end of a ½-yard strip of twill tape and stitch securely to band just above casing at the center of each long edge.

VI-15

Hang a hammock made of Sunbrella® canvas from Glen Raven Mills, Inc., in a secluded corner to get away from it all. The hammock was designed and made by the author.

SEW A HAMMOCK

For centuries hammocks were used as portable beds and couches. Today they are still a backyard favorite and you may have the perfect spot. Basic sewing technique and a few tools are all you need to make one of your own. Be sure to double fabric if making hammock of a lighterweight fabric than canvas.

MATERIALS NEEDED:
3 yards of 31"-wide Sunbrella® canvas
18 small ⅞"–wide D-rings
84' of ¼" no. 5 mason line rope
2 heavy 3"–wide D-rings
9' of galvanized steel wire, gauge no. 16
2 S-hooks

Nylon thread size D/E
Machine needles size 18

Straighten canvas ends. Mark and cut two 3"-wide strips from selvage to selvage for facings and two 8"-wide strips, the same way, for tabs. Mark and cut 18 tabs 3¼" wide from the 8" strips. Remaining canvas will measure about 85".

CONSTRUCTION (figure VI-16): Use the longest stitch on your sewing machine.

1. To make tabs, fold strip in half lengthwise; press lightly.
2. Open and fold cut edges in to meet at crease.
3. Refold along center crease; press.
4. Stitch the two folded edges together.

VI-16

155

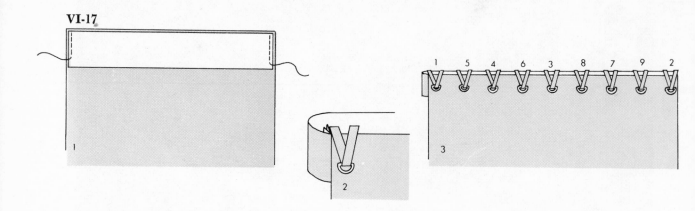

VI-18

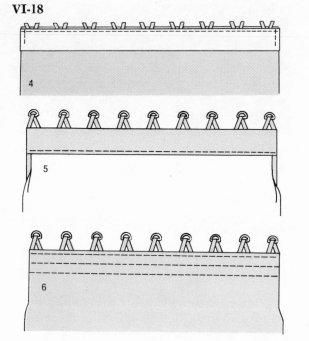

1. With right sides together (figure VI-17), attach facing to each end of the hammock at the side edges only, by stitching from the outer edges to within ½″ of inner edge.

Turn facing to the wrong side to pin tabs in place. The tabs are very thick, so pin from the hammock side catching several layers of the tabs, keeping the facing free while pinning tabs in place.

2. To position tabs, pin one end in place along the facing edge, extending the end 1½″ beyond raw edge of hammock; slip small D-ring over free end and fold at an angle ½″ from hammock edge, making sure ends are even and tabs are not crossed; pin.

3. Position the remaining tabs the same way starting at opposite side, then at the center, working as indicated by the numbers at the top of the sketch.

4. Turn facing (figure VI-18), with right sides together, over tabs; stitch to hammock in a ½″ seam.

5. Turn facing to inside along seam; press. Turn in remaining facing edge ½″, encasing raw tab ends; stitch close to fold.

6. To reinforce tabs on the outside, stitch ¼″ from outer edge and again in the center.

7. Turn in long selvage edges of hammock ½″; stitch in place ¼″ from selvage.

NOTE: The tabs and D-rings may be eliminated if heavy grommets, designed for outdoor use, are available in your area. Use nine grommets at each end and attach rope supports in same manner as instructed below.

To add rope supports, cut two 30′ and two 12′ lengths of rope. Also cut two 18″ and two 36″ pieces of wire.

At one end of hammock, tie 12′ of rope to the first tab's D-ring with a terminal knot (figure VI-19).

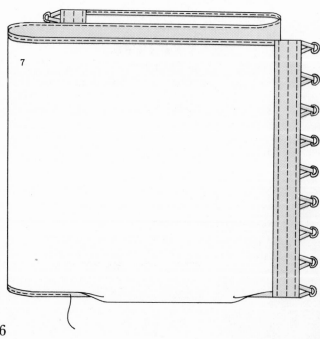

VI-19

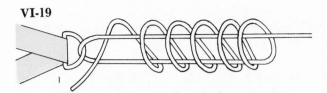

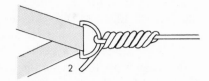

1. To make knot, pull rope through D-ring for 12″. Turn end up and tie in back of rope about 2″ above D-ring; wrap tightly over the two thicknesses five times, pulling end through rope loop that goes over the D-ring.

2. Pull tightly, sliding coil down tightly against ring.

VI-20

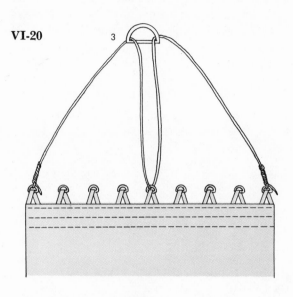

3. Thread free rope end (figure VI-20) through the back of one heavy D-ring, then down through the fifth tab's D-ring, then up over the heavy D-ring and down through the ninth tab's D-ring. Fasten with a terminal knot.

4. Tie 30′ rope to second tab's D-ring with a terminal knot. Thread free end of rope through heavy D-ring, then down through third D-ring, then up over heavy D-ring. Do this on the fourth, sixth, and seventh tabs with small D-rings. Fasten end to eighth tab with terminal knot.

To even up the rope strands, insert a yardstick (or other long, flat object) through the seven center tabs, leaving the tabs at the ends free. Tie heavy D-ring to a secure place (try the shower curtain rod). Slide tabs to center of yardstick and weight it down evenly at both ends (six heavy books of equal weight opened at the center and slipped over the yardstick at each end worked for me). Make the ropes even for the seven tabs. The shorter outer ropes will help form the cocoonlike shape. Keep yardstick and weights in place until ropes are secured by wire.

Secure ropes near heavy D-ring with 18″ wire (figure VI-21).

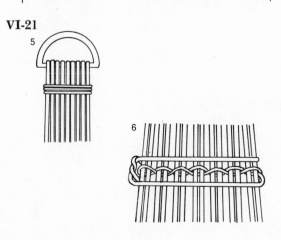

5. Wrap wire tightly around the ropes about three times, pinching wire tightly against ropes at each edge. In the back twist wire together, squeeze flat with pliers, and wrap end around rope tightly.

6. To hold shape of hammock for easier use, make a braided wire clamp over the ropes, using a 36″ piece of wire. Braid wire over the ropes, two at a time. Bend wire in half and slide over the ropes about 12″ below the large D-ring. Keep the ropes in pairs as they emerge from the small D-rings (see figure VI-21). Hold the first two ropes and wire with pliers and make a twist in the wire to hold these two ropes together. Do the same for the remaining six pairs of ropes, ending

VI-21

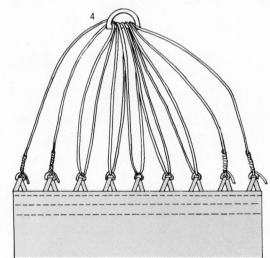

157

with a twist on the opposite side. Squeeze wire firmly with pliers so the twist turns toward the hammock and the twist is hidden. Bring wire ends back across the spread-out braided ropes (one in the front and one in the back). Twist and flatten wire on the underside. Bend both wire ends up, twist and flatten, and then bring wire ends across the top of the spread-out braided ropes to the other side. Twist wires and fasten the ends in the back. Make ends flat with pliers.

Repeat this procedure for the other end of the hammock using remaining rope, wire, and heavy D-ring.

There are many ways to hang a hammock. Screw hooks or eyes, wire, or rope are the most common materials used. Make sure that your anchoring method is secure. Slip S-hooks into D-rings and then fasten to anchors. Using the S-hooks will enable you to remove hammock easily if it's used out-of-doors.

VII
Decorating
Touches

Add visual interest to your home with individualized furniture, wall treatments, and colorful accessories to complement your life-style. With the many building and home furnishing supplies available, anyone who wants to have an original and customized decorated home can see it come alive with careful planning and execution. Most lumber dealers and foam suppliers will cut wood and foam slabs to your measurements. A few pieces of plywood or pinewood, some nails, and a little glue will make frames to support the foam modules needed to make the furniture shown in some of the photographs. And a distinctive table can be made with fabric and polyurethane varnish. Old cracked, plastered walls can be hidden with curtains, frames of fabric, or a wall-to-ceiling wall hanging.

Lamps are often discarded because they are the wrong color or the shade is shabby—they can be restored to look like new. Pictures are easily made with a panel of fabric or your own needlework. Dining room tables can be made to come alive with tablecloths, place mats, and napkins—other tables can be enhanced with fabric, too. Closets may be made bright and colorful with fabric. And bathrooms can be functional for the whole family and colorful as well—there are ways to accomplish this.

FABRIC, FOAM, AND WOOD FURNITURE

You may want to start small by building a hassock or to plunge right in and make a bed or a sofa. Whatever your choice, the basic materials needed are the same; exceptions will be noted for each style given. Plywood or pine strips are nailed together with finishing nails and each joint is strengthened with white wood glue.

You don't need top-grade plywood or lumber for furniture that is painted or covered with fabric. For furniture that is stained or varnished, be sure that the lumber you purchase has at least one good side. Build these stylized furniture pieces yourself or have someone do it for you. I designed and built the pieces described below, so anyone should be able to do it with a little ingenuity.

Sleigh Bed

This couch consists of a wooden frame and foam padding permanently covered with fabric. A round foam bolster was split in half and glued to the outside of each end. The top front, back, and inner edges were padded with $\frac{1}{2}''$-thick foam sheeting glued in place. Each upright end was strengthened with two 4" right-angle braces, and six casters were used for easy moving. Two foam slabs 30" x 74" x 4" were used to make it a comfortable seating height; they also unstack to sleep two guests.

For the platform, a frame was made with two long 2 x 4's and three short ones (see figure VII-1). These were glued and nailed together. A sheet of plywood the same measurement as the frame was glued and nailed in place. For the ends, a frame was made with four 2 x 4's that were glued and nailed together. These end frames were glued and nailed to each end of the

Any creative craftsman can make a sleigh bed from scratch. This sleigh bed will sleep two when one covered foam cushion is placed on the floor. Designed and constructed by the author, the sleigh bed, matching backrest pillows, and bolsters are covered with Bloomcraft's "Sunset." Colorful throw pillows accent the fabric and a color-coordinated floor-length table cover with a recycled lamp complement this contemporary setting.

platform, and both sides of each end were covered with plywood. The braces were then fastened securely with screws.

To pad the frame, cut the foam sheeting about ½" wider than the measurements of the narrow side and top edges of the upright ends (exposed 2 x 4's) and the plywood next to the platform, and glue in place. For the long narrow edges of the platform, make the sheeting 9" wide. Staple or tack it to the underside of the platform edges and bring the foam around (covering the 2 x 4) and staple to the plywood platform, making the edge smooth and flat. Split a round bolster in half lengthwise. Now glue a half bolster to the

outside of each end, making the top edge flush with the sheeting.

After the sleigh bed is built and padded, use the pointers given in Chapter VI for slipcovers and in Chapter III for pillows.

The quick box-edge cushion instructions were used to cover the two foam slabs (see page 83) and the knife-edge pillow instructions were used for the backrest pillows (see page 75).

Make a cover for the bed, cording the end seams that will receive the most wear. Put on the cover, forcing the rounded foam ends into place. Staple or tack the raw edges in place on the underside of the bed. Attach casters with screws.

VII-1

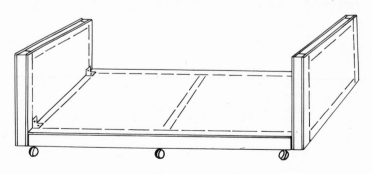

Island Couch

This couch has a box for blanket storage as its base, with six casters so it can be moved easily and a 24″ x 74″ x 4″ foam slab. The box is also 24″ wide, 74″ long, and 8″ deep. The frame and inside support was made from 1″-thick pine with a ½″-thick plywood lid, ⅛″-thick masonite for the bottom; four 1″-square strips were used on the underside of the lid to prevent it from shifting (figure VII-2).

Make the frame by gluing and nailing the three shorter pine sections to the two long ones, forming a box with a divider at the center for support. Glue and nail the masonite to the bottom of the frame and attach the casters with screws. Place the 1″-square strips about 1″ from the long edges of the plywood, making sure the strips clear the end and support the edges of the storage box, and put lid over box. Paint or cover box as desired.

The box was covered with leftover carpet strips

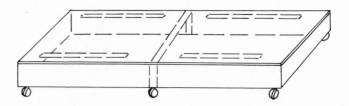

that the wall-to-wall carpet installers left behind. Simply staple or tack the carpet to the box, after you cut the strips to the correct width with a razor blade or mat knife. Butt pieces together tightly and the joinings will be nearly invisible. Only the edge of the lid was covered with carpet. I used a 6″ strip that had been cut by the installers. It was stapled on the underneath side and then wrapped over the edge onto the flat top. Fold corners smoothly and tack if staples won't hold. The foam was covered with an easy box-edge cushion cover (see page 83).

An island couch that can be used from either side was designed and constructed by the author. Bloomcraft's "Sunset" is used for the covered cushion and matching bon bon bolsters. The carpet-covered platform has a storage compartment for bed linens.

Platform Bed

The bed platform was made from ¾″-thick plywood with one good side and it was finished with a walnut stain. This double-bed-size platform is 14″ high, with two supports and eight casters. Since plywood is only 4′ wide, the top had to be pieced (figure VII-3).

To make the platform, glue and nail the two end sections and the two supports to the long side strips. Glue and nail the top in place along all edges and to the supports. Attach the casters

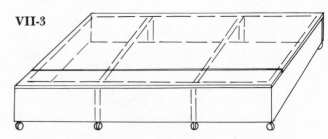

VII-3

with screws. Sand away any rough edges. Finish wood as desired or cover platform to match your bedding.

The platform used in this contemporary bedroom was designed and constructed by the author. It is stained to match the frames of the fabric wall and draped bed-sized canopy. West Point Pepperell sheets, pillowcases, and bedspreads are used to create a perfect corner for relaxing.

Turn a double-windowed wall into a desk–play area for a pair of small-fry occupants. Designer Shirley Regendahl uses Waverly Fabrics' "Plain and Fancy" to make box-edged cushions for the roll-about cube stools, valance, sash curtains, and window shades.

Cube Stool

These two stools are made with six pieces of ¾″ plywood: two 15″ square, two 13½″ x 15″, and two 13½″ square for a recessed top supported by eight angle brackets and a recessed bottom with four casters.

To make the cube, glue and nail the narrower sections to the wider ones, forming a square. Attach the angle brackets to the top with screws. Then glue and attach the top to the cube, about ¾″ below the opening edges, with the brackets and screws. Then glue and nail the bottom onto the square. Fasten caster at each corner.

Use a white latex undercoat to prepare wood before painting—after corners are sanded. Sand after the undercoat dries if wood becomes rough, and fill in any cracks with plastic wood (figure

VII-4), sanding as necessary. Paint as desired and make a basic box-edge cushion cover with self-cording (page 82) for the foam forms.

VII-4

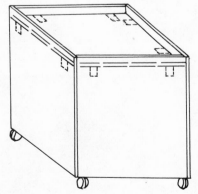

165

Make your own coffee table just like this one designed and constructed by the author. Fabric that matches the cornice and draperies shown in an earlier photograph is used to cover the table and then many coats of polyurethane varnish are added for durability. In the background, notice the Parsons table covered with striped Sunbrella® canvas from Glen Raven Mills, Inc., to match the re-covered director's chairs that are used both indoors and out.

VII-5

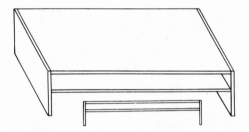

A simple desk made of plywood and covered with a West Point Pepperell "Galleria" striped sheet was designed and constructed by the author. Polyurethane varnish is used to create the high-gloss durable surface. The ruffled borders of the sheets are used for the valance and the opening edges of the matching tieback curtains.

VII-6

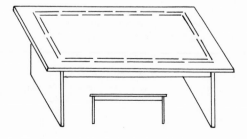

Table and Desk

Cover just about any type of wooden or plastic table—one that has all smooth edges—with fabric. This coffee table was made from plywood and covered with the same fabric that was used for the cornice and stationary draperies in the eclectic living room in Chapter I. The Parsons table was covered with black-and-white-striped Sunbrella® canvas. The desk is covered with a striped sheet that matches the curtains. Many coats of polyurethane varnish were used to protect the fabric.

Coffee Table

This unit is 30″ wide, 48″ long, and 16″ high, with a shelf. The top was nailed and glued to each end, then two right-angle brackets were used at each end to make it strong enough to sit upon. The shelf was glued and nailed and then supported with brackets. Three-pronged metal sliders were used on the bottom edges of each end after the fabric was positioned and had dried.

> MATERIALS NEEDED TO COVER WITH FABRIC:
> Gutoline® wallpaper paste in the yellow box
> Polyurethane varnish
> Paint for the shelf and inside edges
> White latex undercoat
> Fine sandpaper
> Plastic wood

Use tightly woven cotton-and-blend or all-cotton fabric the weight of a sheet or a medium-weight decorator fabric.

Sand all sharp edges; fill in any cracks with plastic wood and paint entire coffee table with a white latex undercoat. Allow to dry thoroughly. Resand and paint if necessary.

Paint the inside edges of the top and ends and both sides of the shelf. Allow to dry. On the outside of the top and ends, brush on a coat of wallpaper paste and allow to dry 24 hours to form a hardened paste glaze. The next day, add another coat of paste and position fabric in place over the wet paste, centering any design motif (the second coat will help the fabric slide more easily). Smooth fabric from the center out to eliminate bubbles (keep checking fabric until it dries) and wrap the fabric over the bottom edges of each end for durability. With a sharp razor blade, cut fabric even with the inner edge of top and ends. Take a sharp pin and pierce any bubbles so you

can force out the air. Allow to dry for 24 hours. NOTE: Fabric will become quite wet, but the colors will be bright and clear when dry.

Start early in the day so you can put on three coats of polyurethane varnish at 6-hour intervals. Allow to dry at least 24 hours; the surface must be completely dry. Sand lightly with fine sandpaper. Repeat this process until you have applied at least six coats of varnish. The coffee table pictured has fourteen coats. Be sure to work in a dust-free, well-ventilated room.

Desk

To make, use ¾″-thick plywood. The top measures 26″ x 48″ and the ends are 22″ x 26″, with 3″ x 42″ supports (figure VII-6). Glue and nail the two narrow support strips to the ends. Then center the top over the frame; glue and nail top in place.

Follow the same procedure recommended for the coffee table, covering both sides of the ends and the outside of the support with fabric. This desk has eight coats of polyurethane varnish.

Parsons Table

To cover a plastic Parsons table with fabric, use a white fabric glue. If you want to make a patchwork top, cut the pieces with a razor blade and a metal ruler so the fabric patch edges are straight.

To cover, brush a coat of glue on the top and two sides. Center fabric over the top, extending it to the rim edge on the two sides. Cover the two remaining rim edges in the same manner. (One long strip may be used to cover the rim, if desired.) With a sharp razor blade, trim away excess fabric at the corners or make tiny cuts so you can make smooth, rounded corners if required. To cover the legs, have the fabric about ¾″ longer and ½″ wider than the leg measurements. Cover leg with glue and center a strip over one leg, extending the fabric about ¼″ over the rim fabric. Smooth fabric on the front of the leg and then to the back, lapping one fabric edge over the other on the inner leg corner. Tuck excess fabric inside the leg and glue. Hold in place with paper clips, if necessary. Cut along the groove where the legs meet the table rim and remove the excess fabric.

NOTE: Contact paper will cover a Parsons table more quickly and easily if you spray it with a blue liquid window cleaner and then wipe nearly dry. Apply same as for fabric, as explained above.

FABRIC FOR YOUR WALLS

Fabric is a great cover-up for the cracked walls and plaster in an old building. It also helps reduce the noise in a poorly insulated room. Walls may be totally covered with fabric from ceiling to floor with simple casement curtains or by wooden frames with casement curtains suspended between the uprights. Decide which type will work best for you.

Use a permanent-press fabric—sheets are the most widely used fabric to create removable coverings for walls, but don't overlook a good buy in a narrower-width fabric. Semisheers and other lightweight fabrics look lovely, too—the softer the fabric, the fuller the casement curtains should be. Don't make panels any wider than two 44" widths or one sheet width so they will launder more easily.

Simple Casement Curtains

Use casement curtain rods or café curtain rods that do not have finials. To make casement curtains, follow directions given in Chapter II, using a casing with or without a heading. Place rods as close to the ceiling and floor as the casing type used dictates, and use as many rods as needed to cover the wall—hemmed side edges can be hidden by the fullness of the curtains.

Frame a Wall

The room shown in the photographs on pages 92 and 164 has two walls covered with fabric and a matching canopy. After the 2" x 2" pine strips were cut to measure, they were finished with a dark walnut stain that matches the platform bed. Nail the casement rod fixtures into position before putting the frame together. The frames fit from floor to ceiling with the upright strips placed so one will fall at each corner of the bed. The remaining space is equally divided by strips. One side has a frame around the closet door, too. Put each frame together with corrugated nails and white wood glue, working in the room where it is to be used. Make a frame for each wall. Place the floor strip next to the baseboard and the ceiling strips out in the room. After one frame is nailed together, push it into place against the wall, hiding the joinings. One strip will go into the corner, so place two uprights on this frame; then you will have a durable, well-matched corner when the next frame is positioned (figure VII-7). Nail frames together at corner.

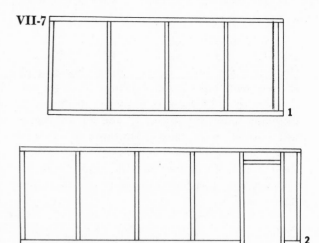

VII-7

Make curtains following the instructions for casement curtains in Chapter II. I hung a casement curtain on the closet door, too, and made a slash for the door knob, finishing the edges with a zigzag stitch.

Canopy (figure VII–8)

This is a rectangular frame the dimensions of the outer edge of the platform bed. Use 2" x 2" pin strips, corrugated nails, glue, a drapery support bracket, and four café or casement curtain rods.

1. To make canopy frame, finish strips to match wall frames, then glue and nail the frame together as shown. Attach the rod fixtures and the support bracket to the canopy before hanging. Nail canopy along one end and one side to the wall frames and anchor the bracket to the ceiling.

2. The curtain for the canopy is constructed just like a casement curtain. Make it the desired fullness and 30"–36" longer than the frame. When the side hems and the end casings are made, two more casings will be needed for the festoons. Divide curtain into thirds and draw a line at the division points. Make casings with a straight strip of fabric the width of the rod plus 1½", and 2" longer than the curtain is wide. Turn in the narrow ends 1" and then make a hem. Turn in the long edges ½" and press. Center casing strip over marks on curtain and stitch both pressed edges in place.

After the canopy curtain is hung, make small pleats over the casings on the inside of the frame and pin so the free ends can be made taut.

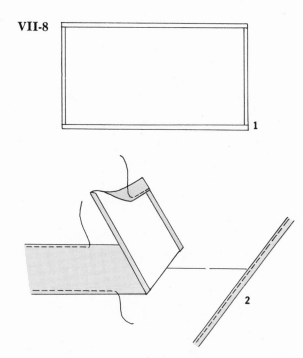

1

2

Fabric Wall Hangings

Create a statement with fabric by making a wall hanging. It may be a panel (purchased by the yard), a sheet, a bedspread, a tablecloth, or your own design made with appliqués. Wall hangings may be as large or as small as you like and they may be used as a divider, as a means of camouflaging structural flaws, or as a focal point. The wall hanging shown in the photograph creates an illusion of space on a wall crowded by a king-size bed and has latticework fabric strips to allow cross-ventilation from a small corner window.

Fabric wall hangings need to be supported when hung. Stretch fabric over plywood or artist's stretcher frames, as explained in this chapter for framing fabric pictures, or make casings at the top and bottom and then insert curtain rods or wooden dowels to hold them flat.

To appliqué a wall hanging, make a paper pattern with newspapers, using the funnies and brown paper bags for contrast. If you are making

Create the perfect wall for a king-sized bed with this colorful wall hanging, matching throw bedspread, and slipcovered headboard designed and constructed by the author. Crompton's uncut pinwale and widewale corduroy are used throughout. The wall hanging's corduroy appliqués are mounted on sheets, and latticework is designed to camouflage a small window that is used for cross-ventilation. The lamps are recycled brass lamp bases with glass chimneys, and flamelike bulbs.

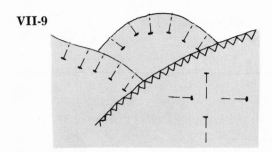

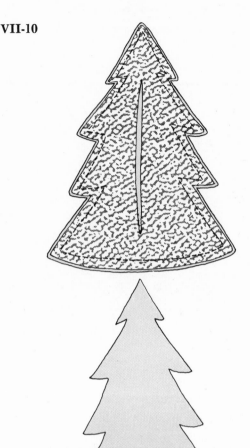

a specific size wall hanging, allow 4″–6″ extra on all measurements, as the appliqué stitching will cause the background fabric to "shrink." Before cutting out the patches, decide how they will be applied to the foundation fabric as the instructions are different for machine and hand sewing.

MACHINE-SEWN APPLIQUÉS (figure VII-9): Seam allowances are not needed for this method. However, if patches will overlap, allow about ¼″ on the edge that will be placed underneath. Pin the entire design securely to the foundation with long thin pins, placing the points about ¼″ from the cut edges so they won't interfere with the machine's presser foot.

To stitch, use the widest zigzag stitch and about twenty stitches to the inch. Stitch each exposed edge of every appliqué patch with matching thread.

HAND-SEWN APPLIQUÉS (figure VII-10): Use a ¼″ seam allowance on all edges. For patches with sharp inward or outward points, it is easier to make a double-layered patch then to turn in the seam allowances and press them flat. Use two layers of lightweight fabric or one layer of heavy fabric (such as corduroy) and a layer of matching lightweight fabric for a lining.

1. Stitch the two layers, right sides together, in a ¼″ seam. Make a slash down the center of the lining only. Trim outward points and clip inward points to the stitching.

2. Turn the patch right sides out through slash and make the points sharp. Press flat, making sure the lining does not show along the seamed edges.

Position the appliqué as explained for the machine method above and baste in place by hand or machine. Slip-stitch patches to the foundation, using method four as explained in Chapter VIII.

Framing Pictures of Fabric

There are many fabrics, rugs, towels, and sheets that would make great pictures, but all of them need support to hang on the wall. Some needlework artists who would like to frame their own

work seem hesitant to try. Perhaps the task seems overwhelming, but it is quite simple with the proper equipment.

At art supply stores or departments you will find artist's stretcher frames in many lengths. These are used to stretch canvas for painting. You will need at least 2″ all around the needlework or fabric so it can be stapled to the underside of the frame. Purchase four strips in the correct length to accommodate your projects.

If piece is too small, make a border in a matching or contrasting fabric (figure VII-11). Allow a ½″ seam allowance on the inner edge and cut a border large enough to be stapled.

1. Reinforce each inward corner with a row of very fine stitches ½″ from the cut edge. Clip corner to the stitching.

2. On the wrong side, turn in all inner edges ½″; press.

3. Center border over your fabric and pin in place. Stitch border in place close to the pressed edge.

VII-11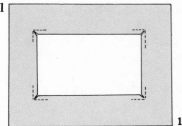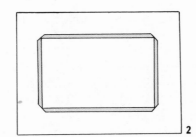

To Make Picture (figure VII-12):

1. Assemble stretcher frame and tack at corners to make it sturdier, if desired.

2. Center frame over the wrong side of the fabric and place a staple at center of each strip, stretching fabric taut.

VII-12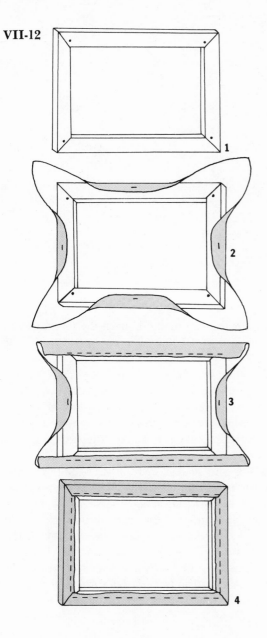

3. Check to make sure design is centered. Then staple the top edge, keeping the raw edge parallel to the inner edge of the frame, working on each side of the center to the corner, ending about 1″ from each corner. Do the same on the bottom edge, making fabric taut.

4. Staple the ends to within 1″ of the corners and then make smooth folds in the fabric, aligning the folds with the narrow edges of the frame. Pull taut across the back and staple. Add hangers and hang, or insert in a decorative frame to hang.

RECYCLE LAMPSHADES

A lampshade is the crowning glory of a lamp—its size and shape are designed to complement the lamp. When a lampshade becomes drab or soiled, it is often hard to find a suitable replacement. Or when you are redecorating, the lamp and shade may no longer fit in because of their colors. Whatever the problem, you can recycle many lampshades. Fabric and paint are the easiest ways to restore them. Try to use the same tint, shade, or color for the lampshade when redoing it so you will have the same lighting effect and efficiency you had from the original lampshade.

When considering the lampshade, make sure the paper- or cloth-covered frames will support a new covering. Bent frames or ripped coverings will not be worth the time you take to cover them. Damaged coverings will show through any smooth covering and bent frames will never hold the lampshade on the lamp satisfactorily.

The following are two types of lampshade covering that are easy to do.

Permanent Fabric Coverings

Just about any stable woven fabric may be used to cover a lampshade: cottons, textured silks, burlap—anything that can be glued to the shade. It's even possible to paint shades and then cover them with eyelet or other openwork fabric. Be sure the shade is worth painting (keep the coat

171

as thin as possible). Do a fabric patch test to make sure the fabric can be glued successfully—use Sobo® glue.

There are three ways to cover a shade permanently. The first is to cover the shade to the edge and then encase the fabric edge and frame with matching or contrasting band trim and plastic tape. The second method is to cover the shade by wrapping the fabric to the underside over the frame. And the third is an addition to the second method—glue any type of fabric trim to the recovered lampshade at the top and bottom edges. The types of trim are unlimited.

In some cases, however, a coat of paint is all that is needed for both lampshade and lamp. The lamp and shade shown with the sleigh bed in the first picture in this chapter were painted with aluminum paint, because the color did not match the new furnishings.

MAKE A PATTERN: In order to cover the lampshade (figure VII-13), make a pattern with newspaper or a large brown paper bag.

1. Lay lampshade on the paper. Starting at the seam, draw a line the length of the shade. Then mark the top and bottom edges. Roll shade over the paper, marking both the top and bottom edges as you move it, ending again at the seam. Make lines smooth.

Cut out pattern with a 1″ margin. Place pattern on lampshade and check fit, lapping the ends ½″. The lines should be even with both shade edges. When pattern is satisfactory, make provisions for the style of covering desired. For the first method, cut pattern along the lines, retaining ½″ for lapping one end. For the second

VII-13

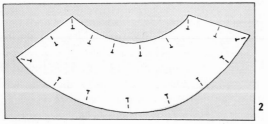
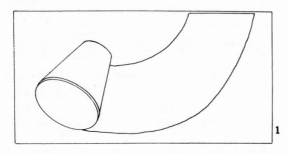

and third methods, add ½″ to the top and bottom edges and to one end for a lap.

2. When adjustments are made, pin pattern to fabric, as shown, so the grains are balanced. Cut out fabric.

TO ATTACH THE FABRIC (figure VII-14): Remove any decorative trim from the shade edges. *Do not* remove the thin paper tape that holds the shade to its frame. Brush on a thin coat of the glue. Center fabric over the lampshade. Starting opposite the seam, smooth fabric around the shade, overlapping and gluing the ends.

VII-14

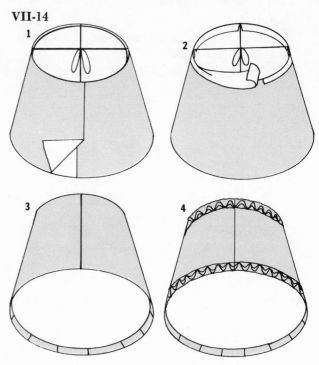

1. For the first method, make the long top and bottom edges of fabric even with the shade edges.

2. When the glue is dry, tape the edges. Center tape over the top of the frame and wrap one edge down over the fabric, keeping the tape even all around. Wrap remainder of tape to the inside, making clips to accommodate the frame, if necessary.

3. For the second method, the long top and bottom edges should extend ½″ above and below the lampshade. When the shade is covered, brush glue on the top edge of the frame and about ½″ deep on the underside of the shade. Wrap the top edge over the frame. If fabric is bulky, make short clips at even intervals so the edges will lie flat on the underside of the lampshade. Do the same for the bottom edge.

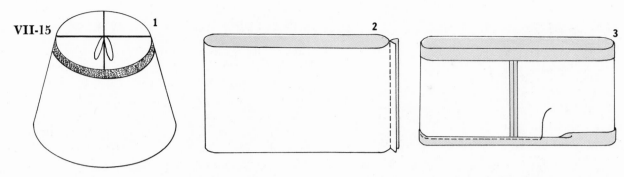

VII-15 1   2   3

4. For the third method, attach fabric same as the second method. Glue trim in place, having the designs match at the ends over the lapped seam if possible by stretching or easing it gradually to make it fit. The lampshade shown in the bedroom photograph on page 92 has narrow strips of satin ribbon and eyelet lace glued at even intervals lengthwise on the shade and then around both edges. The ribbon and lace was salvaged from the sheet hems used to make the framed wall coverings and canopy.

Removable Fabric Coverings

There are several ways to make covers removable for a lampshade. The coverings may be attached to shade with a tape fastener of Velcro® or snaps.

Test the fabric with the light turned on to see if the colors of the fabric and shade are compatible. Light does strange things when it shows through a shade and loosely draped fabric.

Lampshades with the covers attached with tape fasteners may be gathered or pleated. Make the fabric 3″ longer than the shade (½″ is needed at the top and bottom so the shade does not show; 1″ for a turn-back at the top to apply the tape fastener and 1″ for a narrow hem). For a gathered cover, make fabric twice the circumference of the shade bottom; for a pleated cover, triple the bottom circumference of the shade. To each type add 1″ for two ½″ seam allowances.

BASIC COVER (figure VII-15):

1. Glue the hook strip of the Velcro® or the ball section of the snap tape to the top edge of the lampshade.

2. To make covers, cut out a rectangle the required measurements. Stitch the ends together in a ½″ seam, forming a tube.

3. Turn the top and bottom edges to the inside 1″ and press. Make a narrow hem on the bottom edge by turning in the raw edge ½″, then stitch or sew hem in place; press. The loop half of the Velcro® or the socket half of the snap tape are stitched to the inside of the lampshade covering after the gathers or pleats are made.

FOR GATHERED COVER (figure VII-16): Add two or more rows of gathering threads ½″ below the top, the width of the tape fastener. Pin cover to tape, dividing them each in quarters. Pull up threads and distribute gathers evenly along the tape.

1. Stitch cover to tape just inside the top and bottom row of gathering-threads.

2. Decorate with ribbon and a bow tacked to the gathers.

3. There are many beautiful fringe and band trims available, too.

4. Self-fabric ruffles are great for sheer or lightweight fabrics. Apply trim to lower edge as explained for *extended trim as an edge finish* in Chapter VIII.

VII-16

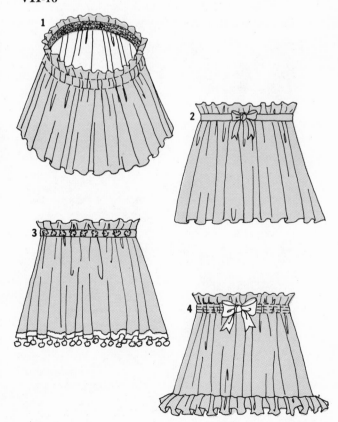

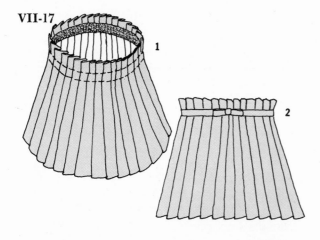

VII-17

1

2

FOR PLEATED COVER (figure VII-17): Make basic cover same as figure VII-15, steps 1, 2, and 3.

1. Then form knife pleats so the tube fits smoothly around the bottom edge of the lampshade. Place the tape fastener ½″ below the pressed top edge. Pin each pleat in place, easing the fabric to fit; stitch cover to tape close to both tape edges.

2. Cover stitching with band trim or ribbon, making a bow for that added touch, if desired.

TABLE TOPPINGS FOR EVERY ROOM

Want to make a drab corner come alive? Cover that old reliable lamp table with a bright color or print, edging it with fringe, ruffles, or other trim for a great look. No longer are tablecloths relegated to the dining room and kitchen; designers have used them in every room in the house over tables of all shapes. The secret to a handsome table topping is in shaping the hemmed edge.

But let's not belittle those wonderful utilitarian table coverings that add just the right foundation for your lovely china, glassware, and silver. The classic tablecloth is a perfect way to show off your needlework skills. Today many linenlike decorator fabrics are available in 54″ width and this is usually wide enough for the average table. The tablecloth shown in the Pennsylvania Dutch kitchen was made from 45″-wide fabric, with a shaped ruffle added to form the drop needed. A gathered ruffle with a heading was used on a cloth for the patio umbrella table shown in Chapter VI, but it will work just as well for the conventional tablecloth.

The Pennsylvania Dutch theme is emphasized in this eat-in kitchen with an oval tablecloth that has a shaped ruffled edge. Designed and made by the author. The tablecloth, made from a calico print from Spring Mills, has middy and soutache braid accents with a corded string hem. Matching curtains are shown in Chapter II, page 56.

Medium-sized checked gingham is used by the author to make the self-fringed place mats, napkins, and runner. Simple, easy-care table covering will add elegance to any dinner party.

Place mats are now acceptable for any type of entertaining—throughout the book you will find simple place mats made from the curtain or wall fabric for a total look. All a handsome fabric needs is a narrow hem or self-fringe. Matching napkins will help create an impact if they are placed where they can be seen.

Fabric selection is important when making table covers—select durable permanent press for all tablecloths, place mats, and napkins if you want covers that require little maintenance. A linen tablecloth and napkins are still the favorite for traditional dining, but take advantage of the soil-release and permanent-press treatments that are given to many linenlook fabrics.

Floor-length table coverings for occasional tables need not be washable. Felt, damask, moiré, velvet, silk, and other dry-cleanable fabrics are great for the traditional living room or bedroom, especially 72″-wide felt. These types of fabric look best with the elegant satin, rayon, and silk trimmings used for draperies and upholstery.

Sheets have become a favorite as they seldom require piecing; they should have washable trimming when used.

MEASURING TABLES FOR YARDAGE REQUIREMENTS

In order to purchase the necessary yardage for any table covering, there are a few measurements needed (figure VII-18).

1. Measure the length of the table.
2. Measure the width at the table's widest point.
3. Measure from the table edge to the floor for a floor-length drop.
4. Measure to within 6″ of the chair seat for the standard drop.

To the length measurement and the width measurement add twice the drop measurement, plus twice the hem allowance measurement needed for the style cover you plan to make. If you want to use a trim along the edge or an extended trim such as a self-ruffle or fringe, see Chapter VIII for how much hem allowance to add.

VII-18

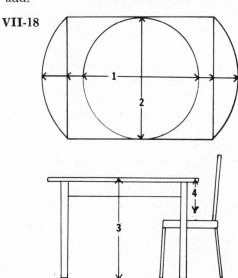

VII-19

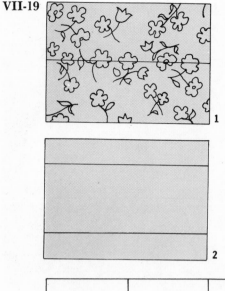

1

2

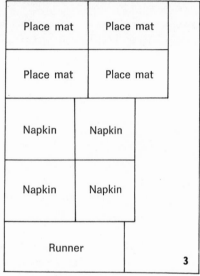

Place mat	Place mat
Place mat	Place mat
Napkin	Napkin
Napkin	Napkin
Runner	

3

For self-ruffles or matching napkins, additional fabric will be needed. Make ruffles 1½ or 2 times the total outer edge measurement, depending on the weight of your fabric. For a shaped ruffle (as shown in the Pennsylvania Dutch kitchen), turn to the instructions on page 177 and see the shape, then allow enough material to cut the number of ruffle sections needed. For napkins use at least a 16″ finished square—narrow hems ½″ wide will require an 18″ cut square. If you want a narrower or wider hem, adjust the cut size of the napkin.

For place mats with matching napkins and a table runner, make a diagram to see how much yardage is needed. The red-and-white self-fringed gingham table coverings shown here were made from 44″-wide fabric. The finished measurement for a place mat is about 12″ by 18″. Allow for hem or self-fringe finishes as desired. The gingham place mats were made 12½″ by 19″ so that they could be cut along the same bar of the check, the napkins were made 17¾″ square for the same reason, and the runner was made 10″ by 31″ so there would be nearly equal spaces of the table showing around its edge.

3. A diagram should look something like this. Allow ¼″ yard extra to straighten ends.

Floor-Length Table Covers
Regardless of the style, all corners must be rounded. Whichever style you are making, seam the pieces together, if necessary, and press the seam allowances open (figure VII-20). Fold fabric equally lengthwise, right sides together, and smooth fabric flat to the fold, keeping cut edges even. Pin cut edges together. Next fold the folded and pinned fabric in half crosswise, matching folds and cut edges. Make all four layers smooth and pin the cut edges together, removing the previous pins as you work.

1. For a round tablecloth, use the folded corners as a pivot point. Using a yardstick (or a string the exact length needed with a push-pin at one end and a pencil tied to the other), mark with a pencil one-fourth the total measurement needed. Move yardstick 1″ at a time, forming a quarter-circle opposite the raw edges. Cut in a smooth line along the markings.

When marking floor-length round table covers, it is recommended that you place the cut and shaped fabric on the table 24 to 48 hours to let the fabric hang so any bias sections that are going to stretch more than the nearly straight grain

The total measurements will tell you how long and wide the fabric must be to cover the table correctly. In most cases, floor-length covers will need to be pieced (figure VII-19). Depending on where the table is placed, you may piece one side if it will not show.

1. For fabric with design motifs that need to be matched, the quickest way to piece the fabric is to make one seam down the center of the tablecloth.

2. For solid colors, make the piecings in the drop where they will be less noticeable. Split one fabric section and stitch a narrow strip to each side of the widest section.

Be sure to allow for at least a ½″ seam allowance on both edges that are to be pieced together.

areas will stretch in length before you finish the hem edges. Mark stretched areas with a row of pins and then recut these sections.

2. For a square or rectangular tablecloth, measure in from the cut edges on both sides of the corner equally; where the lines intersect, make a dot. Using the straight lines as a measurement guide and the dot as a pivot point, mark a rounded end between the lines. Cut off rounded corner in a smooth line along the markings.

3. For an oval table, center the fabric over the tabletop with the wrong side uppermost, making all edges even. Weight fabric securely. With tailor's chalk or the side of the lead on a pencil, draw the shape onto the fabric along one-fourth of the table's top. Fold and pin fabric as directed previously. Using the drawn shape of the table and a yardstick, mark the cutting line for the oval drop. Make marks no more than 1″ apart. Cut along these markings in a smooth line.

For all types of floor-length table covers, finish hem edge as planned, adding any trim along or above the edges for a customized cover. The black cotton floor-length square table cover shown with the sleigh bed in the beginning of this chapter was trimmed with white fringe along the edge with red-and-green rickrack and a strip of white

single-fold bias tape forming the border. The corded hems from the section on couch covers in Chapter II make an elegant custom finish for a floor-length table cover.

Standard-Size Tablecloths

For a total look, make a tablecloth and napkins to match the curtains—or take it one step further and make place mats as well for a change of pace. Tablecloths are usually laundered more frequently and if you have several sets of linens that match or complement your curtains, they will all wear out at the same time.

The yellow calico print shown on page 174 was 44″ wide. For this table a 2″ drop could be made all around the table. To this narrow drop, semicircular ruffles were added. I used the bottom of a gored skirt pattern to get the shape. Each 7″-deep ruffle section was 20″ long on the short, inward curve and 35″ long on the long, outward curve (figure VII-21). NOTE: The same ruffle pattern was used for the calico shaped valance that was made to frame the window shown in Chapter II.

1. Draw a pattern or cut one as I did.

2. Stitch the ruffle sections together in a ¼″ seam and then zigzag the edges together. Finish the outward curved edge with a corded string hem (see how to make hem in Chapter VIII).

3. To attach the shaped ruffle to the tablecloth, stitch the ruffle sections together in one long strip and make the hem. Next, join ruffle to the tablecloth, using a ½″ seam. Start the stitching about 2″ from the end of the ruffle strip and stitch around the cloth until the ruffle ends meet. Break the stitching and stitch the ruffle ends together. Trim this seam to ¼″ and zigzag the raw edges together. Stitch ruffle to tablecloth, connecting the stitches for a more durable seam. Press

VII-20

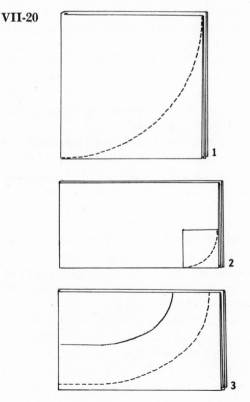

VII-21

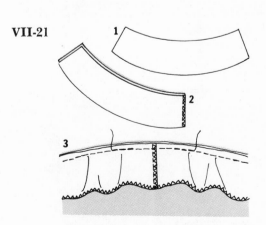

177

seam toward tablecloth and trim as desired. The calico tablecloth was trimmed with one row of blue middy braid placed along the seam and red soutache braid placed ¼″ away.

Napkins, Place Mats, and Runners

These small fabric lengths are often the ultimate touch for a beautifully set table. Napkins do not have to be finished exactly like the tablecloth or even be made of the same color or fabric so long as they complement the tablecloth and setting.

There are many ways to make lovely napkins, place mats, and runners, and all may be finished in the same manner (figure VII-22).

1. Trim the edges with commercial bias tape or decorate with band or fringe trim and/or appliqués.

2. To make a corded string hem, see figure VIII-10 in Chapter VIII; reinforce each side of the corner with a bar tack of three stitches. Stitch to corner, drop feed dog (see your sewing machine manual), and make a bar tack ending with needle on the napkin side of the fabric; raise presser foot and pivot fabric on the needle so the opposite side of the corner is ready to be stitched; make bar tack, then raise feed dog and stitch to the next corner. Repeat the bar tack step until the hem is completed.

3. To make a self-fringed edge, pull a thread where you want the fringe to end (½″ to 1″). Use matching thread; stitch along the line formed by the pulled-out thread, using 20 stitches to the inch to prevent fraying when laundering. The first few threads will pull out easily. Use a pin to pull two or three threads out to the edge, forming a loop. Pull from each side of the loop as you would gather threads. Remove all threads parallel with the reinforcement stitches.

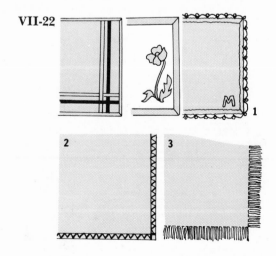

VII-22

CLOSETS COME ALIVE WITH FABRIC

Splash colors into your closet with fabric and protect your clothes, shoes, gloves, and handbags at the same time. Cover shoe boxes and other boxes with fabric to store your accessories. Shoe bags are a way to solve clutter on the closet floor for those who have a door that swings out. Make garment bags to cover seasonal and seldom-used clothes—you may even want to convert one to a carry-on to save excess packing when traveling. Use padded hangers to support knits or to prevent low necklines from slipping off. In most cases there will be enough fabric left over from the boxes, shoe bags, and garment bags to cover the hangers; otherwise use fabric scraps. Corduroy and velveteen are excellent choices to cover hangers you use for garments made of slippery fabrics. The mysteries of closet accessories are solved on the following pages to help you get your closet in order!

Select tightly woven, medium-weight cotton or cotton-and-synthetic fabrics for your closet project. Sheets, denim, and sailcloth are some of the fabric types that work best.

Fabric-Covered Shoe and Other Storage Boxes

If you are like me, you keep your shoes in the original boxes. Sooner or later you will want to make them more attractive—fabric attached with Sobo® glue is an easy way to do it. Identifying the contents is made easy with a clear vinyl pocket and a paper label. If the wording on the box shows through the fabric, paint the box with a coat of latex white undercoat and allow to dry thoroughly. If you are painting a lot of boxes, number the lids and boxes on the inside—it will save time and aggravation.

Measure each box for fabric; all manufacturers have boxes made to their own design and few are the same measurements. Measure the length and width of the box (include both sides and ends), adding 1″ to both measurements for a ½″ tuck-in on all four edges. Measure the length and width of the lid and both lips; add 1″ to both measurements for ½″ tuck-in on all four edges.

To cover a box, cut a rectangle of fabric for both the box and the lid to the required measurements (figure VII-23).

1. Using the longest stitch, stitch a 2″ by 4″ piece of clear vinyl to one narrower end of the box rectangle about 2″ below the raw edges.

2. Brush a thin coat of glue on the sides and bottom of the box. Center box over wrong side

of fabric. Smooth fabric across the bottom and up over the sides and ends, forming triangles at each corner. Trim folds to ½″ and brush a little glue on the fabric. Tuck the side edges under the narrow ends. Then glue the narrow ends over the sides so the seams won't show when stored.

3. Brush glue on top edges and about ½″ down on the inside. Wrap fabric over edges to the inside of the box.

4. If the edges pull up, hold in place with paper clips or bobby pins. Cover lid in the same way.

5. When glue is dry, make labels and insert into pocket; put in the corresponding shoes, gloves, bags, or other accessories and store.

VII-23

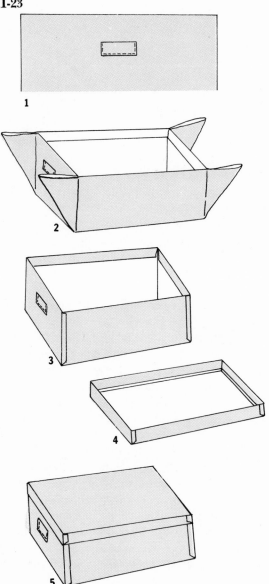

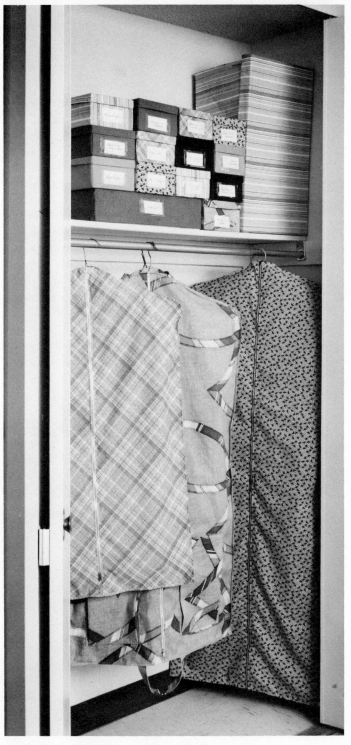

Organize your closet with matching accessories like the ones designed and constructed by the author. Burlington's "Ultra Vino" is used to cover the shoe and boot boxes, the large box to store purses, the jacket-length garment bag and floor-length garment bag. A denimlike fabric is used for the street-length carry-on garment bag.

Garment Bags

Protect your clothing from dust and make a colorful addition to your closet at the same time. You will find these garment bags so durable and convenient that you may want to add handles and use them for carry-on bags—the directions for the street-length bag will have all the details for the additions needed, but the other styles can be adapted the same way. The three types most often used are a jacket or suit size for both men and women, a street-length size for topcoats and dresses, and a floor-length size for jumpsuits and gowns. Garment bags may be made flat or have side extensions for several garments or a bulky one. Use 44"-wide fabric and zippers the length recommended. The jacket or suit bag requires 2¼ yards of fabric and a 36" zipper or two 18" zippers; the street-length bag requires 2¾ yards of fabric and a 45" zipper or two 22" zippers; and the floor-length bag requires 3⅜ yards of fabric and two 22" or 30" zippers.

Flat Jacket or Suit Bag: Cut one rectangle 25" by 40" for the back, two rectangles 13" by 40" for the front, and two patches 1¼" by 5" for the hanger opening.

VII-24

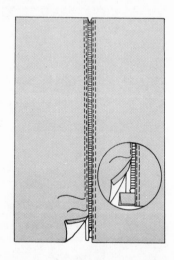

To make the zipper opening (figure VII-24), turn in one long edge of each front section ½"; press. Place pressed edges alongside the zipper teeth with stop 1" below the top of the section. (If using two zippers, have pull tabs meet at the center.) Pin the pressed edges to the zipper tapes. If zippers do not reach the bottom, cut a 2¼"-wide strip twice the length needed. Fold strip in half, wrong sides together, and place under pressed edges over zipper tape ends; pin. Using a zipper foot, stitch pressed edges in place and again about ¼" away through all thicknesses.

VII-25

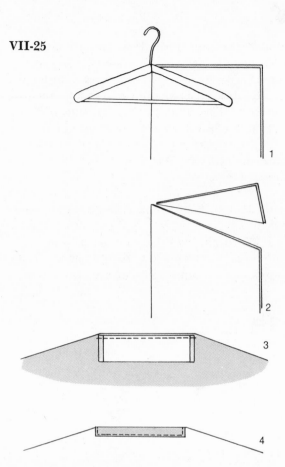

To shape the top (figure VII-25), fold back in half, right sides together.

1. Using a wooden suit hanger, place the center of hanger along fold. Draw a line on the fabric along the upper edge of the hanger. Slide hanger along line and continue line to fabric edge, rounding the corner.

2. Trim away excess fabric at corners along the line.

Pin front to back, right sides together, with sides and bottom edges even. Trim the front top edge to match the shape of the back.

3. Make hanger openings by turning in the narrow ends of the patches ½"; press. At the center of the back and front top edges, stitch one strip to each one in a ¼" seam. Turn patch over the raw edge to the wrong side.

4. Turn in remaining long edge about ¼" and stitch in place through all thicknesses.

To assemble (figure VII-26), open zipper(s).

5. With right sides together, stitch front to back in a ¼" seam, starting and ending at the hanger opening.

6. Turn right side out and press seamed edges flat. Stitch ¼" from pressed edges, forming a welted edge around the bag. Insert hanger and store clothing.

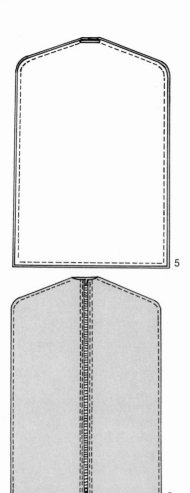

Street-Length Garment Bag (figure VII-27): Cut one rectangle 25″ by 47″ for the back and two rectangles 13″ by 47″ for the front. Cut 3″-wide boxing strips long enough to encircle the bag plus 2″ for narrow hems. Piece strip where necessary, using a ¼″ seam, zigzagging seam allowances for durability. Make zipper opening and shape top edges same as for figure VII-24 and VII-25, steps 1 and 2.

1. To attach boxing strip, first narrow-hem one end of boxing strip. Turn in end 1″; press. Then turn in raw edge and stitch hem in place. Place strip and bag front with narrow hem at center of the front; stitch a ¼″ seam, ending about 2″ on the opposite side of the zipper. Extend strip over the opposite side ¼″ and turn back to form a fold. Trim away 1″ from the fold and narrow hem. Complete stitching.

2. Turn right side out and press seamed edge flat. Stitch ¼″ from the pressed edge, forming a welted edge around the bag, easing the excess strip fabric around the corners to fit the bag.

3. Stitch boxing strip to back same as for the front, forming a welted edge.

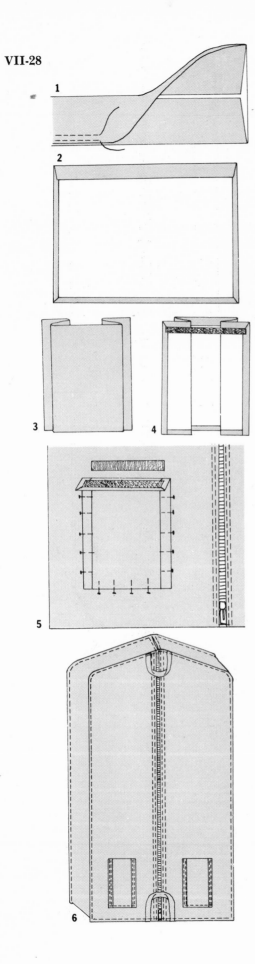

Carry-On: Adapt the street-length garment bag as a carry-on luggage bag. To convert a garment bag, cut two strips 4″ by 12″ for the handles and two rectangles 12″ by 13½″ for pockets. Two 7″-long strips of Velcro® are needed for the pockets (figure VII-28).

1. To make handles, fold strip in half lengthwise, wrong sides together; press. Turn in raw edges to meet crease; press flat. Stitch the two folded edges together and again ¼″ away.

2. To make pockets, turn in the side and bottom edges ½″; press. Turn down the top edge 1″; press. Turn in all corners on an angle so the raw edges won't show when stitched; press.

3. Make 1″-deep pleats on each side of the pocket, placing folds ¼″ from the pressed-under edges; press flat.

4. On the wrong side, center the loop strip of Velcro® over top of pocket and stitch in place.

5. Prepare front and back same as previously explained for the street-length bag. Place a pocket on each side of the zipper near the bottom edge. Pin pockets securely to bag front to within 2″ of the top. Lightly press hook strip to loop strip on pocket, aligning all edges. Pin hook strip to bag and stitch in place.

6. Stitch side and lower pocket edges to bag and again ¼″ away, keeping pocket folds free. Pin handles at the center of the front top and bottom bag edges, extending the ends ⅜″ beyond the edges and making the ends about 5″ apart. Stitch in a scant ¼″ seam.

Complete carry-on bag same as the street-length garment bag. Put garment in bag, fold in half with handles meeting, and you're ready to go!

Floor-Length Garment Bag: Cut one rectangle 61″ by 40″ for the back and two rectangles 13″ by 61″ for the front. Follow the method explained for the shorter-length suit and jacket bag or the street-length bag. There is ample fabric for boxing strips if you choose to make that type.

Hangers

There are many types of colorful hangers available today, but many are slippery and the garments may slip off. Fabric-covered padded hangers are quite easy to make and they help hold garments in place. Use narrow wooden hangers, color-coordinated plastic tape for the custom-made hanger, ½″-thick polyurethane foam or batting for padding 27″ of 1″-wide ribbon for a bow or 16″ for a knot.

To begin (figure VII-29), cut two fabric strips

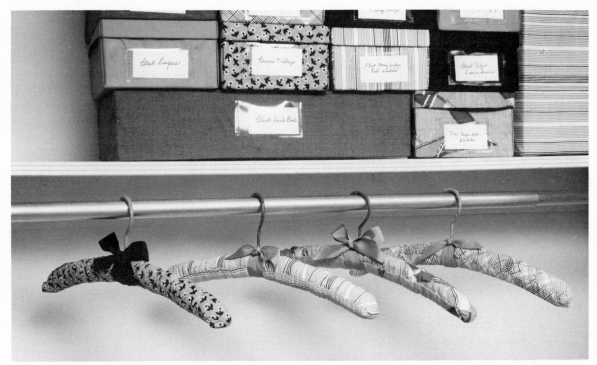

Add matching padded hangers covered with Burlington's "Ultra Vino" and your knits or slippery fabric garments will stay on the hangers. Designed and constructed by the author, the hangers are decorated with ribbon bows or knots.

2½" by 9", two fabric strips 2½" by 13½", and 1 strip of foam 2" by 32" or a 4" by 33" strip of batting for padding. Wrap hook with plastic tape, pulling tightly as you work.

1. To pad hanger, fold batting in half lengthwise—foam is used in a single layer. Wrap padding strips around narrow edges of hanger, having ends meet at the hook. Fold padding over flat sides and staple the three edges in place below the hook.

2. To make covers, add a row of gathering threads ¼" from both long edges of the longest strip.

3. Pin these strips to the shorter strips. Adjust gathers and distribute evenly. Add more pins as needed. Stitch long side edges and one narrow end in a ¼" seam.

4. Turn right side out and slip a cover section over each end of the hanger, crushing padding tightly as you work. Lap raw ends where they meet around the hook.

5. Loop ribbon over hook and wrap down over the raw edges. Bring ribbon up around in the back. Tie into a bow or a knot at the front of the hook.

VII-29

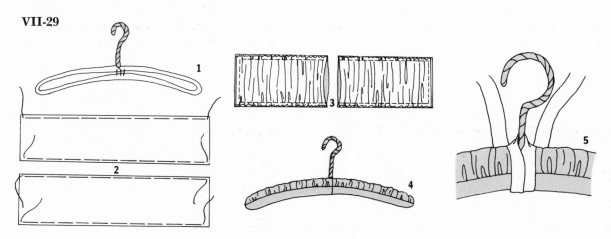

183

Shoe Bags

Make these great organizers for either men or women—the method is the same for both, only the measurements differ. The man's bag is quite large; be sure it will fit on the door or wall where you plan to use it. For each bag, you will need four large eyelets and four cup hooks; a 1″-wide slat or a ¾″-thick dowel to hold the bag straight at the top (18″ long for the women's bag and 22″ long for the man's); 1¾ yards of fabric for the women's bag and 2½ yards of fabric for the man's; a strip of iron-on interfacing 2″ by 18½″ for the women's bag and 2″ by 22½″ for the man's bag; about 2½ yards of double-fold bias tape or foldover braid for the women's and 3½ yards for the man's.

WOMEN's SHOE BAG: Cut a rectangle 18½″ by 33″ for the foundation and three strips 9½″ by 34½″ for the shoe pockets; cut a strip of iron-on interfacing 2″ wide and 18½″ long.

1. To prepare pocket strips (figure VII-30), make a narrow hem on one long edge of each pocket strip. Turn in the edge 1″; press. Turn in raw edge to meet crease and stitch hem in place.

2. On two pocket strips, turn up the remaining long edges ½″; press.

3. Press creases for pocket positions by folding foundation in half lengthwise, wrong sides together; press fold. Pin layers together ½″ from long raw edges.

4. Fold foundation again until pressed fold is ½″ from raw edge; press second fold and remove pins.

5. Press all three pocket strips the same way.

To attach pockets (figure VII-31), start at the bottom of the bag and work up.

6. Using the pocket strip with three raw edges, place wrong side of strip over the right side of the foundation. Match pressed creases. With raw edges even, pin sides in place and at the top and bottom of each crease. Add several more pins along each crease.

VII-30

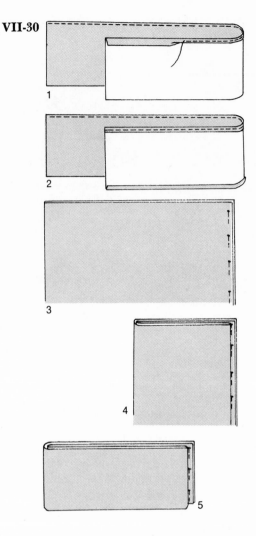

7. Form box pleats for each pocket, having a fold ½″ away from the raw side edges and the remaining folds ¼″ from the crease. Starting on the right raw edge, stitch ¼″ from the edge. At the corner, stitch across the first pocket and the crease to the first fold of the next pleat. Continue by stitching to the hemmed edge ¼″ from the crease, keeping the pleat folds free. Stitch across hem edge ½″ (backstitch to reinforce),

VII-31

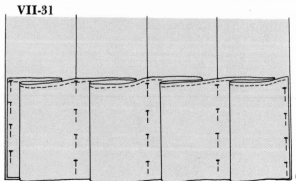

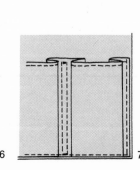

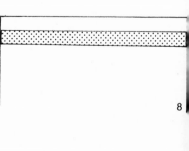

then stitch down to the raw bottom edge ¼″ from the crease. Stitch in the same manner for the remaining pockets, continuing up the left raw edge of the hem.

Position the middle pocket strip ¾″ above the bottom pocket and pin pleats in place the same way. Stitch pockets in place the same way, stitching about ⅛″ from the lower pressed edge so you can catch all the pleat folds in the stitching. Position the top pocket strip ¾″ above the middle strip and stitch in place same as for the middle strip.

8. To reinforce foundation for the eyelets, on the wrong side, place interfacing strip 2″ below the top raw edge and fuse to fabric according to the manufacturer's instructions for the type you are using.

To bind side and bottom edges with double-fold bias tape (figure VII-32), slip tape over the raw edge with the widest edge underneath.

9. Stitch tape in place with straight or zigzag stitches, making sure the raw edges touch the single inner fold of the tape; ending at the corner, break stitches.

10. Form a miter at the corner. Stitch miter in place and continue across the bottom. Miter the remaining corner and continue to the top edge.

11. To finish the shoe bag, turn top down 3″ over the interfacing; press. Stitch 1″ from pressed top edge. Turn in the raw edge ½″ and stitch close to fold, forming a casing for the dowel or slat.

12. Attach four eyelets to the top edge, following manufacturer's instructions. Insert dowel or slat in casing. Secure cup hooks to door or wall and hang shoe bag.

MAN'S SHOE BAG: Cut out a rectangle 22½″ by 45″ for the foundation and three rectangles 12″

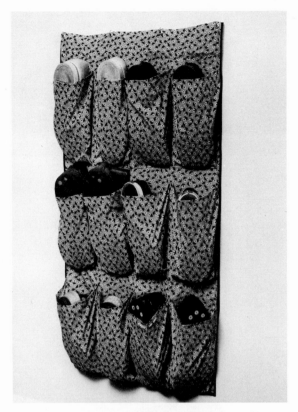

A shoe bag will have your shoes in easy reach. Designed and constructed by the author, this man-size shoe bag is made from Burlington's "Ultra Vino" and bound with double-fold bias tape.

by 42½″; cut a strip of iron-on interfacing 2″ wide and 22½″ long. Make shoe bag as instructed for the women's shoe bag, leaving a 1½″ space between the pocket strips. If foundation is too wide for the space where it is to be used, make it narrower, pleating in excess pocket fabric.

VII-32

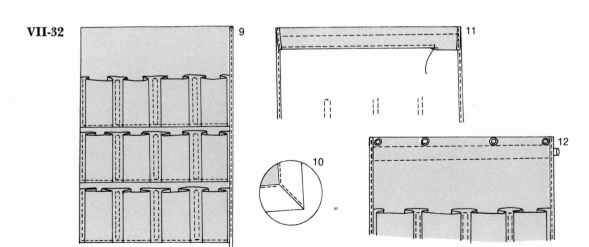

An old-fashioned bathroom is brought up to date by designer Bobbi Stuart with Josephson's wall covering and white percale. Gingham ribbon is used to hold back a stationary curtain over the shower stall and on the inexpensive white stock shade used with classic Priscilla curtains. A design motif is cut out of the wallpaper and glued to the shade, too. The sink skirt is added to create storage space.

BATHROOMS WITH PIZZAZZ

Most of us are stuck with the bathroom arrangement that we have—we had little to say about its design. However, there are many ways you can improve a bathroom to make it work for you and your family. Decorate your bathroom with efficiency in mind. Even if you live alone, a boxlike bathroom can be made attractive with a little bit of fabric and some creative effort. Perhaps all that is needed is a splash of color for the shower curtain and the window, if you have one. Wall-to-wall washable carpet is another source of color that will add a touch of class as well.

BATHROOM SINK SKIRT: For those who need additional storage space, a skirt around the sink is the perfect solution. Make a pair of free-hanging curtains (see glass curtains, Chapter II). Use two cup hooks and ½"-wide elastic to hang the skirt. Fasten a hook to the wall at either side of the sink, and stitch loops at each end of the elastic, making it quite taut. Insert elastic into heading and hang.

NOTE: To use Velcro®, gather skirt top and stitch to the loop strip. Fasten hook strip to the sink with waterproof glue. When glue is dry, hang skirt.

Organize the bathroom to meet the needs of the entire family. Have a place for everyone's towels, washcloth, toothbrush, etc., and an easy-reach hamper (made from towels or fabric) on the wall or the back of the door if you do not have floor space for one. The bathroom shown in these photographs is a standard development-house style that was not planned adequately for a family of six. As a starting point, fabric in the form of sheets was selected for the shower curtain, valance, and Austrian shade; it had enough colors to give each person his or her own color of matching towels.

Appeal to the children's natural instinct for tidiness by giving each one a specific color towel to call his own. Then add a silhouette cut from contact paper of the same color and secure it to the wall. Install hooks for everything: bath towel, hand towel, and face cloth—you'll be pleasantly surprised to find that all the things have been hung up when they don't have to be folded "just so."

The shadow box frame shown was made so each child would have a place for his own cup and toothbrush and so the parents could have a place for their towels, too. Pine boards ½" thick and 3½" wide were used for the frame and two 1"-thick dowels were used for the towel bars; all of these were cut to measurement at the lumber yard. The boards and dowels were stained in a shade to complement the vanity and medicine cabinet. They were then nailed together with finishing nails and each joint was glued with Elmer's® glue. The frame was then nailed into the wall at each end. NOTE: The board at the end that holds the towels extends from the top shelf to the floor.

Shower Curtain

To make a shower curtain from a sheet, use the double-bed size. You will also need a clear plastic liner and large metal eyelets. Use the decorative border from the bottom hem and allow 3" for

These development-house bathroom accessories were designed and constructed by the author to meet the needs of a family of six. Burlington's matching sheets and towels are used for a color-coordinated bathroom. On the right are an Austrian shade, valance, and shower curtain made from sheets with a set of towels over the toilet for each of the parents. On the left below is a simple way to have children hang up wet towels and to find out who doesn't. Silhouettes of contact paper are cut out and pasted to the wall, then hooks are added to hold matching colored bath and hand towels and face cloths. A large hamper made from four colored towels is hung on the wall with Velcro® to dispose of soiled clothes since the builder did not allow floor space for one. The photo below right gives you a good view of the shadow box frame showing each of the four children's toothbrush and glass (the same color as the towels) in easy reach.

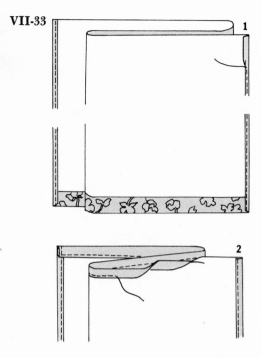

VII-33

1

2

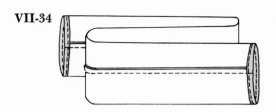

VII-34

the top hem. The finished length measurement should be ½" above floor or carpet to the top edge of the hook, below the shower curtain ring.

To hem the side edges (figure VII-33):

1. Turn in the edges 1" and stitch in place. If the selvage edges seem shorter than the sheet proper, trim them away. Turn in side edge 1½" and then turn under the trimmed edge ½" and stitch hem in place.

2. To hem the top edge, turn down the cut edge 1" and press. Turn down the pressed edge, encasing the raw edge; press. Stitch inner folded edge in place.

To mark position for the eyelets, place liner on top of the shower curtain and trace around the holes. (If shower curtain is slightly wider than the liner, distribute the extra width evenly across the curtain.) Attach eyelets according to the manufacturer's instructions. Hang shower curtains with the liner in back extending into the tub and the curtain on the outside of the tub so it doesn't get wet.

Tube Valance

To make a simple valance to match the shower curtain, make a tube of fabric from another sheet (figure VII-34). The tube valance should be made twice the depth needed to cover the space between the ceiling and about 1" below the shower curtain rod, plus 3" (1" for two ½" seam allow-

ances and 2" to go over each rod). Make the tube the length of the indentation of the tub plus 4" (2" for a narrow hem at each end and 2" for ease).

Open the border and restitch to sheet fabric, if necessary. Then stitch long edges together forming the tube. To narrow-hem the ends, turn in the raw edges 1" and press. Turn in the raw ½" and stitch hem in place. Turn right side out. Hang valance with two presser rods over the tub and shower curtain, making it as smooth and taut as possible.

Wall-to-Wall Carpet in the Bathroom

To lay carpet in a bathroom you will need a pattern. Tape newspaper together to fit the floor, with an inch or so extending up the wall and around the fixtures (figure VII-35). Weight paper so it doesn't shift as you work.

1. With a mat knife or razor blade, cut around the walls, door opening, and tub, forcing the paper into the crack as you work so every bit of the floor is covered no matter how irregular the edges may be. Cut the pattern carefully for the toilet base and any sink supports that cannot be removed.

With a bright-colored pen or crayon make several big X's on the newspaper to mark the top of the paper. This is most important—otherwise you may find that the holes needed for the fix-

1

188

tures are not in the right spot after the carpet has been cut. Slit paper pattern from the wall in back of the toilet to the opening and remove pattern carefully.

2. Spread out carpet with tufted side down and the backing facing you. Place pattern on top with the X's next to the backing. Weight pattern to hold in place and draw outline on the backing. Cut out carpet with razor blade, mat knife, or scissors, being careful not to cut away any more of the tufts than necessary, cutting on the outside of the line.

3. Make the same slash to the holes from the fixtures and place the carpet on the floor. The rubberized backing will keep it from shifting.

VII-35

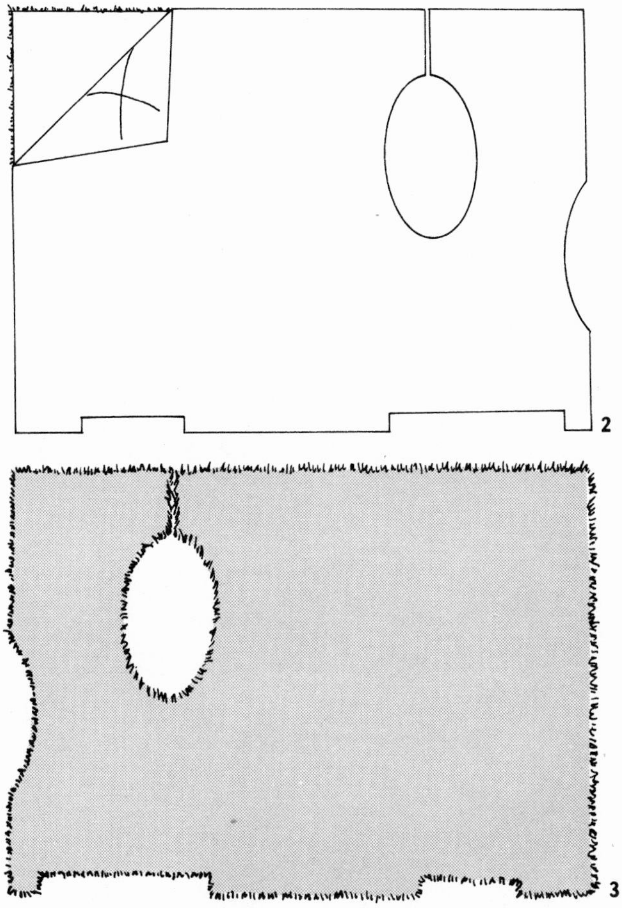

Clothes Hamper

A place for dirty clothes is a must for everyone— make a fabric hamper as large or as small as is needed. The one shown on page 187 is made with four bath towels, about 2½ yards of trim, and two strips of Velcro® 30″ long for easy removal to empty.

To Make Hamper (figure VII-36):

1. Stitch the towels together in a narrow seam, leaving a 10″ opening on each seam where the towels intersect.

2. Turn back the triangular edges, forming a diamond. Pin trim to these edges, then pin both trim and triangles to fabric underneath. Stitch trim and triangles in place through all thicknesses. Stitch ¼″ from diamond shape to hold folded edge in place.

3. Make a pleat at each side of the opening, adjusting the depth so the hamper will fit in the space allowed. Fold towel strip 2″ above the trim edge, right sides together. Mark fold with pins. Stitch pleat in place for 6″ on each side of the marked fold.

VII-36

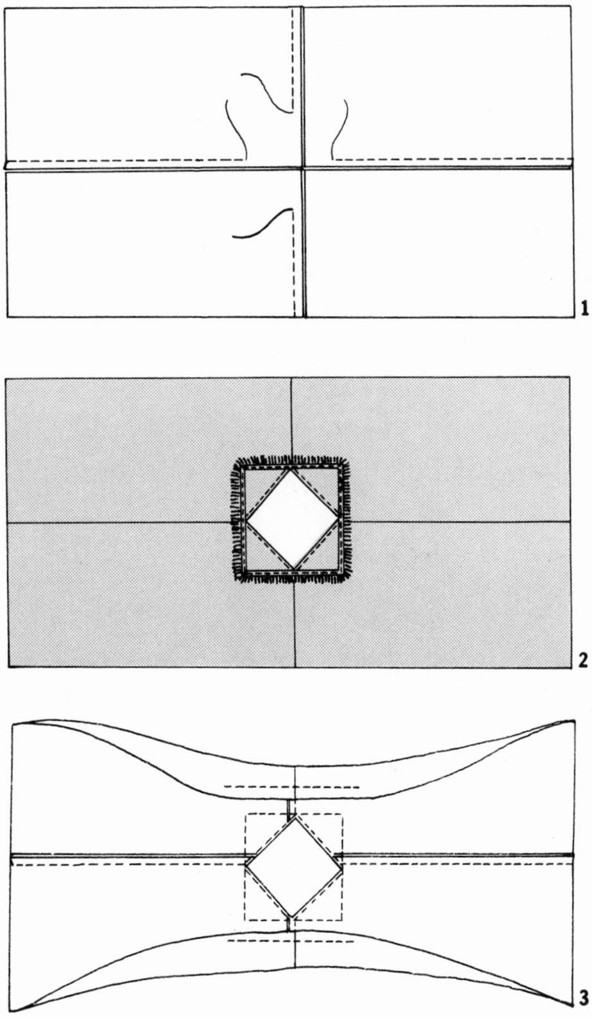

4. Attach Velcro® on the outside. Stitch one loop strip to the fabric just below the fold and the other loop strip 2¼″ away.

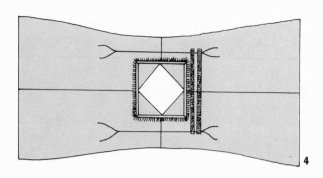

5. To shape hamper, stitch ends together, forming a tube. Next stitch the sides to within 2″ of the bottom fold. Mark fold with pins. Make a square bottom by bringing the fold and seam together forming a triangular end. Make a 6″-long seam across the triangle with 3″ on each side of the seam and fold. Stitch again ¼″ away. Trim away excess fabric and zigzag raw edges together. Turn right side out through opening.

Attach hook strips to wall with glue or molly bolts or whatever type of hardware is needed for your walls and hang the hamper.

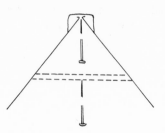

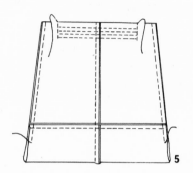

VIII
Terms and Techniques

Many of the sewing terms and techniques that are used for dressmaking and tailoring are used for home decorating, too. Throughout the first seven chapters, the step-by-step procedures refer to specific terms and general sewing methods. These techniques are explained on the following pages in alphabetical order. They will serve as a reminder for the experienced and help to make each project a little easier for the novice.

Applied (apply)

Ruffles and other trims are sewn or stitched onto the fabric for a decorative accent (see decorative band trim and ruffles).

Backing

An additional layer of fabric used under sheer or semisheer fabric to make it opaque so other colors (such as the blankets on a bed) won't show through or make shadows on the light color or lightweight bedspread. Use muslin, sateen, sheets, or any tightly woven fabric that has the same cleaning requirements as the decorative fabric.

Cut backing the same measurements as the decorative fabric. Place backing right side up on a flat surface and place the wrong side of decorative fabric over it; pin raw edges together as they fall. Machine-baste 1/4″ from all raw edges and handle the two layers as one throughout the construction procedures.

Band Trim

See *decorative band trim* and *extended trim*.

Basting

There are three types of basting you may use when sewing for your home; each serves a purpose and there may be times when two basting methods are used for one seam (figure VIII-1).

PIN-BASTING:

1. Hold fabric layers together or hold trim in place with pins. Place pin at right angle to the raw edges so you stitch over them with a hinged presser foot. Use as many pins as needed to control the fabric or match simple fabric designs.

2. For trim or seams that are bulky, place pins parallel with the heads facing you. Remove pins as you machine-baste trim in place.

MACHINE-BASTING:

3. To hold fabric layers or trim in place temporarily, use the longest machine stitch. Reduce the tension on the top thread a few points in order to remove threads more easily.

VIII-1

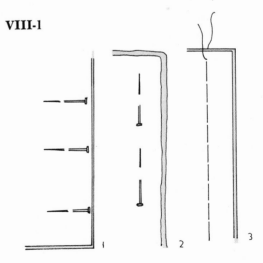

SLIP-BASTING: This technique is one of the custom decorator's best tools. It is used to hold

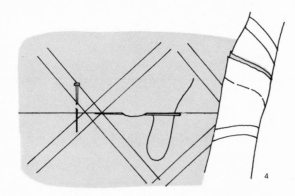

fabric design, plaid, stripes, or prints in place while you stitch.

4. Turn in one edge along the seam line; crease and pin. Lap creased edge over the other section, matching the design along the lower layer's proposed seam line; pin. Insert needle through crease on top layer, then through the lower section, making stitches on each layer about ¼" long. Open out seam allowances and stitch along basting.

Bias and Straight-Grain Strips

Dressmakers are sure that bias-grain strips are best for cording, but upholsterers are most likely to use straight-grain strips. After testing both, let the fabric dictate the type of strip to use—a plaid looks great cut on the bias, but for a plain color or weave it doesn't matter. Heavy, unyielding fabric should be cut on the straight grain.

BIAS STRIPS: Use leftover fabric or purchase at least ½ yard of extra for continuous strips.

To use leftover fabric (figure VIII-2), straighten one corner so the crosswise grain is perpendicular to lengthwise grain or selvage. Fold corner diagonally to find true bias; mark fold with a ruler and pencil on the wrong side of fabric.

1. Mark as many strips of the desired width as needed, allowing ¼" at each end for piecing.

Mark all ends along the straight grain. Cut along the markings.

2. Stitch ends of strip by placing right sides together along the straight-grain edge. Pin with long edges meeting as shown. Stitch where strips intersect, usually about ¼" from ends.

3. Make strip as long as needed; press seam open.

Continuous strips (figure VIII-3). Straighten raw fabric edges along crosswise threads. Fold one corner at a time at a 45° angle so the crosswise grain is perpendicular to the lengthwise grain. Mark folds on wrong side of fabric and then mark strips the necessary width until you meet the second fold line.

1. Cut away corners along first and last strip lines. With right sides together, pin strip ends together, matching lines with one strip extending beyond the ends at each side. Stitch in a ¼" seam; press seam open.

2. Start cutting along marking at one end. When cutting is completed you will have one continuous strip.

VIII-3

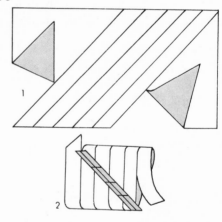

VIII-2

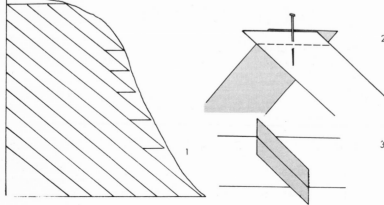

Straight strips (figure VIII-4). Use leftover fabric or purchase at least ¼ yard of additional fabric. On the wrong side of fabric, make a straight line near the selvage, then mark strips the necessary width.

1. Cut along markings. Ends must be cut at a 45° angle to eliminate bulk at seam.

2. Fold end of one strip diagonally with corner up, and one end of another strip at opposite angle with corner down. Cut along folds.

Stitch ends together same as for leftover bias strips, figure VIII-2, steps 2 and 3.

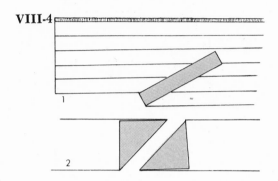

VIII-4

Binding

An easy way to finish an edge without using a hem is with bias binding. Use commercial wide or double-fold bias tape or make your own. Binding may be as narrow as ¼" and as wide as 2".

To cut bias strips, see figures VIII-2 and VIII-3. Make strips four times the desired width, plus ⅛" to ¼" for shaping (thicker fabric will need the most). Cut enough strips to cover the edge(s) to be bound, piecing as needed. Allow 2" to finish the ends. Example: For a 2"-wide binding you need 8"-wide strips, plus ⅛"–¼" for shaping. For a ¼" binding you need strips 1" wide plus ⅛"–¼" for shaping.

To form binding (figure VIII-5).

1. Fold strips in half; press stretching gently to remove slack.

2. Open strips, and turn in cut edges toward the crease, making the bottom layer a scant ⅛" wider than the top layer; press lightly.

VIII-5

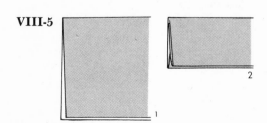

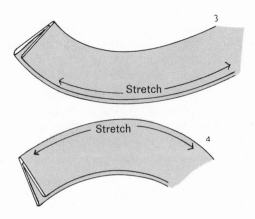

Before binding curved edges, shape binding (either commercial or self-made) to match the curve on the bedspread, ruffle, etc. Use a steam iron and press lightly.

3. For an inward curve, stretch the two folded edges while easing the single folded edge.

4. For an outward curve, stretch the single folded edge while easing the two folded edges.

To stitch binding to an edge (figure VIII-6). Open binding and pin narrowest edge to the right side of the edge to be bound, making the raw edges even.

1. Stitch binding in place along crease. Turn binding to the wrong side along the stitching, encasing the raw edge. Make sure the remaining folded edge covers the seam, stitching a scant ⅛"; pin.

2. On the right side, stitch in the groove where the binding joins the fabric, catching the remaining free edge in the stitching.

VIII-6

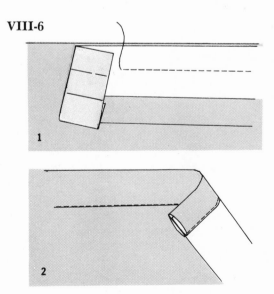

To join binding in a continuous strip (figure VIII-7). Stitch ends in a seam or lap them.

For a seam, keep 1″ of the strip free at the beginning of the stitching.

1. When you have stitched to within 1″ of the beginning, stop and break threads. Fold edge so the binding ends are at right angles. Stitch ends along the straight grain where they meet, keeping the edge being bound free. Trim seam allowances to ¼″.

2. Press seam open and complete stitching. Finish binding same as figure VIII-6, steps 1 and 2.

For lapped ends,

3. turn in the beginning ends ½″ and stitch in place. When you come to the turned-in end, allow ¾″ to lap over it and complete stitching. Finish binding same as figure VIII-6, steps 1 and 2.

VIII-8

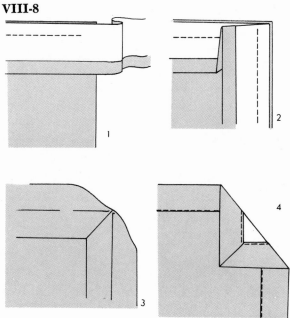

VIII-7

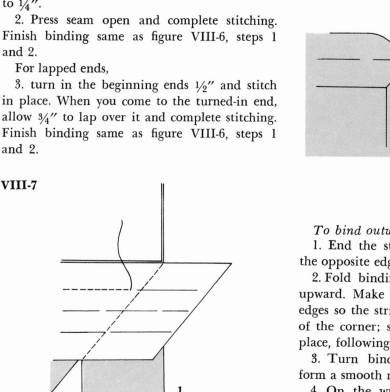

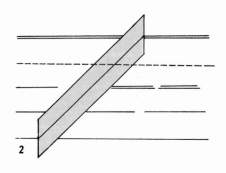

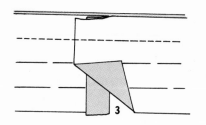

To bind outward corners (figure VIII-8).

1. End the stitching the same distance from the opposite edge as the binding is wide.

2. Fold binding diagonally and extend strip upward. Make another fold at the upper raw edges so the strip is even with the opposite side of the corner; stitch folds and binding strip in place, following the crease.

3. Turn binding to inside along stitching; form a smooth miter on front.

4. On the wrong side, form another miter, placing the folds in the opposite direction of those on the right side so you won't have a lumpy corner. Pin and stitch entire free edge in place, following figure VIII-6, steps 1 and 2.

To bind inward corners (figure VIII-9).

1. Make a row of reinforcement stitches the same distance as the finished binding width. Use 20 stitches to the inch and stitch about 1″ on each edge of the corner. Clip to stitching at corner. When stitching the binding in place, open the corner so the reinforcement stitches are in a straight line.

2. Stitch along the outside of the stitches so they won't show when the binding is completed.

3. On the wrong side, pull miter folds through clip.

4. Make another miter, placing the folds in the opposite direction on the remaining edge. Pin and stitch entire free edge in place, following figure VIII-6, steps 1 and 2.

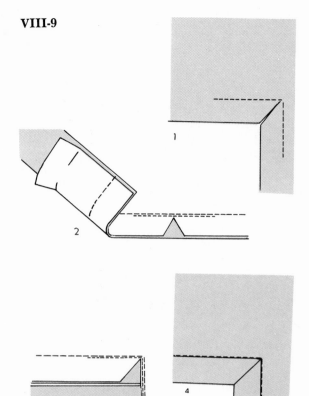

margin about ½″ from its raw edge with rust-proof staples or tacks. Now gently stretch the piece over the opening until it is smooth and the top left corner and the bottom left corner are square; secure bottom edge to the frame. Anchor one side and then the other the same way, keeping corners square and needlework free from puckers.

For runproof threads and yarns. From the wrong side, wet the foundation fabric (the bathtub is the best place for large pieces). Shake off the excess water and allow to dry thoroughly. Sometimes it will take several days, depending on atmospheric conditions.

For threads or yarns that are not runproof. Hold steam iron over the wrong side of the needlework, allowing the steam to penetrate the foundation, never resting the iron on the needlework. Allow to dry and repeat three or four times. Do not oversteam. A small amount of steam at more intervals is safer for threads or yarns that may run, damaging the needlework.

Casing
A term used for a tunnel formed with fabric so a curtain rod, elastic, or drawstring may be inserted.

Corded String Hem
Use sheer, semisheer, light, or medium fabric that is crisp and tightly woven and does not ravel easily. For cord, use a heavyweight crochet cotton that matches or contrasts and use thread the same color as the cord.

To make hem (figure VIII-10). Use a medium-width zigzag stitch and 20 stitches to the inch. Lay cord on the right side of the fabric under the presser foot. Drop presser foot and pull cord up through slot. Hold cord slightly off the fabric as you zigzag over it, keeping one edge of the presser foot close to the raw fabric edge (cord will be

VIII-10

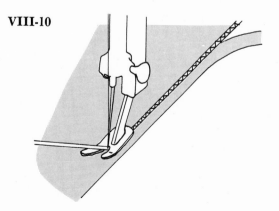

Blind Stitch
There are two ways to make stitches nearly invisible on the outside. To make blind stitches by hand, see *slip-stitching,* figure VIII-29, method 1. To make them by machine, see *machine blind-stitch hem,* figure VIII-24.

Blocking
When the foundation fabric or the canvas of your needlework does not lie flat without puckers or does not have square corners, it must be blocked. The easiest way to do blocking is with an artist's stretcher frame. Purchase stretcher strips according to the raw edge measurements of the foundation. The strips come in lengths from 6″ to several feet long in 2″ graduated measurements. If your needlework piece does not match the standard stretcher strip measurements exactly, don't be too concerned. These strips are about 1½″ deep and will accommodate pieces up to 1″ smaller than the outer edge measurements.

Center the needlework piece, right side up, over the frame. Starting at the top edge, secure about ¼″ from the edge). Trim away excess fabric alongside the cord, being careful not to cut the zigzag stitches. Also see the corded hem in Chapter IV, figures IV-5 and IV-32.

Cording
To make cording, use cable cord the desired thickness and bias or straight-grain strips, figures VIII-2, VIII-3, and VIII-4. The strips should be wide enough to encircle the cord, plus 1″ for two ½″-wide seam allowances. Remember to double the amount needed for length when trimming two edges on a cushion or valance.

To prepare cording (figure VIII-11). Cut a piece of cable cord and a fabric strip as long as needed. Use a zipper foot, placing machine needle to the right of the foot edge indented as far as possible. Fold fabric, wrong sides together, over cord with long raw edges even. Stitch close to cord using the longest stitch, but do not crowd the cord.

VIII-11

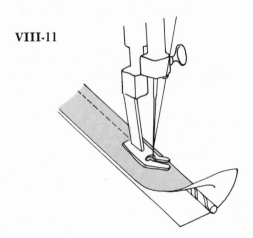

Crosswise
A term used to denote the thread that runs across the fabric from selvage to selvage, indicating the crosswise grain of the fabric.

Decorative Band Trim
Indent trim or apply to the edge for a custom touch. To indent (figure VIII-12), make a line with chalk the desired distance from the finished edges.
1. Stitch both edges of trim in place. To miter, end stitching at opposite line.
2. Fold trim back at line; crease. Then fold to make a right angle; crease. Lift up trim; stitch along diagonal crease.
3. Reposition trim and stitch both edges of trim in place along remainder of markings.

VIII-12

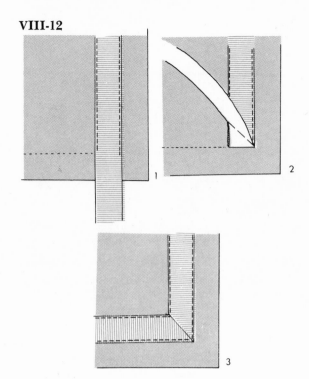

To apply to an edge (figure VIII-13). Use in place of a hem. Turn up the raw edge ½″ and press. Lap trim over the raw edge, making trim even with the pressed edge.
1. Miter a corner same as figure VIII-12, steps 1, 2, and 3, covering the raw edge.
2. For a rounded edge, ease inner edge to fit.

VIII-13

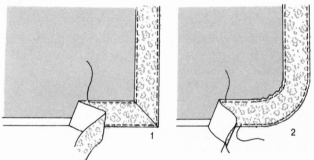

Decorative Seams
A small roll of fabric filled with cord, a ruffle, and any of the decorative trims available today are just right for pillows, slipcovers, bedspreads, curtains, and many other items featured in this book. These handsome seam accents will increase the value of your decorating project and make the seam more durable and visually more pleasing, especially if the fabric design cannot be matched on the seamed edge. See *corded seam,* *ruffled seam,* and *purchased trim in a seam* on the following pages in this category.

CORDED SEAM: This classic trim has been a favorite for years—sometimes it's called piping or welting. Make it with bias or straight-grain strips of either matching or contrasting fabric and a filler or cable cord in any size desired, from a tiny $\frac{1}{16}''$ to a plump $1''$ in diameter. Test various sizes with a fabric sample to determine which is the best one for your decorating project. To cut bias strips, see figures VIII-2 and VIII-3; for straight strips, see figure VIII-4; and to make cording, see figure VIII-11.

To stitch a corded seam (figure VIII-14): Use a zipper foot.

1. Place cording on the right side of one fabric section with raw edges even; machine-baste in place, being careful not to crowd cording. NOTE: If cording has wider seam allowances, stitch along the proposed seam line.

To complete seam, move needle slightly toward the left to the edge of the foot. With raw edges even, pin remaining section over basted cording section.

2. With the basting section uppermost, stitch seam to the left of the basting, crowding the cording slightly.

3. *To turn cording at a corner or point.* Stitch to within $\frac{1}{2}''$ of next side. With needle in fabric, raise presser foot and clip cording fabric only to needle. Pivot fabric on needle until next side is lined up with presser foot. Make sure cording seam allowances and fabric sections are flat, keeping raw edge even. Drop presser foot and continue stitching. NOTE: For heavy fabrics, round the corners slightly.

4. *For a sharp curve or rounded corner.* Stitch to within $1''$ of curve. Lay cording around curve,

clipping cording seam allowance only as needed to make it lie flat. Then continue stitching.

Inward curves do not cause a problem when stitching, but you may want to notch out excess folds on heavy fabric when seam is completed.

To make cording continuous (figure VIII-15).

1. Start at the center of one edge, leaving about $1''$ of cording free. When the ends nearly meet, extend cording $1''$ over first end; cut off. Open this end of cording fabric; cut cord only so it is flush with first end.

2. Turn in fabric end $\frac{1}{2}''$, wrapping folded edge over cord at starting end, having cord ends meet.

3. Stitch remainder of cording in place, connecting with previous stitches.

To end cording at an intersecting seam that will not be corded.

4. Taper cording to nothing where it meets the intersecting seam line.

VIII-14

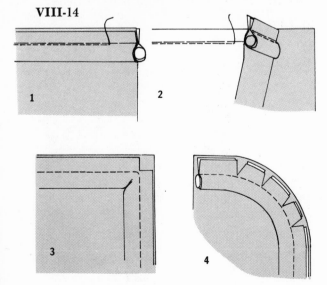

VIII-15

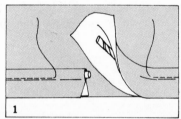

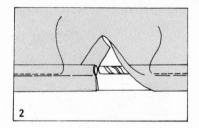

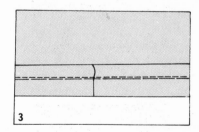

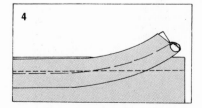

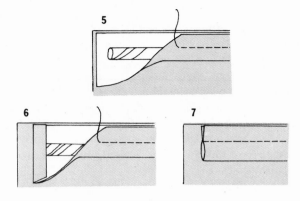

To end cording at an edge.

5. Open cording fabric 1″. Trim away ½″ of the cording.

6. Turn fabric over cord, making fabric flush with the intersecting seam line, and then pull down the seam allowances over it.

7. Machine-baste cording in place.

RUFFLED SEAM: See instructions under *ruffles* (*extended trim edge finish*). There are two ways ruffles are used in a seam: One is continuous and the other has finished ends. For self- or contrasting ruffles, cut a straight-grain fabric strip for a single thickness or double thickness as directed in figure VIII-4, step 1.

CONTINUOUS RUFFLE (figure VIII-16): Cut fabric strip as desired. Example: For a 15″-square pillow with a 1½″-wide double-thickness ruffle, cut a strip 4″ wide and 65″ long, piecing where necessary.

1. Stitch ends in a ½″ seam; press open. Fold strip in half, wrong sides together, press.

2. Divide ruffle in quarters and mark with pins. Gather raw edges, breaking stitches at pins (see *gathers*, figure VIII-23). Divide each edge in half or divide a circle into quarters; mark with pins. Pin ruffle to right side of fabric, matching pins. Adjust gathers to fit evenly, allowing extra fullness at corners so ruffle will lie flat when extended beyond seam edge; pin in place.

3. Machine-baste ruffle in place along inner gathering thread line. Press gathered edge of seam allowance only. Pin remaining layer over ruffled section and stitch seam with basted layer uppermost, stitching alongside the inner edge of the basting thread. To stitch pillows, see Chapter III.

RUFFLE WITH FINISHED ENDS (figure VIII-17): Cut fabric strips as directed. Example: For a rectangular pillow 22″ long and 16″ wide with a 2″ double-thickness ruffle at each end, cut two strips 5″ wide and 33″ long, piecing if necessary.

1. Fold strip right sides together, stitch ends in a ½″ seam. Turn right side out, fold in half lengthwise with raw edges even; press ends and fold flat.

Gather raw edges of ruffle (see *gathers*, figure VIII-25). Divide ruffle in half; mark with pins.

VIII-16

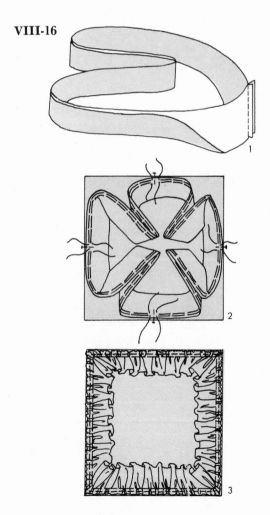

VIII-17

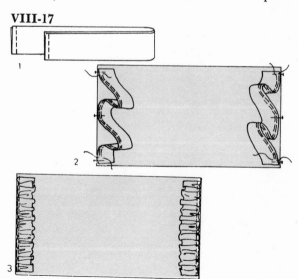

Divide fabric ends in half; mark with pins.

2. Pin ruffle to fabric matching pins and place finished ends of ruffle along intersecting seam line (½″) of long edge.

3. Adjust gathers to fit evenly. Pin in place. Machine-baste ruffle in place along inner gathering thread line. Press gathered edge of seam allowance only. Pin remaining layer over ruffled section and stitch seam with basted layer uppermost, stitching in planned seam width and alongside the inner edge of basting thread. To stitch pillows, see Chapter III. NOTE: Make sure ruffle ends are not caught in remaining seams when stitching.

PURCHASED TRIM IN A SEAM (figure VIII-18): Trims available to the home sewer have never been more interesting—the wide variety of fringe, ruffles, and heavy lace are still the favorites.

Trim should always be flat when it extends beyond the seamed edge. Lay the straight edge of trim along a curve, corner, or point to see how much extra trim is needed so the outer decorative edge will lie flat. Place straight edge of trim about ⅛″ over the ½″-deep seam line on the right side of the fabric. Keeping decorative edge free, machine-baste ½″ from raw edge along seam line.

VIII-18

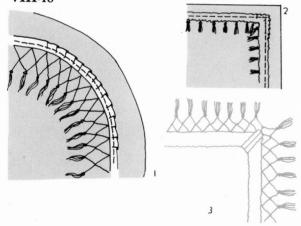

For curved edges.

1. Ease trim to fit as you stitch by pushing tiny folds of trim against the machine needle with a pin.

For straight edges with corners or points.

2. Ease in trim at corners by forming tiny pleats. Or

3. form a miter and stitch it in place. Cut off excess fold of trim and press seam open. Zigzag raw edges to prevent fraying. Then stitch trim in place along seam line as instructed above.

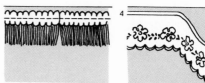

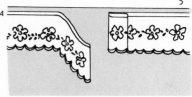

To join trim ends where they meet.

4. Butt ends together for fringe, making sure each end has a finished loop at the top. Or

5. turn back first end ½″ when starting and extend remaining trim over turned-back end ¾″ as you complete machine-basting.

Drop

A term used to describe the fabric that extends from the top of a bed or table to the floor or any other planned spot. A fabric strip may be stitched around the edges to form a fitted, gathered, or pleated drop, or one large fabric section (pieced if necessary) will have extensions that hang loosely from the edges, such as on a throw bedspread or a tablecloth.

Extended Trim as an Edge Finish

Decorative trims of this type may have a band with scallops and tassels, ball fringe, looped fringe, flat-cut fringe, or knotted-cut fringe. If your band is narrower than ½″, turn under the raw edge so it won't show and press. Do not trim; it will weaken the edge. Also see *ruffles (extended trim edge finish).*

VIII-19

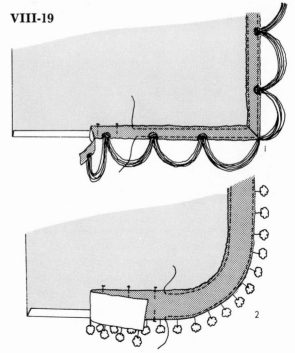

To prepare the edge (figure VIII-19), turn up the raw edge ½″ and press. Pin solid edge of trim over the raw edge so it won't show. Stitch close to both band edges.

1. Miter corners or
2. ease inner edge of band to fit along a curve.

Facing

A term used to denote a layer of fabric stitched in a seam, then turned to the inside to finish an edge. Inner edge of facing should be held in place with slip stitches or machine stitches.

Festoon

A term used to describe the draped, curved folds of fabric that form between two stitched areas, such as those that form between the shirred ring tapes of Austrian shades or a draped valance.

Finial

A term used for the decorative ornaments inserted at each end of a drapery or café curtain rod.

Flat-Felled Seam

This seam is used as a finish for fabrics that fray easily, such as denim. To stitch seam (figure VIII-20), pin layers, wrong sides together. Stitch in a ⅝″ seam. Trim one seam allowance to ⅛″. Press both seam allowances in the same direction with the longer one on top. Turn in the top seam allowance ¼″ and stitch in place close to fold.

VIII-20

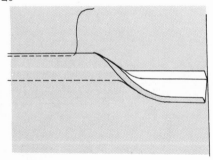

French Seam

Use this seam to enclose raw edges so the wrong side is smoothly finished with no raw edges showing. Use on curtains, unlined draperies, or for other seam allowances that may show or to prevent fraying during cleaning (figure VIII-21).

To make a classic French seam.

1. Pin layers wrong sides together. Stitch in

VIII-21

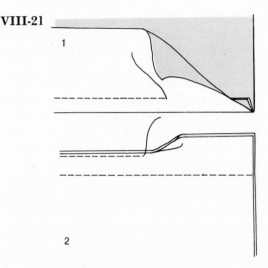

the desired seam width. Turn right side over the seam allowance; crease along stitching and press. Stitch again, just deep enough to enclose raw edges. For sheers stitch about ⅛″ from raw edges, making the second row a scant ¼″ deep. For other fabrics stitch ¼″ from raw edges, making the second row about ⅜″ deep.

To make a mock French seam.

2. Stitch layers in a regular seam, with right sides together. Tuck in the raw seam allowances to meet the seam and stitch folded edges together (2).

French Tack (figure VIII–22)
VIII-22

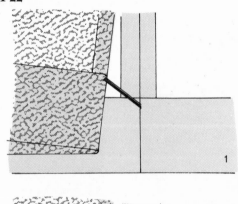

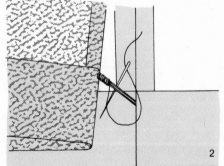

1. Make several 1″-long thread loops between lining and draperies at each seam.

2. Then, using the same thread, work closely placed blanket stitches over the loops. To make blanket stitches, slip needle under loops, working from right to left; bring needle out over the thread. Pull up tightly and make remaining stitches in same manner.

Gathers

These soft folds of fabric that extend beyond a seam require some careful planning to achieve the best results. Select light- to medium-weight fabric—stiff or heavy fabrics will not fall in soft, cascading folds but will bell outward, puffing rigidly. The fullness of the gathers will depend on their use. Some fabrics will look better a little skimpy—just 1½ times longer than the edge to be joined. The favorite amount is double the length, but then some very soft lightweight fabrics look smashing when the length is tripled.

To ensure that threads will not break when pulling up the gathers, use heavy duty or button and carpet thread on the bobbin.

Two rows of gathering threads are needed (figure VIII-23). Place the first row alongside the seam line in the seam allowance and another row ¼″ away, closer to the raw edge.

When gathering long edges, divide fabric strip into quarters (or eighths); mark with pin and break stitches at pins. The heavier the fabric, the shorter the gathering threads should be.

Make a test on a fabric scrap to see what procedures to follow.

For a seam with one layer gathered. Stitch from the right side of the fabric so the bobbin thread will be on wrong side.

For a decorative ruffle. Stitch from the wrong side of the ruffle so the bobbin thread will be on the right side. Remove the gathering threads after the ruffle is stitched in place.

To join a section to be gathered to a shorter edge. Divide both the shorter and the longer edge into quarters or eighths; mark with pin. Make gathering stitches on longer section as previously directed. Pin to shorter section, matching pins. Pull gathering threads at each end until they fit shorter edge. Fasten thread ends securely by knotting or making a figure eight over a pin. Adjust gathers by sliding folds along thread so they fall evenly between pins; add more pins and machine-baste in place along inner gathering thread. Press gathered folds in seam allowance only.

Heading

A term used to describe an edge made above a casing that forms a ruffled edge when a rod, elastic, or drawstring is inserted and the fabric is gathered along the inserted object. It also is used to describe the narrow free edge found on some ruffles.

Lambrequin

A shaped covering at the top of a window or door. Used at a window with or without curtains or draperies, a lambrequin may be padded and covered with fabric the same as a cornice, or it may be painted.

Lap

A term used when one layer of fabric or trim is placed over another layer so the edges cover each other for a short distance.

Lengthwise

A term used to denote the threads that run parallel with the selvages down the length of the fabric.

Machine Blind-Stitch Hem

Most sewing machine manuals give instructions

VIII-23

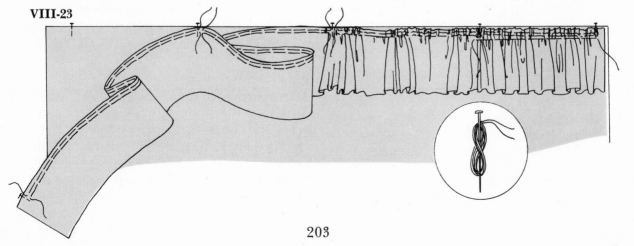

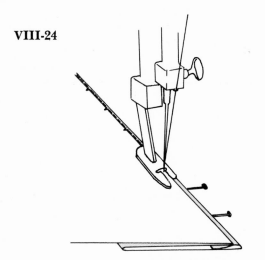

for this type of hem. However, there are several tips that will make it easier (figure VIII-24).

Insert pins about ⅛″ from the inner hem fold. Turn back hem along the pins so the hem edge extends ⅛″ beyond the fold. Using the blind-hem stitch, stitch alongside the fold, catching just a thread or two with extended stitch. Pull hem down and press gently.

Miter

There are two ways to miter a corner for a smoother finish (figure VIII-25).

To miter seam allowances.

1. Turn in corner at a 45° angle where they intersect.

2. Fold in long edges to meet at an angle at the corner.

VIII-25

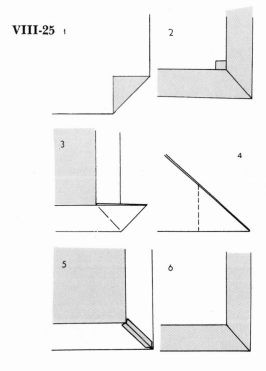

To miter a hem.

3. Turn hem allowances to the outside at the corner. Pinch the edges together where they meet. Make diagonal creases at the corner.

4. Bring creases together and stitch them together in the crease.

5. Trim away excess to within ¼″ of the stitching; press seam open with tip of iron, being careful not to press hem edge.

6. Turn hem allowances to the inside; press. Complete hem as desired.

Nap

A general term used to indicate the pile on fabrics. Such fabrics must be cut in a special way so that all pieces will reflect light in the same manner. Corduroys and velvets are the best-known napped fabrics, with tiny tufts woven into the foundation fabric. To see if your fabric will reflect light, hold fabric over your body under your chin and look down over it in a well-lighted room. Reverse the fabric so it falls in the opposite direction. If one way is bright and the other way is dull, the fabric has a napped finish. Other fabrics such as satin and gabardine also should be handled as a napped fabric. One-way printed designs should be handled this way too.

When cutting napped fabrics, be sure to mark the top edge of all panels for curtains, draperies, bedspreads, etc., to save time. For fabrics that can be marked safely on the wrong side simply print "top" with a soft lead pencil. If pencil marks will show through or damage the fabric, pin a safety pin at the top of each panel on the wrong side of the fabric.

Piping

Another term used for cording (figure VIII-10). Usually piping is made with ¹⁄₁₆″–⅛″ size cable cord.

Preshrunk

A term used for fabric that has been pretreated to avoid shrinkage after the fabric is washed or dry-cleaned. To shrink fabric before cutting see *shrinking fabric.*

Pivot

A term used when stitching corners and points. To pivot, stitch to corner or point where intersecting seam lines meet (usually ½″ or ⅝″ from the raw edges). With needle still inserted in fabric, raise presser foot. Pivot (swing) fabric on needle so you can stitch the remaining side along the seam line. Drop presser foot and continue stitching.

Reinforcement Stitches

A row of fine machine stitches (20 to the inch) is placed a scant 1/2″ from the raw edge of one fabric layer so the edge can be clipped and then stitched to another layer. Clip to stitching at even intervals; pin in place, spreading clips so the raw edges will lie flat. Stitch alongside the inner edge of the reinforcement stitches so they can't be seen from the outside when the fabric is turned right side out.

Ruffles (Extended Trim Edge Finish)

Long a favorite garment trimming for both men and women, ruffles are used to add a custom touch by decorators—deep dust ruffles or several tiers for the bed; framing the edges of a pillow and as a trim for curtains or draperies. Plain ruffles have one free edge, with the gathered edge stitched in a seam or enclosed with a lining or facing or a hem allowance. Ruffles with a heading have two free edges; one is very narrow and is applied on top of the fabric along the gathers. Double ruffles have two free edges of equal measurement and are applied the same as a ruffle with a heading.

CUTTING STRIPS FOR RUFFLES: Ruffles may be made with a single or double thickness of fabric. Cut fabric strips on straight grain, piecing where necessary. Seam allowances that are not exposed do not need to be finished. Make a narrow French seam in single-thickness ruffles if the seam will be seen. Determine the desired finished width of the ruffle.

To make single-thickness ruffles. Add 7/8″ to the desired width (1/2″ for seam allowance and 3/8″ for a narrow hem) for the plain ruffle; add 3/4″ to the desired width (3/8″ for each narrow

hem) for the ruffle with a heading and the double ruffle.

To make double-thickness ruffles. Double the desired finished width and add 1″ for two 1/2″ seam allowances for the plain ruffle; the ruffle with a heading and the double ruffle do not need seam allowances.

Add gathering threads to all types of ruffles as indicated following instructions in *gathers*, figure VIII-23.

PLAIN RUFFLE (figure VIII-26):
1. For a single thickness, narrow-hem one long edge and gather the other;
2. For a double thickness, fold long edges of fabric wrong sides together; press. Gather raw edges.

To stitch a plain ruffle to an edge. A 1″ hem allowance is needed. Narrow-hem ruffle ends or join in a seam, see figures VIII-16 and VIII-17.

3. Pin ruffle so its raw edge is 1/2″ below the edge to be finished. Adjust gathers and distribute evenly. Stitch along inner gathering thread. Trim ruffle seam allowance only to a scant 1/4″. Turn in raw edge of hem allowance, then turn the edge over the raw ruffle edge. Stitch inner fold in place.

4. Turn ruffle down; press. On the outside, if desired, stitch 1/8″ from the seam, catching the enclosed ruffle seam allowance in stitching.

RUFFLE WITH A HEADING (figure VIII-27):
1. For a single thickness, narrow-hem both long edges and gather about 1/2″ from one edge.

2. For a double thickness, fold one long edge to the wrong side 5/8″; press. Fold remaining long edge up to meet narrow edge; press. Gather 1/8″ from each raw edge. (See next page.)

To stitch a ruffle with a heading to an edge. Use a 1/2″ hem allowance for the application.

VIII-26

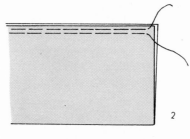

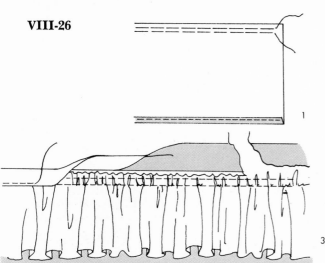

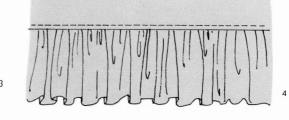

205

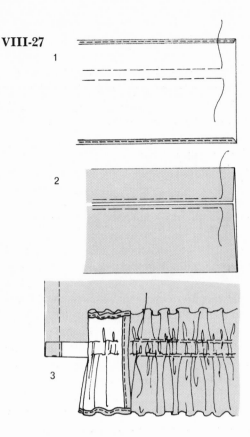

VIII-27
1
2
3

Narrow-hem ruffle ends or join in a seam, see figures VIII-16 and VIII-17. Turn edge to be finished to the outside ⅜″, right sides together; press. Pin ruffle over raw edge with fold ⅛″ below lower gathering threads. Adjust gathers; allow extra fullness at any corners so ruffle will lie flat when extended beyond the edge.

3. Stitch ruffle in place alongside both the gathering threads as indicated.

DOUBLE RUFFLE (figure VIII-28):

1. For a single thickness, narrow-hem both long edges; gather at the center.

2. For a double thickness, fold long edges to the wrong side so they meet at the center of the strip; press. Gather ⅛″ from each raw edge.

To stitch a double ruffle to an edge.

3. Use a ½″ hem allowance and apply same as a ruffle with a heading. Be sure to use crisp fabrics so the upper ruffle edge will stand up.

Sew

A term used throughout this book to indicate the need to use a hand-sewn stitch to complete a procedure.

Shirring

A design feature in which two or more rows of gathering threads are used below a seam as a decorative touch.

Shrinking Fabric

Make sure fabric will not shrink after bedspreads, slipcovers, curtains, or draperies are made. To shrink washables, lay fabric in a large vessel of water (the bathtub works great) until thoroughly wet. Squeeze out water (do not wring) or hang over a towelrack until the fabric stops dripping. Dry fabric in a dryer at correct setting, or hang it on a line in a protected area free of wind, without pins, with selvages even. To shrink dry-cleanables, take uncut fabric to a reputable establishment or use one of the do-it-yourself dry-cleaning machines. NOTE: Remove fabric from dryer as soon as it is dry to eliminate the need for excessive pressing.

Slip-Stitching

There are several ways to make these durable hand-sewn stitches work for you (figure VIII-29).

To use as a hemming stitch. Work from right to left. Knot thread and hide under fold.

1. Slip needle through folded edge; swing needle to pick up a fiber thread of the fabric alongside the hem edge. Pull thread up and repeat this step, making the tiny stitches about ¼″ apart.

To join two folded edges. After anchoring thread, slip needle through one fold; swing needle to pick up a fiber thread of the fabric on the opposite fold. Pull thread up and repeat this step, making the tiny stitches about ¼″ apart. Join

2. two flat edges or

3. two extended edges.

To attach trims and appliqués. Anchor thread,

VIII-28

1

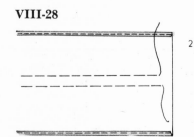

2

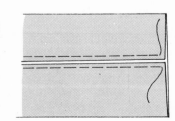

3

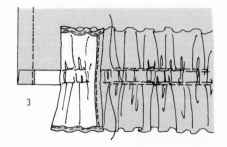

VIII-29

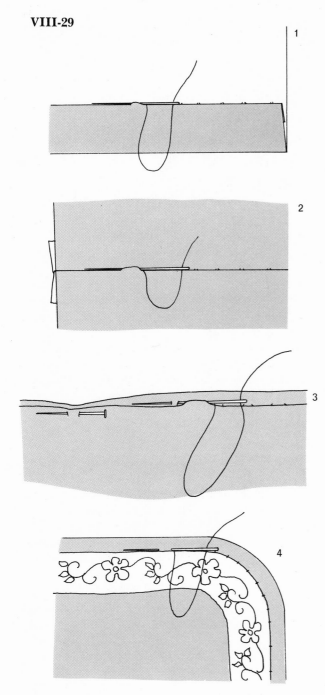

selvage edge. Pick up one thread and pull it gently, forming puckers along it. Work puckers across the thread so a line is formed.

1. Cut along the thread. If the thread breaks, cut as far as possible and then pull the same thread again.

For fabrics that are treated, matting the threads together so a thread cannot be pulled,

2. mark a line at right angle to the selvage with a T- or L-square. Cut along marked line.

VIII-30

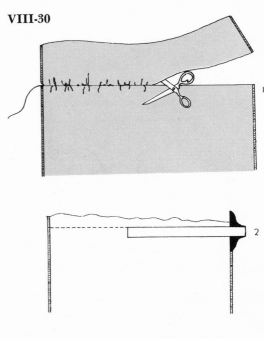

Welting

Another term sometimes used for cording. However, it is used incorrectly. Welting is formed by stitching a narrow seam (right sides together). The item is turned right side out and the stitched edge is pressed flat. Another row of stitches is made an even distance from the pressed edge, encasing the raw edges. Welting was used to finish the edges of the garment bags in Chapter VII.

slip needle up through the foundation fabric.

4. Pick up a fiber thread of the trim and reinsert needle. Repeat this step, making tiny stitches about 1/4″ apart. Curved edges may need tiny stitches as close as 1/8″.

Straightening Fabric Ends

There are two ways to straighten fabric ends (figure VIII-30). For fabrics that are woven, so that a thread may be pulled make a snip at one

Yardage Key

Use this simple guide when calculating yardage:

- 1/8 yard = 4½″
- 1/4 yard = 9″
- 3/8 yard = 13½″
- 1/2 yard = 18″
- 5/8 yard = 22½″
- 3/4 yard = 27″
- 7/8 yard = 31½″

Index

211